INDIA PARTITIONED
The Other Face of Freedom

———— • ————

The Partition of India cast its lengthy shadows on two generations in the subcontinent. Ordinary people across borders were sucked into its vortex as unconscious and innocent actors, as maddened mobs. The first of two volumes, this book draws upon short stories, poems, and satirical pieces, to represent the voices of anguish and the sense of betrayal at the freedom gained.

———— • ————

MUSHIRUL HASAN (born 1949) is the author of *Legacy of a Divided Nation: India's Muslims since Independence* (1997); *Nationalism and Communal Politics in India, 1885-1930* (1991); *A Nationalist Conscience: M. A. Ansari, the Congress and the Raj* (1987), and *Mohamed Ali: Ideology and Politics* (1981). He has edited *India's Partition: Process, Strategy and Mobilization* (1993); *Islam and Nationalism: Reflections on Abul Kalam Azad* (1992); *Communal and Pan-Islamic Trends in Colonial India* (1985); and co-edited *India's Colonial Encounter* (1993)

———— • ————

INDIA PARTITIONED
The Other Face of Freedom

OTHER LOTUS TITLES

AMRITA PRITAM	*The Other Dimension*
ASHISH KHOKAR	*Baba Allauddin Khan*
A.S. PAINTAL	*Ustad Amir Khan*
DHANANAJAYA SINGH	*The House of Marwar*
GANESH SAILI	*Glorious Garhwal*
GIRISH CHATURVEDI	*Tansen*
IRADJ AMINI	*Koh-i-noor*
JAIWANT PAUL	*'By My Sword and Shield'*
JAIWANT PAUL	*Rani of Jhansi, Lakshmi Bai*
JOHN LALL	*Begam Samru*
JYOTI JAFA	*Nurjahan*
KHUSHWANT SINGH	*Kipling's India*
LALI CHATTERJEE	*Muonic Rhapsody and Other Encounters*
L.K. PANDIT	*Krishna Rao Shankar Pandit*
MAGGI LIDCHI-GRASSI	*The Great Golden Legend of the Mahabharata*—2 vols
MANJARI SINHA	*Ustad Bade Ghulam Ali Khan*
MANOHAR MALGONKAR	*Dropping Names*
P. LAL	*The Bhagavad Gita*
RUSKIN BOND	*Ruskin Bond's Green Book*
V.S. NARAVANE (ed.)	*Devdas and Other Stories by Sarat Chandra*
V. S. NARAVANE	*Best Stories from the Indian Classics*

FORTHCOMING TITLES

AMRITA PRITAM	*Fire in the Mirror*
ARJAN SINGH	*Tiger Anthology*
C. M. NAIM	*Zikr-e-Mir*
J.C. WADHAWAN	*Mantonama*
K. M. GEORGE (ed.)	*Best of Thakazhi Sivasankara Pillai*
LAKSHMI SUBRAMANIAN	*Medieval Seafarers*
SHOVANA NARAYAN	*Kathak: A Journey through the Ages*
SUDHIR KAKAR (ed.)	*Indian Love Stories*
V. N. RAI	*Curfew*

—a multi-volume series—
India: Fifty Years Before and After 1947
MUSHIRUL HASAN: General editor

INDIA PARTITIONED
The Other Face of Freedom

———— • ————

Volume I

Edited by
MUSHIRUL HASAN

Revised & Enlarged Edition

LOTUS COLLECTION
ROLI BOOKS

Lotus Collection

© Mushirul Hasan 1995, 1997
Selections and Introductions

© Roli Books Pvt Ltd 1995, 1997
for the following:
'How Much is the Difference?'; 'The Divine Law'; 'It's Voting Day: Let's March . . . Mukhiaji' by Mehboob Ludhianvi *et al*; 'Independence ' by Makhdoom Mohiuddin: 'Azadi', *Zabt Shudah Nazmen*; 'Black Margins' by Saadat Hasan Manto: 'Siyah Hashiye', *Atish Pare aur Siyah Hashiye*; 'So the Witnesses Stated' by Fikr Taunsvi: 'Gavahon ne Bayan Diya'; 'The Book of Divine Knowledge' by Fikr Taunsvi: 'Aasmani Kitab'; 'The Wagah Canal' by Fikr Taunsvi: 'Wagah ki Nehar', *Satvaan Shastra*; 'We have arrived in Amritsar' by Bhisham Sahni: 'Amritsar aa Gaya hai', *Mere Priya Kahaniya*; 'My Native Land' by Vishnu Prabhakar: 'Mera Vatan', *Kitne Toba Tek Singh*; 'The Last Wish' by Badiuzzaman: 'Pardesi', *Chautha Brahmin*; 'How Many Pakistans?' by Kamleshwar: 'Kitne Pakistan': *Kohra*; 'Asylum' by Agneya: 'Sharandata', *Ye Tere Pratirup*; 'The Dunghills' by Mumtaz Mufti: 'Gobar ke Dher' and 'An Impenetrable Darkness' by Mumtaz Mufti: 'Ghor Andhera, *Ismaraiyaan*; 'Lord of the Rubble' by Mohan Rakesh: 'Malbe ka Malik', *Kitne Toba Tek Singh*.

This edition first published 1995
Revised and enlarged edition 1997
The Lotus Collection
An imprint of
Roli Books Pvt Ltd
4 Ansari Road
New Delhi 110 002
Phones: 3276325, 6442271, 6462782
Fax: 6467185
Also at
Varanasi, Agra, Jaipur and The Netherlands

ISBN: 81-7436-011-5 (set)
ISBN: 81-7436-012-3 (Vol. I)
Price: Rs. 595.00 for the set of two volumes

Typeset in Galliard by Roli Books Pvt Ltd and
printed at Print Perfect, New Delhi

'For a long time I refused to accept the consequences of the revolution, which was set off by the partition of the country. I still feel the same way; but I suppose, in the end, I came to accept this nightmarish reality without self-pity or despair. In the process I tried to retrieve from this man-made sea of blood, pearls of a rare hue, by writing about the single-minded dedication with which men had killed men, about the remorse felt by some of them, about the tears shed by murderers who could not understand why they still had some human feelings left. All this and more, I put in my book, *Siyah Hashye*.'

—*Saadat Hasan Manto*

*For Javed Anand, Ajit Bhattacharjea,
Praful Bidwai, Mohan Chiraghi, Vinod Mehta,
Seema Mustafa, Kuldip Nayar, Saeed Naqvi,
Dileep Padgaonkar, Amrik Singh
and Hasan Suroor.*

—In appreciation of their support and solidarity

Contents

Preface	9
Introduction MUSHIRUL HASAN	15
How Much is the Difference? HUMAYUN AKHTAR	45
The Divine Law HARI CHARAN LAL	48
It's Voting Day: Let's March ... Mukhiaji	49
Aadha Gaon RAHI MASOOM REZA	53
India, My India! SHAMIM KARHANI	80
The Land of Moon and Stars MAKHDOOM MOHIUDDIN	83
The Morning of Freedom FAIZ AHMAD FAIZ	86
Black Margins SAADAT HASAN MANTO	88
The Book of Divine Knowledge FIKR TAUNSVI	102
We have Arrived in Amritsar BHISHAM SAHNI	114
My Native Land VISHNU PRABHAKAR	127

The Last Wish BADIUZZAMAN	136
The New Regime KRISHNA SOBTI	147
How Many Pakistans? KAMLESHWAR	154
Asylum AGNEYA	169
Lajwanti RAJINDER SINGH BEDI	179
Pimps RAMANAND SAGAR	192
The Dunghills MUMTAZ MUFTI	200
An Impenetrable Darkness MUMTAZ MUFTI	210
The Alien BADIUZZAMAN	225
His Heap of Rubble MOHAN RAKESH	238
The Wagah Canal FIKR TAUNSVI	249
So the Witnesses Stated FIKR TAUNSVI	256
Shadowlines SURINDER PRAKASH	267
Roots ISMAT CHUGHTAI	279
The Vultures of the Parsi Cemetry ALI IMAM NAQVI	290

Preface

This collection stands as a witness to the hypocrisy, barbarity, recklessness and ultimately the absurdity of communalist thought and action—a testimony no less pertinent today than in 1947. It is designed to support and supplement the historical literature on India's partition. Its aim is to unfold certain aspects of this epic tragedy with the aid of stories, poems, diaries, eye-witness accounts and excerpts from novels and autobiographies. The two volumes do not provide an episodic narrative. Rather, they form a cultural archive of first-hand information, experiences and vivid impressions. The idea is to let poets and writers reflect on the social, cultural and political upheaval on the eve of and in the aftermath of the country's division. In a nutshell, to give them a voice in the scholarly debates on independence and partition.

Those who speak through these volumes do not occupy centre stage in national or provincial arenas of formal and institutional politics. By conventional political standards they are not 'influential'. Yet they must be heard and their views and impressions need to engage scholars and citizens alike. They articulate, in varying degrees, the mood and the sensitivities of large numbers of aggrieved and tormented people who had no say in the actual transfer of power to two sovereign nations. Even if this was not so, their writings stand out as invaluable contributions to India's cultural and literary heritage.

Those who speak through these volumes do not always echo the same feelings and sentiments. It is not surprising why this is so. The country's vivisection, after all, symbolized different things to different people and conveyed several meanings in various regions. Yet there is an unmistakable commonality of concerns, an underlying coherence and unity of thought. Most writers share and convey to us the agony, pain, sorrow and indignation of a generation that was unwittingly caught up in the internecine 'communal' conflicts of the 1940s. This is indeed the dominant strain in the writings of Saadat Hasan Manto in *Thanda Gosht* (Cold Meat), *Khol-do* (Open Up) and *Toba Tek Singh*, in Krishan Chander's *Ham Wahshi Hain* (We Are Brutes), and in Kartar Singh Duggal's *Ujla Anchal* (Clean Mantle).

Many of the contributions do not bear an 'Indian' or a 'Pakistani' imprint. Nor can their authors be designated as 'Hindus', 'Sikhs' or 'Muslims'. It would be a mistake, nay a grave error, to categorise them as such. What distinguishes a Manto or a Bedi from contemporary political commentators and analysts is their ability to repudiate 'communal' categories and transcend religious, regional and territorial barriers. Their creative energies were released not because their co-religionists alone were mercilessly slaughtered, but because their humanity was wounded and the civilizational rhythm of the subcontinent was being irreparably destroyed. This is why Manto, Josh Malihabadi, Intizar Husain, Krishan Chander, Ismat Chughtai and Faiz Ahmad Faiz are 'Indians' as much as 'Pakistanis'. We turn to them not to discover fresh 'insights', 'analysis' and 'interpretation', but because they stir the individual and collective conscience of sensitive and discerning readers anywhere and everywhere. In Lahore and Delhi; in Pyongyang and Seoul; in Berlin and Bonn; and in the war-torn cities of the former state of Yugoslavia. To divide such authors and their writings into narrowly-defined religious, sectarian or geographical entities implies the partitioning of a common as well as a vibrant cultural, intellectual and literary heritage. Manto was concerned that this might well be the outcome of partition. When asked to write for the Urdu daily *Imroze*, he wondered: 'To whom will now belong what had been written in undivided India? Will that be partitioned too?'

The fact is that Manto is today widely read in India and Pakistan. If ill-informed critics from the left or the right still find him an embarrassment, as indeed they did during his lifetime, he would have reiterated his response in 1951 to the publication of *Siyah Hashye*. He had written then:

> If after my death, the official media and the country's libraries welcome my works and my stories are accorded the same kind of high-minded reverence that is reserved for the poet Allama Iqbal, my soul will not find peace. I am quite content with the treatment given to me until now. May God protect me from

PREFACE 11

posthumous recognition which will eat like a mould through my dry bones in the grave.

Why Rajinder Singh Bedi and not Krishan Chander? Why Kamleshwar and not Intizar Husain? Why Faiz and not Firaq? Why Josh and not Qudratullah? Why Krishna Sobti and not Jilani Bano? This selection is, some might say, arbitrary. I do not deny this is so. Moreover, I also concede that there are many other stories, poems and autobiographical accounts, some of greater literary merit and historical value, that could have been part of such a compendium. Some have already figured in published anthologies, such as *Writings on India's Partition*, edited by Ramesh Mathur and M. Kulsaresth; *The Best of Manto: A Collection of His Short Stories*, translated and edited by Jai Ratan; *Breakthrough: Modern Hindi and Urdu Short Stories*, edited by Sukrita Paul Kumar; *Saadat Hasan Manto: Partition*, translated by Khalid Hasan; *Kitne Toba Tek Singh* (People's Publishing House, 1988); *Fasadaat Ke Afsane*, compiled by Zubair Rizvi; others form part of a three-volume anthology compiled by Alok Bhalla. I expect readers would turn to them for a rounded and more comprehensive view of the partition story. I also hope this compilation would be read along with and as a sequel to my edited work on *India's Partition: Processes, Strategy and Mobilization* (Delhi: Oxford University Press, 1993).

With the notable exception of Amrita Pritam's Punjabi poem, this collection is limited to Hindi, Urdu and English writings. This is because I read no other language. I have not been able to include some works in English, such as Attia Hosain's *Sunlight on a Broken Column* or Nirad C. Chaudhuri's *Thy Hand, Great Anarch*! because of copyright restrictions.

The translations were specially commissioned for this volume and this process was not easy. According to Rukmani Bhaya Nair, who has helped translate some Urdu poems, 'although translation gives us access to new linguistic and cultural worlds, the terrain the translator inhabits is always hazardous. This is not only because a translator is torn between the demands of faithfulness to an 'original' and readability in a 'target' language. It is also because, as a conscientious translator, one has to respond to recent theories of translation. Among such theories are those which favour the retention of a certain quality of 'roughness' of 'unreadability' in translated pieces, so as to resist absolute homogenisation and remind the reader of the fact that the writing before a translator is indeed a translation.' In the translations, some concession has been made to this new perspective.

I agree with a number of reviewers that the translation of some stories is inadequate, though the publisher has done his best to marshal the resources available in Delhi. The effort has not proved rewarding in some cases. In this edition, however, a number of stories have been translated afresh; others have been brushed up in the light of various suggestions. More readable and authentic translations of the stories by Bhisham Sahni and Mohan Rakesh are included.

There are other significant additions as well. Manto's *Siyah Hashye* has been translated in full owing to my dissatisfaction with the efforts of Khalid Hasan. I have also included the stories of Ismat Chughtai, Surinder Prakash and Ramanand Sagar, a poem 'Divine Law', and an extract from a pamplet. The revised introduction is an abridged version of a chapter in my book *Legacy of a Divided Nation: India's Muslims since Independence.* Finally, a glossary is appended for the benefit of the readers.

Thanks to Mr Purushottam Aggarwal, Associate Professor, Centre of Indian Languages, Jawaharlal Nehru University, New Delhi, for the introductory notes on Agneya, Mohan Rakesh, Vishnu Prabhakar, Badiuzzaman and Kamleshwar; to Ritu Menon for notes on Kamaladevi Chattopadhyay and Aruna Asaf Ali; to M. Asaduddin for his notes on Ramanand Sagar, Ismat Chughtai, Surinder Prakash; and to Urvashi Butalia for her note on Begum Anis Kidwai. Mr L. Deevani of the Nehru Memorial Museum and Library furnished biographical information on A. D. Mani, Ganda Singh and D. F. Karaka.

A special word of gratitude to Krishen Khanna, renowned artist and witness to the partition, for his drawing, included as frontispiece. Dating back to 1948, it represents a document of the times.

Ms Jehanara Wasi, Dr. M. Asaduddin and Ms Raj Kamini Mahadevan helped to prepare the final version. I am grateful to them and the translators. Mr Pramod Kapoor came up with the idea of such an anthology. He sustained my interest and supported this endeavour.

SEPTEMBER 1996   M. H.

Acknowledgements

The editor and the publisher are grateful to the copyright owners for permission to reproduce texts. Every endeavour has been made to contact copyright owners. We apologise for any omission:
To Penguin Books India Pvt. Ltd, Mrs Nayyar Reza and Gillian Wright for the excerpts from *The Feuding Families of Village Gangauli*, Viking, New Delhi, 1994, pp. 149-50, 237-51, 255-6, 273-6, 283-5, 292-5; to Prof. M. U. Memon for 'The Vultures of the Parsi Cemetery', *Colour of Nothingness: Modern Urdu Stories*, ed. M. U. Memon, Penguin Books, New Delhi, 1991, pp. 138-43; to Baidar Bakht and Kathleen Jaeger for 'The Land of Moon and Stars', by Makhdoom Mohiuddin, *An Anthology of Modern Urdu Poetry*, Educational Book House, Delhi, 1984, pp. 10-12; to Khaleeq Anjum and Mujtaba Husain for 'Independence' by Makhdoom Mohiuddin, *Zabt Shuda Nazmen*, Delhi, 1975, pp. 253-4; to Faiz Foundation for 'The Morning of Freedom', *Journal of South Asian Literature*, vol XXV, no 2, pp. 128; to Phool Kumar for 'Aasmani Kitab', 'Wagah ki Nehar', 'Gavahon ne Bayan Diya' by Fikr Taunsvi, *Satvan Shastra*, Delhi, Burki Press, 1950, pp. 185-202, 57-66, 67-86; to Bhisham Sahni for 'We have arrived in Amritsar', *The Penguin Book of Modern Indian Short Stories*, eds. Stephen Alter and Wimal Dissanayake, Penguin Books, New Delhi, 1989, pp 180-192; to the People's Publishing House (PPH) for 'Mera Vatan' by Vishnu Prabhakar, *Kitne Toba Tek Singh* ed. Bhisham Sahni, PPH, New Delhi, 1987, pp. 24-32; to Indian Institute of Advanced Study, Shimla, for 'His Heap of Rubble', *Breakthrough: Modern Hindi and Urdu Short Stories*, ed., Sukrita Paul Kumar, Indian Institute of Advanced Study, Rashtrapati Nivas, Shimla, 1993, pp. 223-26; to Begum Sayeeda Khatoon for 'Antim Ichcha' and 'Pardesi' by Badiuzzaman, *Chautha Brahmin*, Delhi, 1982, pp. 118-28, 31-46; to Kamleshwar for 'Kitne Pakistan?' *Kohra*, Rajpal & Sons, Delhi, 1994, pp. 89-106; to Trustee, Vatsal

Nidhi Trust for 'Sharandata', *Ye Tere Pratirup*, Rajpal and Sons, Delhi, 1961, pp. 47-60; to Sahitya Akademi, New Delhi, for 'Lajwanti' by Rajinder Singh Bedi, *Contemporary Indian Short Stories* (Series III), ed. Bhabhani Bhattacharya, (1st edn 1957, 5th edn 1991) pp. 172-83; to Mumtaz Mufti for 'Gobar Ke Dher', and 'Ghor Andhera', *Ismaraiyaan*, Feroze Sons, Lahore, 1993, pp. 268-79, 226-45; to PPH., for 'Sikka Badal Gaya' by Krishna Sobti, *Kitne Toba Tek Singh*, PPH., Delhi, 1987, pp. 92-7; to *Indian Literature* (170) for 'Shadowlines' by Surinder Prakash, pp. 93-103; to *Zahn-i Jadid*, for 'Jarein' by Ismat Chughtai and 'Bhaag in Burdafarushaon Se' by Ramanand Sagar, *Fasadaat ke Afsane*, ed. Zubair Rizvi, Delhi, 1995, pp. 55-61, 88-94.

Introduction

Kaho dair-o-haram walo ye tum ne kya fusoon phoonka
Khuda ke ghar pe kya guzri sanamkhane pe kya guzri

Jagan Nath Azad

Rehmat Ali's 'Pakistan scheme', published in Cambridge in January 1933, caused much political embarrassment back home and was summarily dismissed as 'chimerical' and 'impracticable'.[1] For nearly a decade afterwards Pakistan remained a pipe-dream and the League a paper body. But when the dust settled after the Lahore meet in March 1940, Pakistan was no longer an elusive goal, the League no longer a benign organization. Having refurbished its image, reorganized its structure at various levels and formulated a strategy to deepen its popular base, the League picked up seats in by-elections, increased its membership, secured a firm foothold in Muslim-majority provinces, and commanded widespread support from various groups and social classes. Sixty-one by-elections were held for Muslim constituencies during 1937-43 and out of this the League bagged 47 seats. The Congress managed to secure only 4 seats. The League polled about 4.5 million or 75 per cent of the Muslim votes in 1945-46 and won 460 out of the 533 Muslim seats in the central and provincial elections.

The League, according to W. C. Smith, then researching in India, had conquered the bulk of the middle class as well as the lower middle class.[2] By 1942, Jinnah 'actually assumed a position like Gandhiji so far as Muslims were concerned'.[3] He was 'a sword of Islam resting in a secular scabbard'.[4] His Pakistan idea 'appeared a thing to laugh at five years ago: now, though I think it is impracticable, it has become the slogan and watchword of the Muslim masses'.[5] Jinnah, commented another writer, was the incarnation of one idea, 'but the idea can be fertile once it has succeeded'. He continued:

> Therefore Moslem Leaguers are in earnest when they believe that Pakistan is the inviolable prelude to their communal well-being and prosperity. They may or may not be deluded in this, other elements may adulterate their zeal, but in the emotional fervour of the two thousand or so students who greeted us with green flags chanting Pakistan in unison at Lahore; in the frenzied cries that met Jinnah when he spoke to thousands in the same town when we were there; in the long elaborate exposition I heard at a Moslem tea gathering at Allahabad; in the somewhat confused utterances of three opulent and corpulent Muslim spokesmen at Peshawar; in the persistence of those who pursued me at the last Indian gathering; and in a score of other instances, *I perceived that Pakistan had caught on with large numbers of Moslems and had become an intense political-religious faith* (emphasis added).[6]

The picture in the provinces gives credence to these impressions. The League's prospects in Punjab, always a matter of concern to Jinnah and his lieutenants, improved vastly after the collapse of the Jinnah-Sikander Pact in April 1944. Its political strategy, coupled with an intensive propaganda campaign along religious lines, paid off. The landlords and the *pirs*, whose directives were widely disseminated by means of small leaflets and wall-posters, deserted the Unionist Party for reasons that are now known through the scholarly researches of David Gilmartin, Ian Talbot, Ayesha Jalal and Imran Ali. Their overwhelming support enabled Jinnah to raise his party's flag in the 'cornerstone' of Pakistan. Before the War, Hindus, Muslims and Sikhs lived, for the most part, as neighbours in rural Punjab. With the intensive propaganda which accompanied the elections of 1945-46, communal politics burst into the village, setting Muslim against non-Muslim, and giving both a new and exciting word—freedom.[7] M. A. H. Qadiri, Professor of Zoology at the Aligarh Muslim University, found in rural Punjab a great change in the mentality of the Muslim masses. They were 'aroused and inspired by the message of Pakistan'.[8] Though some areas were untouched by and beyond the League's sphere of influence, 'responsible' and 'influential' leaders toured the province, educated the masses, established League branches and enlisted primary members.[9] Malcolm Darling commented during his tour of the Punjab:

> If only propaganda had not poisoned the air with hatred and distrust, Hindu, Muslim and Sikh could have continued to live happily together in the village, as they had done for over a hundred years. . . . We met Muslims who for generations had their genealogies kept and horoscopes cast by Brahmins, and passed villages owned by Muslim and Sikh, or by Hindu and Muslim, sprung from a common ancestor, and we even came across one village where Hindu, Muslim and Sikh were of the same tribe. Without neighbourliness there can be no comfort in village life, but, alas, propaganda with its ghastly brood— mutilation, massacre and rape—has turned Jinnah's two-nation creed in the village from a theory into a bloody fact.[10]

Similar processes were at work in Sind. The League projected its image as the defender of Islam, exploited the Shahidganj mosque affair which resulted in strife and violence, toppled Allah Bakhsh's pro-Congress ministry, replacing it with by one headed by a League sympathizer, Mir Bandeh Ali Khan Talpur.[11] This was not enough! 'In every mosque', reported a Leaguer, 'the principle underlying the "Buy from Muslim" campaign was explained and the pulpits (*sic*) were asked to exhort the congregationists to take to trade. . . . A day was fixed as the "Muslim Trade Day" and an appeal was issued to the Muslims . . . to observe the day. As many as 200 places in the province observed and celebrated the day'.[12]

An additional bonus was that *pirs* and other religious men were cultivated, drawn into the political arena, catapulted into public prominence, reassured that their interests would be firmly secured under a League-led government and paid thousands of rupees in offerings to take part in canvassing.[13] By the time of the Quit India movement, in a province where political activity had been sporadic even during the Khilafat enthusiasm, the League had set up 450 branches comprising, at least on paper, 126,484 members.[14]

The League bandwagon also rolled on in the Central Provinces and Berar, Bombay, and Madras. Towards the end of 1941 Madras claimed to have 112,078 members. By 1944-5 Bengal had branches in eighteen out of twenty-eight districts with 550,000 primary members.[15] These figures 'exceeded the number ever scored by any organization in the province not excluding the Congress.'

The League started off unsteadily in U.P. [United Provinces], though it began making substantial gains after the adoption of the Lahore Resolution. The province's chief secretary thought that 'the Pakistan scheme now seems to be an accepted part of the tenets of the League'.[16] The Allahabad and Muzaffarnagar district branches scored substantial gains in membership. 'Everyday we eagerly wait for *Dawn*', wrote the president of the Muzaffarnagar branch to Jinnah, 'to see if you have issued any fresh statement or instruction. How glorious it is to be in communion with you. . . .'[17] In Deoria, the League gained a foothold by taking advantage of estranged Hindu-Muslim relations. Patrick Biggie, a police officer, commented: 'Any district in the west of the Province will seem like child's play after the many complex problems of Deoria—its dacoities, its communal trouble, murders and political activity.'[18]

The same was true of Kanpur during 1939-41. Worker unrest was widespread. Christians were agitated over the sale of church land, and the Shias over police firing on their brethren in neighbouring Lucknow.[19] Hindu-Muslim strife was heightened by disputes over the ownership of Parade grounds and the Ramnarain Bazaar, the kidnapping of a young boy by Shahid Ali, and the outbreak of riots in June 1939. Tension mounted when the Kanpur Hindu Sangh observed 'Hyderabad Day' and 'Anti-Pakistan Day' to express solidarity with the Arya Samaj movement in the princely state of Hyderabad. Jinnah provided the healing touch to the beleaguered Muslims, travelled to Kanpur, hobnobbed with influential Muslims and addressed a public meeting. Nearly 25,000 people turned up to listen to this rising star on the Indian political firmament.[20]

Aligarh's Muslim University was, as Jinnah once said, 'the arsenal of Muslim India'. But this was not so until the late 1930s, when the liberal-socialist combine dominated campus politics. The mood changed with the founding of the All-India Muslim Students' Federation (AIMSF) and the Students' Union adoption of the Lahore Resolution as its 'official creed'. The AIMSF launched a quarterly journal in English and Urdu; students and teachers churned out pamphlets on Pakistan, such as 'The Nature of Islamic Political Theory' by Jamiluddin Ahmad; 'Industrial Pakistan' by

Mohammad Yunus and 'The Herculean Task' by Farzand-i-Raza. League stalwarts visited Aligarh periodically. The citadel of Syed Ahmad Khan, who had urged his co-religionists to stay clear of politics, was breached. 'The walls of the Stratchey Hall', wrote an AIMSF activist, 'had echoed with the voices of great men right from the days of Sir Syed. These voices are now silent. A new voice had begun to be heard in the late 1930s and during the last decade before Independence it was the only political voice that mattered in Aligarh: it was the voice of Mohammad Ali Jinnah.'

In September 1942, members of the Muslim University Duty Society toured some princely states, carrying 'the torch of League ideals' and discovering 'signs of life and awakening' in the Muslim masses. Jinnah's stirring speech at the University's Stratchey Hall on 2 November 1942 must have disturbed Syed Ahmad Khan lying in his grave in the nearby mosque. It certainly caused panic in pro-Congress circles. Aligarh's grand old man, steeped in the feudal traditions of a passing era but keeping pace with the changing world around him, had not been by any means the architect of Muslim nationalism. He was a modernizer, a reformer and an educationist who tried bridging the gulf that separated the colonial government from the remnants of the Muslim elite of north India. His efforts were not wasted although his death in 1898 brought profound changes. For one, the legacy of compromise and accommodation with the Raj was repudiated by the radicals at Aligarh during the first decade of the twentieth century. The University, modelled on Oxbridge and designed to produce loyalists serving the government, turned into a storm-centre of nationalist activities during the heady days of the Khilafat and Non-Co-operation enthusiasm. But in the early 1940s the clock was turned back. Memories of the Khilafat days faded away. The political message of Ajmal Khan, Mohamed Ali, Ansari, Hasrat Mohani, Shibli, Azad and Maulana Mahmud Hasan, which had once stirred the imagination of students and teachers alike, was lost. Aligarh discovered a new set of heroes, created new symbols to embrace and pinned their hopes on the evolution of a specifically Muslim nationhood. The University, caught up in the communal cauldron, was called upon to endorse the League's demand for a Muslim state.

The broad direction and course of politics at Aligarh was clear in the early 1940s but the underlying driving force was the Communist Party of India (CPI) and the change in its attitude towards the League generally, and the AIMSF at Aligarh. The Germans were pounding the gates of Stalingrad and the Japanese were pushing their way through the forests of Imphal and Kohima to India's eastern border. It was feared that if India were to fall into the hands of the Axis powers it would be an utter global disaster for the antifascist allies. That had to be prevented at all cost. In India itself there was a political deadlock. A desperate search was made for a solution to the 'Indian problem'. According to the new CPI line, it lay in 'Congress-League Unity' to be realized through Gandhi-Jinnah talks. This became the new CPI slogan and was echoed in Sajjad Zaheer's articles in *People's War*. To justify theoretically this new turn in politics, the Comintern and the CPI argued that there were not one but two 'National Bourgeoisies' in India—the Indian National Bourgeoisies and the Indian Muslim Bourgeoisie. The Muslim League was characterized as the party of the Indian Muslim Bourgeoisie and not a stooge of the British, as it was being described a short while ago.[21] A way was thus opened, ideologically, for the formula of Congress-League unity and a settlement with the British on the basis of a deal between the two parties who were the supposed standard bearers of the 'National Democratic Revolution'.

As a sequel to this new policy, the CPI instructed the 'Muslim' communists to join the League. Thus Danial Latifi, having just been called to the Bar, was asked to become the office-secretary of the Punjab Muslim League—the 'feudals' in the person of Mian Mumtaz Daulatana held on to the Secretaryship. The change was also apparent at the Aligarh University campus, where as Hamza Alavi informed me, an 'order' came 'from above' 'instructing us to disband the AISF (All India Students Federation) branch at Aligarh. Each one of us was required to join the AIMSF individually. I was outraged by the undemocratic manner in which it was imposed on us without the slightest attempt to engage us in a discussion. I was quite appalled by that dictatorial method. But for that, who knows, I might have even joined the CPI.'

Most fell in line with the 'Adhikari thesis'. The communists have openly come out in the field', reported Jamiluddin Ahmad from Aligarh in early 1943, 'preaching communist doctrines, distributing communist literature and their organ of the People's War, and enrolling members of the League. They have established a regular centre at the house of a professor and some other professors are secretly supporting them.'[33] Jinnah could not figure out why this was so. He expressed his disdain for the communists and exhorted the correspondent to 'face any attempts to disrupt the Aligarh solidarity'. 'I should have thought', he continued, 'Aligarh is not strong, well-knit and organized enough to resist any mischief that may be created against us.'[22]

Jinnah's speech in early November 1942, followed by the League's mobilization drive, sealed the fate of the liberal-left combination on the campus. In October 1944, the Raja of Mahmudabad set up a 'League Camp' at Aligarh, and a year later the *Aligarh Magazine* published a 'Pakistan Number'. Aligarh was chosen as the venue of the seventh AIMSF conference held from 1 to 3 March 1945.[23] An atmosphere of 'mystic frenzy' prevailed.[24] An American student recalled how his fellow-students perceived Pakistan 'as a bright dream, a passionate goal, the vision of a Muslim paradise on earth'. A great many—though not all—shared their fancy.[25]

The much-awaited 1945-46 elections were 'a matter of life and death' for students and faculty members,[26] most of whom poured their 'idealistic zeal into the emotionalism of Pakistan'.[27] They were organized into a cohesive force by Dr. Ziauddin, the Vice-Chancellor, a Wrangler from Cambridge; his deputy A. B. A. (Abba) Haleem; M. A. H. Qadiri, a Cambridge graduate who had built a reputation at the Cavendish Laboratory for his doctoral work; and Manzar-i-Alam, president of the University Muslim League. By 15 November 1945, 650 students were despatched to coaching centres. It was an unforgettable experience for them. For the first time they received lessons on Islam and Islamic history. For the first time they were acquainted with the Pakistan movement's religious background. For the first time they knew what distinguished the League from the Congress.[28] By November 1945, they were sent to canvass in the NWFP, Punjab, United Provinces, Bengal, Sind and Assam. 'Imagine', wrote the University League's President, 'this large number of educated young men celebrating their Id festival in unfamiliar villages and away from their friends and relatives.'[29]

Kalim Siddiqui, then living in his ancestral village in north India and now known as the main spokesman of Muslim fundamentalist groups in England, happily remembered how three young men from the university planted the League flag in the square, how within an hour his quiet village was turned into a 'Pakistan village'. His mother made League flags out of every piece of green material. A few months later his parents along with others walked to the polling booth four miles away, to vote for Pakistan. 'This was repeated all over India. Seldom in history have so few inspired so many with so little effort.'[30] Siddiqui could well have added that never before in South Asian history did so few decide the fate of so many.

Much of what the students said was not specific to Siddiqui's village but in tune with the religio-fundamentalist tenor of the League activity throughout the country. Some talked of the wrongs done by the Congress ministries, of Muslim children being made to sing the *Bande Mataram*, of Hindi's exaltation and the accompanying attack on Urdu, of Muslim exclusion from local bodies and government service, and being hapless victims of communal riots. Some harped on the Wardha and the Vidya Mandir schemes endangering Islamic practices and threatening to destroy the traditional system of Muslim education.

For some, the chief spur was the fear of Hindu domination: Jinnah's 'Two Nation' expressed the 'ideology' of the weaker Muslim 'salariat' *vis-a-vis* the dominant high caste Hindu 'salariat' groups.[31] For others such as Omar Ali Siddiqi, who led the Aligarh contingent in Punjab, the battle lines were drawn between Islam and Hinduism. Raising the spectre of a bloody civil war, reminiscent of the Battle of Karbala, he called upon his audiences to save the imminent destruction of the Muslim nation.[32]

The martyrdom of Imam Husain, the grandson of Prophet Mohammad, was invoked to draw a parallel between the endangered position of Islam in A.D. 680 and its status in contemporary India. The Muslim brethren were asked, as at Allahabad, to defend Islam just as Husain and his seventy-two companions did so on the banks of the Euphrates river. 'We are Indians not Hindus. Our religion, history, traditions, civilization are separate from the Hindus. . . . This is the moment to be inspired by the life of and emulate the example set by Imam Husain. This is the moment to vote for the Muslim League candidates in the provincial elections. This is the time to rescue the *millat* from the clutches of the enemies.'[33]

The entire campaign was coloured by and gathered sustenance from religious symbols and idioms. Shias in general deployed the emotive symbols of martyrdom, associated with Ali, Prophet Mohammad's cousin and son-in-law, and his son, Husain. Sunnis, on the other hand, turned to the more fundamental tenets of Islam for legitimation and rationalization. What was common in both was the portrayal of a besieged and beleaguered community fighting for its right of survival in a world dominated by unfriendly and hostile forces. The movement, starting with Jinnah's Lahore proclamation, rested on the notion of two warring communities, one using its brute majority to suppress the other. 'Islam in Danger' was the war cry, with the guns pointing towards those who opposed the League. They were threatened with hell and damnation and even with exclusion from burial in a Muslim cemetery.[34] Much the same crudity and viciousness marked the RSS and Hindu Mahasabha mobilization techniques. Muslims were not their sole target. They attacked, with equal vehemence, the liberal and secular-minded leaders in the Congress.

The dominant strain of the League campaigns is vividly described in Rahi Masoom Reza's novel *Aadha Gaon* (Half-a-Village). Gangauli village in eastern Uttar Pradesh was the microcosm of what was happening everywhere. What was said there by the motivated Aligarh students was being repeated and echoed all over India. For this reason, their dialogue with the rural folk, parts of which are reproduced here, is most illuminating.

'If Pakistan is not created the eighty million Muslims here will be made, and made to remain, untouchables', said the other [student]. . . .

One of the young men proceeded to deliver a complete speech which Kammo didn't understand in the least because the young man was mentioning matters not one of which had any connection with him or with Gangauli.

'I can't believe all that, *sahib*', said Kammo after listening to the whole speech. 'Why should this Gaya Ahir, this Chikuriya or Lakhna Chamar or this Hariya *Barhai* become our enemies, for no reason, after Hindustan gets free? Is that what you people learn over there [Aligarh].'

'At this moment you may not be able to comprehend this fact, but that is indeed what is going to happen. Cows will be tethered in our mosques [student].'

'*Eh, sahib*, if all the Muslims go to Pakistan, what difference does it make if horses are tied in them or cows? It's not as if Hindus are going to say prayers there. It's a fine old bit of nonsense that we all go to Pakistan and then expect the Hindus to look after our mosques.'

At first the young men [Aligarh students] tried to persuade the peasant in front of them, but then gradually they became angry—and rightfully so. . . . One of them said hotly, 'Very well, but don't you complain when the Hindus come and carry off your mothers and sisters. . . .'[35]

'You must all be aware that at the present time, throughout the country, the Muslims are engaged in a life and death struggle for existence. We live in a country where our position is no more than equivalent to that of salt in *dal*. Once the protective shadow of the British is removed, these Hindus will devour us. That is the reason that Indian Muslims require a place where they will be able to live with honour [student] . . .'

It was a very rousing speech. The brothers in Islam even interrupted from time to time to cry out *Allah-o-Akbar*! As a result, a large section of the traders and weavers decided that they should vote for the League as a religious duty. Haji Ghafoor tried to speak several times but the young men wouldn't allow him the opportunity.

'So you people go ahead and fuck your mothers!', he fumed. In his rage he even forgot that he was in a mosque. The visitors from Aligarh took full advantage of this foul language. Even the men who were wavering became absolutely solid in their conviction.

The Haji *Saheb* stormed out of the mosque. The speech had been quite beyond his comprehension. He didn't even understand why all of a sudden Muslims needed a place of refuge. And where was the protective shadow of the British that these boys had made such a song and dance about? No Englishman had ever been seen in Gangauli. And why then hadn't the Hindus killed the Muslims before the British came to India? And what about the fundamental question—was life and death in the hands of God or the British and Jinnah *Sahib*?

'And we'll still be just weavers. Will the Saiyids start marrying their children to weavers in Pakistan?'[36]

What emerges from this discussion is conflicting perceptions, a sense of impatience and urgency on the part of those who tried to impose their codes on Gangauli and the stout resistance to a discourse that conveyed no real meaning to, say, the Haji *Saheb*. There were many Gangaulis in India, with their Ghafoors and Hajis, where people did not quite understand the logic behind Muslim nationalism. Hindus and Muslims living in harmony and goodwill could not understand the ill-will and hostility that was conveyed through speeches and pamphlets. That is why one can spot so many Gangaulis on India's map where the League's message reached but failed to impress. Indeed, there were many Gangaulis where the enthusiasts from Aligarh encountered bitter opposition in their bid to win over a following.

Gangauli was a bitter pill to swallow. Yet the scale and depth of intervention from Aligarh tilted the balance in the League's favour in a few constituencies. More than 500 students 'saved the honour' of the party in Meerut and 'won laurels' for its candidate, Liaquat Ali Khan, in 'the already lost battles of his constituency'.[37] They also thwarted, so they claimed, 'the Congress-cum-Nationalist intrigues' at various polling stations in rural areas,[38] and surpassed, as *Dawn* of 1 December 1945 commented, 'all expectations by their tireless energy and unflinching courage'. 'I have been following the wonderful work that the Aligarh boys have done', he wrote. 'You have proved what I said, that Aligarh is the arsenal of Muslim India'.[39]

Some on the Aligarh campus challenged the underpinnings of the League ideology and tried in vain to counter its activities. Their protests were drowned by the thunderous applause with which Jinnah was greeted during his frequent forays into Aligarh. Their criticism was blunted by the more vociferous League spokesman in the teaching faculty. In effect, Aligarh pronounced in favour of political separatism and an independent 'Muslim personality', divorced from its history, culture, and traditions. Most voted for a traditionalist-fundamentalist theocracy, an imaginary haven for Muslims.

The decision was fraught with serious consequences for a premier educational institution, as also for the future of Indian Islam. But then, who could explain to the students and teachers that their fears were exaggerated and that their fanciful theories rested on questionable assumptions? There was a time when liberal, socialist and anticolonial sentiments had gripped the campus. Photographs of Mustafa Kemal, hero of Turkish revolution, Jawaharlal Nehru, Marx and Lenin formed a part of the ideological furniture of hostel rooms. There had been a time when people had turned to an Ajmal Khan or Ansari for political inspiration, but no longer. Public life lacked men of such charisma, stature and political sagacity. How, then, were the Aligarh students to know that religious fervour was blurring their vision, that for the millions who would need to stay behind in India, Pakistan would divide families and friends and destroy the sociocultural fabric built over centuries of close relationships.[40]

Some League activists in Aligarh and elsewhere discovered, belatedly, that all that glitters is not gold, that the architects of Pakistan had different ideas and that a modern nation-state could not be modelled on medieval theocracy or run on strictly religious lines.[41] Confronted with Muslim rioting and the appalling misery of innocent people, they sought to argue that religio-political conflicts, howsoever endemic they might have appeared in the India of the 1940s, should be resolved through means other than seccession, separation or partition. But it was too late to change the course of events. Great numbers of people had already set out on the dangerously long trek to the imagined *dar al-Islam*. Many had already lost their lives before reaching their destination.

Kammo, Haji Ghaffoor Ansari and Phunnan *Miyan* in Gangauli village had sensed the impending danger long before. The Haji had exhorted the Aligarh boys: 'No *Miyan*, I'm an illiterate peasant. But I think there's not the slightest need to make Pakistan-*Akistan* for the sake of our prayers. Lord God Almighty said quite clearly, "*Eh*, my Prophet. Tell these people that I am with people of the Faith." And someone was saying that this Jinnah of yours doesn't say his prayers.'[42] Phunnan Miyan shared these words of wisdom, adding: 'Is there true Islam anywhere that you can have an Islamic government? *Eh, bhai* (brother), our forefathers' graves are here, our *tazia* platforms are here, our fields and homes are here. I'm not an idiot to be taken in by your 'Long live Pakistan'. '... You're talking as if all the Hindus were murderers waiting to slaughter us. *Arre*, Thakur Kunwarpal Singh was a Hindu. Jhinguriya is a Hindu. *Eh, bhai*, and isn't that Parusaram-*va* a Hindu? When the Sunnis in the town started doing *haramzadgi* (behaving like a bastard), saying that we won't let the bier of Hazrat Ali be carried in procession because the Shias curse our Caliphs, didn't Parusaram-*va* come and raise such hell that the bier was carried? Your Jinnah-*Sahib* didn't come to help us lift our bier.[43]

II

Individual or collective experience can be drawn upon to comment on the *meanings* of Pakistan and what it *symbolized* to different people at different historical conjunctures. The political and religious drive behind the Muslim League movement has been discussed at length. In this section are highlighted the sensitivities of large numbers of people (give them any name or description; I have preferred not to), their sense of hurt, anger, indignation and despair. The variety of perceptions and the several different *meanings* attached to 'nation', 'nationalism', and 'community' are obliquely commented upon. The resource persons relied upon are not 'major' actors in public life; they are not even 'minor' players by conventional political standards. Some are creative writers and poets, many of whom enjoyed fame and reputation but carried no weight in influencing the course of events. Some are passive but interested observers. Some represent the elites, but most are 'ordinary' folks, whose fortunes and destinies were changed without taking into account their feelings and interests. They speak in different voices, express varying concerns and choose separate and distinct points of identification. But there is a thematic unity, a point of convergence as well, a link that binds their seemingly dissimilar discourse. A common discourse is there, waiting to be discovered and underlined.

At a conference held in London in 1967, M.A.H.Ispahani boasted how, after achieving their homeland, Muslims received 'all the encouragement and opportunity to pull themselves up by the bootstraps and they did'. After listing their achievements in industry, banking and insurance, he concluded:

> The Hindu *bania* and the foreigner are no longer in a position to monopolize our economic life, and this is the fruit of the freedom which we won in the form of our separate state. Muslims, having been afforded the opportunity, have fully availed themselves of it and proved their worth. They have also given the lie to the notion that had been spread by hostile elements that Pakistan would not prove to be economically viable. Need I say anything more?[44]

Yes, Mr Ispahani, those directly affected by partition had a lot more to say. It is no doubt true that tangible material benefits accrued to some of the migrants, chiefly from among the 2 million Urdu-speaking refugees (still categorized as *muhajirs*) from UP and Bihar, many of whom monopolized the army, civil service and the professions. The grand bourgeoisie of West Pakistan, originally from Gujarat and Maharasthra, reaped the rewards of supporting the Pakistan demand. People like Habib Ibrahim Rahimtoola, president of the Bombay provincial Muslim Chamber of Commerce, and Ispahani himself, director of his own and other companies, held key diplomatic positions in London and Washington. The great landlords of Punjab and Sind also flourished. Their jealously guarded estates remained intact; in fact, in accordance with the 1950 Act passed in West Punjab, a tenant could be ejected if found guilty of reading out at a public or private meeting the Punjab Muslim League Manifesto of 1944, drafted by Danial Latifi and others. The draft was blasphemous because it advocated land reforms.[45] The nexus of the landowners with the bureaucratic and military establishment enabled them to retain their hegemony in the countryside.

It would be simple enough if the Pakistan story began or ended with the improved fortunes of certain individuals and groups. But that is not so. One must record the immediate and long-term impact on the silent majority, uprooted from home and field and driven by sheer fear of death to seek safety across a line they had neither drawn nor desired. They speak loud and clear through Saadat Hasan Manto's characters.[46] They convey to us how blissfully unaware they were of the deals taking place in Delhi, of Mountbatten's ultimatum that if he did not hear from Jinnah by midnight the Partition Plan would come into effect *in any case*. Fourteen hours to decide the destiny of a nation!

There must also be a place for the harrowing experiences of countless Zahids who boarded the train that would take them to the realization of their dreams, but of whom not a man, woman or child survived the journey.[47] The narrative must also incorporate the symbolic significance of the crumbling houses in Hasanpur or Gangauli. *Havelis* collapsed and occupants went away, but memories lingered—as also did the sense of loss and deprivation. Those who left were part of the *biradari*; their absence was bemoaned not by one or the other denominational group but by the whole community. The passing of an era did not change everything everywhere. Take Hasanpur: the shadow of litigation to abolish landlordism hung over the estate, yet it did not dampen the enthusiasm of the rural people to welcome those who chose to return to their villages after partition. 'It seemed time had not really moved towards the inevitable end.'[48]

The Pakistan story has many facets, but it is surely incomplete without the anguish of those devotees who thought that destiny was taking them far away from the shrines of Nizamuddin Auliya or Muinuddin Chishti—important symbols of a specifically Indian Muslim culture—the *dargahs* of Rudauli, Kakori, Bansa Sharif and Dewa Sharif, the great *imambaras* of Lucknow, Jaunpur and Matiya Burj, and the sites of pilgrimage dotted on India's map. Pakistan would no doubt have its share of mosques, *imambaras* and *dargahs*, but there was no shrine more sacred than that of *Gharib-Nawaz* in Ajmer, nor counterparts to the splendid *imambaras* of Lucknow, symbolizing the high noon of Nawabi rule in Awadh. The pilgrims knew this; year after year they approached the Indian and Pakistani governments for permission to attend the annual congregation (*urs*) at the shrines of venerable Chishti saints buried in Delhi, Fatehpur Sikri and Ajmer. Between 1955 and February 1959, at least 3,973 'officially-sponsored' individuals performed pilgrimage. Many more came on their own, including 3,925 devotees who travelled to the shrine at Ajmer in 1958-9. Pakistan's existence had not lessened their devotion.

One of Rahi Masoom Reza's characters is Saddan, who migrated to Pakistan. But he still claimed to be the same Syed Saadatul Hasnain Zaidi of Gangauli. How could Gangauli be another country! 'All these faces, plants and trees, these ponds and these indigo godown, these *imambaras* and *tazias* [replicas of Husain's tomb] ... and this Karbala, and these bundles of *marsiyas* [elegies] wrapped in red cloth, lying on pulpits ... all these things could only belong to his own village.' In Pakistan he would miss the *majalis* [Shia congregations during the month of Muharram] of Abbu Miyan and Maulvi Bedar in Gangauli, remember Husain Haidar Miyan's *soz* [dirges] recitations and Masshu-*bhai*'s *nauhas* [a short chanted lament accompanied by breast-beating]. "These memories were of no particular importance, they were extremely foolish memories, but still Saddan embraced each one of them again and again and wept. He yearned for Gangauli ...."

One must also not consciously neglect, like most standard histories of partition, the woes of divided families, the deepening nostalgia for places people lived in for generations and forcibly abandoned, the misery of parting from friends and neighbours. Abdul Qaiyum, who quit the Congress to join the League in 1945, was touched by the sight of friends departing with their families and their moveable property, from a land where they had lived for generations and to which they were devoted. He was distressed to bid farewell to friends with whom he worked for years.[49]

Tears began to flow, wrote a distraught eye-witness of the killings in east Bengal during 1946-7, when she realized that

> ....the part of Bengal which had been my home was no longer my home. It was a foreign land and I was not very safe in those difficult days. [...] I was more angry than sorry and vowed never to enter the country and see the people who tore me away from my home. The underlying feeling was that we were being driven from our own country. Bengalis are first and foremost Bengalis—then Indian. We were angry with both Nehru and Jinnah for not handling the situation properly.[50]

Mussarat Husain Zuberi, senior civil servant in the communications ministry, was not angry but deeply anguished:

> As I was leaving Delhi with its centuries-old hallowed memories of Muslim triumphs, its agonized shameless defeats and dishonour are the phoenix-like birth from its ashes of a new Muslim dominion...I decided to pay a farewell visit to the monuments which enshrined the souls and bodies of those who had marched under their own banner to make us at least a shadow of theirs. They were part of me, my inherited leanings, my history, my culture, part of being known and unknown, conscious and visible

Manto went to Pakistan in January 1948. He was filled with sorrow when he left Bombay, where he had spent much of his working life. He was not tied to the city for historical, cultural or intellectual reasons, but deeply attached to it because it 'had asked me no questions. It had taken me to its generous bosom, me, a man rejected by his family, a gypsy by temperament.' His Hindu and Muslim friends lived in Bombay and encouraged his creative genius. He earned from a few hundred to several thousands rupees—and spent it all. He married in Bombay. His first two children were born there. 'I was in love with Bombay. I still am.'[5] Manto's agony or *karb* and sense of loss troubled the family of Dwarkada Prasad, uncle of Prakash Tandon:

As dawn was breaking, they caught the last view of Gujrat through the *shisham* trees by the road; a view they had so often seen when going to the river Chenab at Besakhi. They looked at the weathered dark brown mass of the city rising as a flat-top cone. My aunt's ancestral house was in the highest *mohalla* inside the fortress, and she could see almost the spot where twenty-seven years ago her palanquin had descended the narrow lanes to our old house inside the Kalri Gate. She wondered what would happen to her house, to her cupboards and trunks full of clothes, linen and utensils, and above all to the buffalo and its calf that she had left tied in the yard. [...] As the truck passed the barrier into 'India', they looked back at Pakistan, their homeland which did not want them.

Today we have no one left in Gujrat. All the Hindus came away at partition. It is strange to think that in all the land between Ravi and Chenab, from Chenab to Jhelum, from Jhelum to Indus, in the foothills and in the plain down to Punjab, where the five rivers eventually merge, land which had been the home of our *biradaris* since the dawn of history, there is no one left of our kinds.[52]

The first generation of Urdu poets and writers, many of whom performed the *hijrat* from UP and Bihar, raised a wide range of issues.[72] To which country did they belong? Where did their cultural roots lie? Was their newly-acquired nationality more vital than their larger identity as a civilization? What would be the cultural symbols of their new identity? Should they take pride in their language, their religion or their regional identity? How would they strike a symbiotic balance between contending identities in a society where religious sensitivity was so greatly heightened by the Pakistan movement? What were their links with their erstwhile homeland? Were these to be severed or renewed after the Indian and Pakistani governments had resolved their differences?

There were no straightforward answers. There were just a few preliminary explorations. Compare the poet Josh Malihabadi's autobiographical reflections with some other contemporary writings. He lived in Lucknow, edited the Urdu journal *Ajkal* (1948-55) in Delhi, and left for Pakistan in 1956 against the advice of his numerous friends and admirers, including Jawaharlal Nehru and Abul Kalam Azad.[73] Compare, too, Qurratulain Haider's short novel *Housing Society* with Mohammad Ahsan Faruqi's novel *Sangam*

(Confluence).⁵⁴ Or her first novel *Mere bhi Sanam Khane* with the works of Intizar Husain, perhaps the most perceptive creative writer of Pakistan.⁵⁵

Mere bhi Sanam Khane, published in 1947, portrays how the sparks of partition blew up the pathways of a composite culture, leaving a yawning gap of burning dust. Intizar Husain's story *Ek bin-likhi Razmiya* (An Unwritten Epic), on the other hand, succeeds in gathering a whole era within its fold by presenting partition and Hindu-Muslim violence against a 'fair-sized social and political backdrop'.⁵⁶ Some of his other works reflect the way an onging cultural process was stalled in 'a very unnatural way' by a few Muslims and Hindus who, with their puritan frame of mind, contributed to the tragedy that afflicted the subcontinent.

What, according to Intizar Husain, was the cultural process all about? For one, it was not denominational. The 'Indian-Muslim culture' did not bear a religious stamp. It had its own unique history and individuality, and was, above all, distinctively *Indian* and refreshingly different from the cultural mores and paradigms of Muslim countries. Intizar Husain is proud of being a product of such a cultural tradition, one 'which has shaped the history of which I am a part'. Muslims came to Hindustan and formed close and indissoluble ties with its soil. 'Indian Muslim culture is that creative amalgam which came about in response to the intellectual and emotional climate that was here ... the feel of its seasons ... these ties with the land. Much in it is Indian and much was brought from outside.'⁵⁷

Cultural alienation, combined with nostalgia, also struck 'A Muslim' from Delhi who migrated to Dhaka, 'a strange land'. He wrote to a Lucknawi friend that he joined the Pakistan civil service not because of religio-communal considerations but because of Hindu-Muslim rioting in his locality. But he wondered, in retrospect, if it made sense to live in Dhaka amid people with whom he had so little in common and whose manners, customs, language, culture, diet and dress were 'totally different from ours'. He was perturbed that non-Bengalis were shabbily treated by their own co-religionists as intruders and exploiters. Most Bengalis believed that the Punjabi had 'stepped into the shoes of the outgoing masters'.⁵⁸

Living in Karachi, Mohammad Ahsan Faruqi captures the same mood and in *Sangam* sums up the dilemma of those *muhajirin* who migrated to Pakistan from northern, central and western parts of

India. He wonders how a country created for the Muslims could be so hostile to the *muhajirin*. Ibn Muslim, the central character in the novel, is attracted to Pakistan by the dream of Islamic brotherhood which he sees in Iqbal's poetry and in the actions of Jinnah. But his enthusiasm is dampened when he and others like him are treated as intruders, as aliens, whom 'everyone is bent upon swallowing'. 'The Quaid-i-Azam died and so did his party. And now there is a dispute between the English and Islamic concepts of the nation, and it is we who are the sufferers.'[59]

The *muhajirin* were drawn from diverse socioeconomic backgrounds. Their experiences in Pakistan were mixed. Some achieved high levels of affluence the fortunes of others did not change so dramatically—yet they all had a common refrain in their daily conversations, in mosques, *dargahs* and *imambaras*, the undying memories of their homeland and the consequent nostalgia. This was true of the troubled correspondent from Dhaka, the bureaucrat in the communications ministry, the writer Faruqi and the novelist Ahmed Ali,[60] who made this poignant comment:

> Seldom is one allowed to see a pageant of history whirl past, and partake in it too. Ever since becoming the capital in the early thirteenth century, imbibing knowledge and ideas and imparting cultures, becoming homogenous and cosmopolitan in spite of the origins and ethnicity of its rulers and inhabitants, it [Delhi] had remained the embodiment of a whole culture, free of the creedal ghosts and apparitions that haunt some of modern India's critics and bibliographers chased by the dead souls of biased historians of yesterday.[61]

Ahmed Ali could not return to Delhi from Nanking where he was on a deputation from the government of undivided India. He thus concluded an interview on a highly melancholy note. The poet he cited was the irrepressible Mir Taqi Mir (1772-1849), one of the great love poets of world literature:

> What matters it, O breeze,
> If now has come the spring
> When I have lost them both
> The garden and my nest?[62]

Ahmed Ali did not return to the land he loved, and died in 1994.

For the gentlemen living in Dhaka or Karachi the cultural journey from Delhi was disconcerting. But for the millions in India and Pakistan the professed ideology of nation-state itself had no great relevance or immediacy. Take the Muslim weavers of Panipat. They were not fascinated by Pakistan, which they neither understood nor approved of, except as a remote place where Muslims would go, as on a pilgrimage. On the other hand, the few white-collar government employees left hoping to secure rapid promotions but not to set up permanent homes there.[63] Did it really matter to the Mymensingh peasants and the Kanpur mill-workers whether they were to be physically located in 'India' or in 'Pakistan'? What of the employees of the East India Railway in Kanpur who, having opted for Pakistan, subsequently changed their minds.[64] Or the 8,000 government servants who, having provisionally opted for Pakistan, finally returned to their homes in India in March 1949.[65] Or Yaqub Ali, an assistant-engineer in Nadia district? He would not have left but for the fact that his family was 'eyed in silent menace' by his Hindu neighbours. So when politicians in Lutyen's Delhi resolved to partition India and Bengal, Yaqub collected 300 rupees, boarded the train to Calcutta to buy air tickets, and retuned to Dhaka to fetch his family and his possession.[66]

Most people, Hindus, Muslims and Sikhs alike, were largely unconcerned with the newly-created geographical entities or indifferent to them. They were needlessly caught up in the cross-fire of religious hatred. Some were driven out of their homes; others drifted from one place to another out of fear, panic and a sense of hopelessness. Most were hapless victims of a triangular game plan, worked out by the British, the Congress and the League without care or consideration for a vast number of people who were committed neither to a Hindu homeland nor to an imaginary *dar-al-Islam*. They had no destination to reach, no mirage to pursue. They were unclear whether Lahore or Gurdaspur would be in India or Pakistan. This was the unmistakable message in Bhisham Sahni's story. They did not know whether Gangauli or Hasanpur would remain in Gandhi's India or Jinnah's Pakistan.

In fact, 'India' and 'Pakistan' were mere territorial abstractions to people who had no sense of the newly-demarcated frontiers, and little or no knowledge of how Mountbatten's Plan or the Radcliffe

Award would change the destinies of millions and tear them apart from their familiar social and cultural moorings. 'The English have flung away their Raj like a bundle of old straw', an angry peasant told Malcolm Darling, 'and we have been chopped in pieces like butcher's meat.[67] This was a telling comment by a 'subaltern' on the meaning attached to the Pakistan movement.

Imagine the plight of Hindus and Muslims in Malda district. Between 12 and 15 August 1947 it was unclear where it would finally go to East Pakistan or to India. Till 14 August the Pakistan flag fluttered over the collectorate, but three days later the district, now reduced to ten pre-partition *thanas*, went to India. It pleased Asok Mitra, the newly-appointed district magistrate, to discover that very few of the Muslim staff in the collectorate had opted for Pakistan.

We are told that in those days of inglorious uncertainties the rank and file of the League hoped against hope for a last-minute confederation or a Congress-League agreement that would rule out the division of the country.[69] Whether this is true or not, expectation of what partition would be were curiously mixed. Some longed for Lahore's inclusion in India; others wished that the partition line in Punjab would be drawn below Delhi. 'For millions of people like myself', wrote Begum Shaista Ikramullah, to whom Delhi was synonymous with Muslim culture, 'a Pakistan without Delhi was a body without heart.'[70] She 'never even dreamt' that she would have to leave the city which she loved in its every mood. The frontiers of Pakistan had not been defined and it never occurred to her that Delhi would not be included within it:

> How sure we were that Delhi was ours and would come to us can best be illustrated by this incident. We were having a picnic on the terrace at Humayun's tomb when my sister-in-law remarked: 'Do you think you will get Delhi if Pakistan is established?' My husband replied pointing to the domed and turreted skyline of Delhi: 'Look at it—whom do you think it seems to belong to?' and Dina could not deny that the essentially Muslim character of its architecture seemed to proclaim that Delhi belonged to the Muslims. And so it did, in every way, except population. No, that is not true, even by counting the heads it would have been ours, had the dividing line come below and not above Delhi. But by dividing Punjab,

our overall majority was lost, so we lost Delhi. And today its mosques and minarets join the minarets and mosques of Cordova and Grenada in saying: The descendants of Arabs, they were, those who created me. I stand here, a memorial to their vanished glory.[71]

Pakistan was won, but people on both sides of the fence were tormented by gruesome killings, by the irreparable loss of friends and families and by the scale and magnitude of an epic tragedy. There were memories on both sides of living in close proximity with friends and neighbours, of a shared cultural and intellectual heritage, and of fighting together for independence and raising the banner of revolt against colonial rule. The birth of Pakistan, a prized trophy for some, destroyed Iqbal's melodious lyric of syncretic nationalism—*Naya Shivala* [New Temple], once the ideal of patriots and freedom-fighters. It severed or fragmented cultural ties and undermined a vibrant, composite intellectual tradition. The birth of freedom on that elevated day—14 August for Pakistan and 15 August for India—'did not bring India any such ennobling benediction. On the contrary, the country was shaken by a volcanic eruption.'[72] There was not much to celebrate at the fateful midnight hour or at the dawn of independence.

> This is not that long-looked-for break of day
> Not that clear dawn in quest of which those comrades
> Set out, believing that in heaven's wide void
> Somewhere must be the star's last halting place
> Somewhere the verge of night's slow-washing tide,
> Somewhere an anchorage for the ship of heartache.[73]

The Raja of Mahmudabad, who had devoted many years fighting for his 'Islamic state', was an unhappy man. He recalled 'the general sense of gloom and despondency that pervaded the two newly-created nation states. Instead of the joy and expectancy which should have been ours after these years of struggle there were only premonitions of impending conflicts and a promise of future struggle.'[74] The Raja hurried to Pakistan, leaving behind vast estates, his wife the Rani of Billhera, his young son, and his dear brother Maharajkumar Mohammad Amir Hyder Khan. The *Baradari* in Qaiser Bagh, where his father had hosted the Lucknow Congress in December 1916, was still there to remind citizens of its nationalist associations. But the Mahmudabad House nearby, with dusty portraits of Motilal Nehru, Tej Bahadur Sapru and Sarojini Naidu, looked desolate. The beautiful but crumbling fort and *imambaras* at Mahmudabad in Sitapur district were mostly abandoned. They came alive only during the ten days of Muharram, when the Raja's son, brother and his family travelled to Mahmudabad to mourn the martyrdom of Imam Husain.

For Intizar Husain partition was 'a complex and convoluted human tragedy'. He tried to comprehend, in the light of India's rich ancient and medieval history, how the 'new man—cruel, violent and ruthless—appeared on the scene in 1947. 'How and why did this occur? What historical process gave rise to it? And what has happened to that history which, for example, had produced the Buddha? What new era of history had ushered in? Or is it that mankind is such a creature who can build a movement over centuries, can construct diverse philosophies, but when the crisis comes, when some critical moment occurs, his animal emerges from within to overwhelm him?'[75] Many of his stories reflect isolation, uncertainty, deprivation, grief, and a sense of being cut off from a better and richer past—just the kind of experience, in short, that partition might be expected to create.[76]

Jameel Jalibi, a former vice-chancellor of Karachi University, lamented how the Indo-Muslim cultural heritage, the pride of the *muhajirin*, had ended at the Wagah border and how access to it was controlled by passports and visas. 'This is where our national tragedy begins'. He argued: 'We cannot afford to commit the error of excluding from our cultural history the cultural heritage that has accrued to us as the accumulation of a thousand years of Indo-Muslim culture. Can we be daring enough to begin our new history with 1947 as a turning point where we turned our back on this heritage because of geographical demarcation and a new-born sense of statehood?'[77] Ahmed Ali, who 'never opted for Pakistan', identified himself with the civilization of Delhi that came into being through the mingling of two different cultures, Hindu and Muslim. 'That civilization flourished for one thousand years undisturbed until certain people came along and denied that great mingling had taken place.'[78] His poignant introductory comment in his novel, which was edited and blotted out because it was based in Delhi, the 'forbidden' city across the border, sums up the predicament of a generation which was decidedly unsure of its cultural and intellectual moorings.[79]

So which country did Ahmed Ali, Attia Hosain, Faiz, Josh, Sajjad Zaheer or Manto belong to? India or Pakistan? Manto for one tried in vain to 'separate India from Pakistan and Pakistan from India'. He asked himself: 'Will Pakistani literature be different—and if so, how? To whom will now belong what had been written in undivided India? Will that be partitioned too?' He continued:

> What my mind could not resolve was the question: what country do we belong to now, India or Pakistan? And whose blood was it that was being so mercilessly shed every day? And the bones of the dead, stripped of the flesh of religion, were they being burned or buried? [...]
> Everyone seemed to be regressing. Only death and carnage seemed to be proceeding ahead. A terrible chapter of blood and tears was being added to history, a chapter without precedent. India was free. Pakistan was free from the moment of its birth, but in both states man's enslavement continued: by prejudice, by religious fanaticism, by savagery.

The uppermost question in Manto's mind was: 'Were we really free?' Both Hindus and Muslims were being slaughtered. Why? There were different answers: the Indian answer, the Pakistani answer, the British answer. Surely 'every question had an answer, but when you tried to unravel the truth, you were left groping.'[80] And there was no answer.

Manto's postcript on a colossal human tragedy must not be overlooked, for his anguish and dilemma were not of an individual alone but shared by the silent majority on both sides of the fence, including those 1,000 persons who, after eighteen months of separation, met at the Husainiwala customs barrier in February 1949. They did not pull out daggers and swords but 'affectionately greeted and embraced one another with tears rolling down their cheeks'.[81] Their sentiments can neither be reflected in the elegant exchanges between the viceroy and secretary of state nor in the unlovely confabulations between the Congress and the League managers.

III

Aaj Shabbir pe kya alam-i tanhai hai
(Mir Anis: 1802-1875)

'What a world of loneliness lies upon Shabbir [Imam Husain] this day! Everyone who heard these words in Gangauli started crying and lamenting. They did so to mourn Imam Husain's martyrdom in Karbala centuries ago, but also because 'the cut umbilical cord of Pakistan was around their necks like a noose, and they were all suffocating.' Now they knew what 'a world of loneliness' meant! Life was not the same any more with friends and relatives across the border. People were worried about their kith and kin. They were alone and depressed throughout the day. And the nights became intolerable. 'There was a desire to dream, but what was there safe to dream about?' The atmosphere was foul and murky all around. It was such that 'the blood of one's veins was wandering hopelessly in Pakistan, and the relationships and mutual affections and friendships ... were breaking, and in place of confidence, a fear and deep suspicion was growing in people's heart'.

In short independence and partition brought varied moods of loneliness. Every individual in Gangauli had found himself suddenly alone. All of them turned, just as they did every day of their existence, to Husain and his seventy-two companions for strength, confidence and spiritual comfort.

NOTES

1. Abdullah Yusuf Ali and Zafarullah Khan, quoted in K. K. Aziz, *Rehmat Ali: A Biography* (Lahore: Vanguard, 1987), pp. 93-4.

2. W. C. Smith, *Modern Islam in India: A Social Analysis* (Lahore: Minerva Books, 1943), p. 312. Humayun Kabir, *Muslim Politics 1906-42* (Calcutta: Gupta Rahman and Gupta, 1944), pp. 26-7.

3. Ashraf in Horst Kruger (ed.), *Kunwar Mohammad Ashraf: An Indian Scholar and Revolutionary, 1903-1962* (Berlin: Akademie-Verlag, 1966), p. 414.

4. R. W. Sorenson, *My Impression of India* (London: Meridian Books, 1946), p. 109.

5. J. D. Tyson to Folk, 17 November 1946, Mss. Eur., file no. E 341/41, Tyson papers, India Office Library, (IOL), London.

6. Sorenson, op. cit., p. 111.

7. Malcolm Lyall Darling, *At Freedom's Dawn* (London: Oxford University Press, 1949), p. 299.

8. To Jinnah, 8 February 1946, UP, vol. v, Shamsul Hasan Collection (SHC), Karachi.

9. Inspection Report, 26 February 1945, Committee for Action, 1945, vol. 201, part 1, Freedom Movement Archives (FMA), University of Karachi, Karachi.

10. Darling, op. cit., pp. 302-3.

11. Sarah F. D. Ansari, *Sufi Saints and State Power: The Pirs of Sind, 1843-1947* (Cambridge: University Press, 1992), pp.118-20.

12. Honorary Secretary, Sind Provincial League, to Liaquat Ali Khan, 6 November 1943, Box no. 31, FMA.

13. In one contest the local *pir*, with a fine impartiality, preached in favour of the League at one end of the constituency and for the Unionist Party at the other. Darling, op. cit., p. 85.

14. Box no. 31, FMA.

15. Inspection Report, 29 March 1949, Committee for Action, 1945, vol. 201, part 1, FMA.

16. Fortnightly report (FR), first half of September 1940, Mss. Eur., file no. 164/6, R.F. Mudie papers, IOL.

17. M. Saleem Jan to Jinnah, 21 August 1945, correspondence general, UP., vol. 1, SHC.

18. Patrick Biggie papers, Centre for South Asian Studies, Cambridge (CSAS).

19. Diaries, 10 June 1939, Mss Eur., file no. E. 255/14, Harold Charles Mitchell papers, IOL. He was Superintendent of Police, Kanpur, from 1938 to 1939.

20. Scrapbook (Kanpur), ibid; *Pioneer*, 21 May 1939; FR, second half of April 1941, Mudie papers, IOL.

21. P. C. Joshi, in his policy statement of February 1942, referred to the League as an emerging 'mass party'. Quoted in Gene Overstreet and Marshall Windmiller, *Communism in India* (Berkeley: California University Press, 1960), p. 201.

22. Jinnah to Jamiluddin Ahmad, 9 January 1943, Aligarh file, SHC.

23. Mushirul Hasan, 'Nationalist and Separatist Trends in Aligarh 1920-1947', in A. K. Gupta (ed.), *Myth and Reality: The Struggle for Freedom in India 1945-47* (Delhi: Vikas, 1987).

24. Smith, *Modern Islam in India*, pp. 181-2.

25. Philips Talbot, 'I am a Pakistani', 28 November 1956, Ian Stephens Papers, CSAS.

26. Iqbal Masud to Jinnah, 24 September 1945; M.A. Humayun to Jinnah, 16 August 1945, SHC.
27. Smith, *Modern Islam in India*, pp. 181-2.
28. Ziauddin Ahmad to Jinnah, 29/31 October 1945, vol. 5, SHC; Manzar-i-Alam to Q. M. Isa, 15 November 1945, vol. 237, FMA; Hasan, 'Nationalist and Separatist Trends in Aligarh', op. cit., p. 131, and f.n. 93-4, p. 140.
29. Manzar-i-Alam to Q. M. Isa, 19 November 1945, vol. 237, FMA.
30. Kalim Siddiqui, *Conflict and War in Pakistan* (London: Publishing House, 1972), pp. 50-1.
31. Hamza Alavi, 'Pakistan and Islam: Ethnicity and Ideology', Fred Halliday and Hamza Alavi (eds.), *State and the Ideology in the Middle East and Pakistan* (London: Macmillan, 1987), pp. 68-70.
32. *Dawn*, 19 December 1945.
33. Dr Najmuddin Jafri, *Suniye Hazrat Imam Husain kya dars dete hai* (Pay heed to Imam Husain's Message), box no. 151, FMA.
34. Darling, op. cit., p. 86.
35. Rahi Masoom Reza, *The Feuding Families of Village Gangauli*. Translated from the Hindi by Gillian Wright (Delhi: Viking, 1994), p. 238. I am grateful to the translator and the publisher for permission to reproduce excerpts from the book.
36. Ibid., p. 241.
37. Ahmad Faziel to Jinnah, 2 December 1945, SHC; Begum Shaista S. Ikramullah, *Huseyn Shaheed Suhrawardy* (Karachi: Oxford University Press, 1991), pp. 46-7.
38. Manzar-i-Alam to Q. M. Isa, 4 December 1945, vol. 237, FMA.
39. Jinnah to Zahid Husain, 5 December 1945, SHC.
40. Jameel Jalibi, *Pakistan: The Identity of Culture* (Delhi: Alpha & Alpha, reprint, n.d.).
41. Jahanara Shah Nawaz, *Father and Daughter: A Political Biography* (Lahore: Nigar-i-shaat, 1971), pp. 301-2.
42. Rahi Masoom Reza, op. cit., p. 240.
43. Ibid., p. 149.
44. M. A. H. Ispahani, 'Factors Leading to the Partition of India', in C. H. Philips and M. D. Wainwright (eds.), *The Partition of India: Policies and Perspectives 1935-1937* (London: Allen & Unwin, 1970), p. 39; see also, Firoz Khan Noon, *From Memory* (Lahore: Feroze Sons, 1969), p. 216.
45. Ibid., Chapter 7; Stanley Kochanek, *Interest Groups and*

Development: Business and Politics in Pakistan, (Delhi: Oxford University Press, 1983).

46. *Another Lonely Voice: The Life and Works of Saadat Hasan Manto*. Introduction by Leslie A. Fleming (Lahore: Vanguard, 1985), pp. 77-86.

47. Attia Hosain, *Sunlight on a Broken Column* (Delhi: Penguin Books, 1992).

48. Ibid., p. 299.

49. Abdul Qaiyum Khan, 'Reflections on Some of the Causes of the Partition of the Indo-Pakistan Subcontinent', in Philips and Wainwright (eds.), *Partition of India*, p. 380.

50. 'The Memsahib I could never be', H. Ghoshal papers, CSAS.

51. Saadat Hasan Manto, 'Not of Blessed Memory', *Annual of Urdu Studies*, 4, 1984, pp. 88-9.

52. Prakash Tandon, *Punjab Century, 1985-1947* (London: Chatto and Windus, 1961), pp. 246-7, 249.

53. Josh Malihabadi, *Yadon ki Baraat* (Delhi: Shaan-i Hind Publishers, 1992, enlarged edition).

54. Qurratulain Hyder, *Patjhar ki Aawaaz* (Delhi: Maktaba-i Jamia, 1965).

55. Muhammad Umar Memon, 'Partition Literature: A Study of Intizar Husain', *Modern Asian Studies*, 14, 3, 1990, p. 377.

56. Ibid., pp. 402-3; and Intizar Husain, 'A Letter from India', in Alok Bhalla (ed.), *Stories About the Partition of India*, vol. 1 (Delhi: Indus Publishers, 1994).

57. Intizar Husain, Interview, *Journal of South Asian Literature*, vol. 18, no. 2, summer/fall 1983, p. 167.

58. *Hindustan Times*, 19 September 1947.

59. Munibur Rahman, 'Political Novels in India', *Contributions to Asian Studies*, vol. 6, 1989, p.150.

60. 'Seldom is one allowed to see a pageant of history whirl past, and partake in it too. Ever since becoming the capital in the early thirteenth century, imbibing knowledge and ideas and imparting cultures, becoming homogeneous and cosmopolitan in spite of the origins and ethnicity of its rulers and inhabitants, it [Delhi] had remained the embodiment of a whole culture, free of the creedal ghosts and apparitions that haunt some of modern India's critics and bibliographers chased by the dead souls of biased historians of yesterday. Enmeshed in the prejudices of ruled and rulers, they gainsay by the very nature of their studied silence, his rightful place to the author among his contemporaries; and in their self-seeking

separateness deny the city of the novel its Indianness and wider cultural view and representational character, against the verdict of history.' *Twilight in Delhi* (Delhi: Oxford University Press, 1991). p. viii.

61. Ralph Russell and Khurshidul Islam, *Three Mughal Poets: Mir, Mir Sauda, Mir Hasan* (London: George Allen and Unwin, 1969), p. 260.

62. William Dalrymple, *City of Djinns: A Year in Delhi* (Delhi: Harper-Collins, 1993), p. 65.

63. Khwaja Ahmad Abbas, *I am not an Island: An Experiment in Autobiography* (Delhi: Vikas, 1977), p. 295.

64. *Hindustan Times*, 8 October 1947.

65. Nehru's note to Minister of Home Affairs, 16 March 1948, S. Gopal (ed.), *Selected Works of Jawaharlal Nehru*, second series, vol. 5 p. 459.

66. Diary, p. 2, Mss. Eur., file no. C/188/8, A.J. Dash papers, IOL.

67. Darling, op. cit., p. 307.

68. Asok Mitra, *The New India 1948-1955: Memories of an Indian Civil Servant* (Bombay: Popular Prakashan, 1991), p. 2.

69. Ikramullah, *Huseyn Shaheed Suhrawardy*, p. 51.

70. Ibid., p. 59.

71. Begum Shaista S. Ikramullah, *From Purdah to Parliament* (London: The Crescent Press, 1963), pp. 135-6.

72. Kamaladevi Chattopadhyay, *Inner Recesses Outer Spaces* (Delhi, 1986), p. 306.

73. V. G. Kiernan (ed.), *Poems by Faiz* (London, 1971), p. 123.

74. The Raja of Mahmudabad, 'Some Memories', in Philips and Wainwright (eds.), *Partition of India*, p. 389.

75. Intizar Husain, op. cit., p. 161.

76. Francis W. Pritchett, 'Narrative Modes in Intizar Husain's Short Stories', op. cit., p. 192.

77. Jameel Jalibi, op. cit., p. 8.

78. Dalrymple, op. cit., p. 63.

79. *Twilight in Delhi*, op. cit., pp. vii-viii.

80. *Annual of Urdu Studies*, op. cit., pp. 89-90; see also Saadat Hasan Manto, *Kingdom's End and Other Stories*. Translated from the Urdu by Khalid Hasan (Delhi: Penguin Books India, 1989), pp. 5-7.

81. *Hindustan Times*, 28 February 1949.

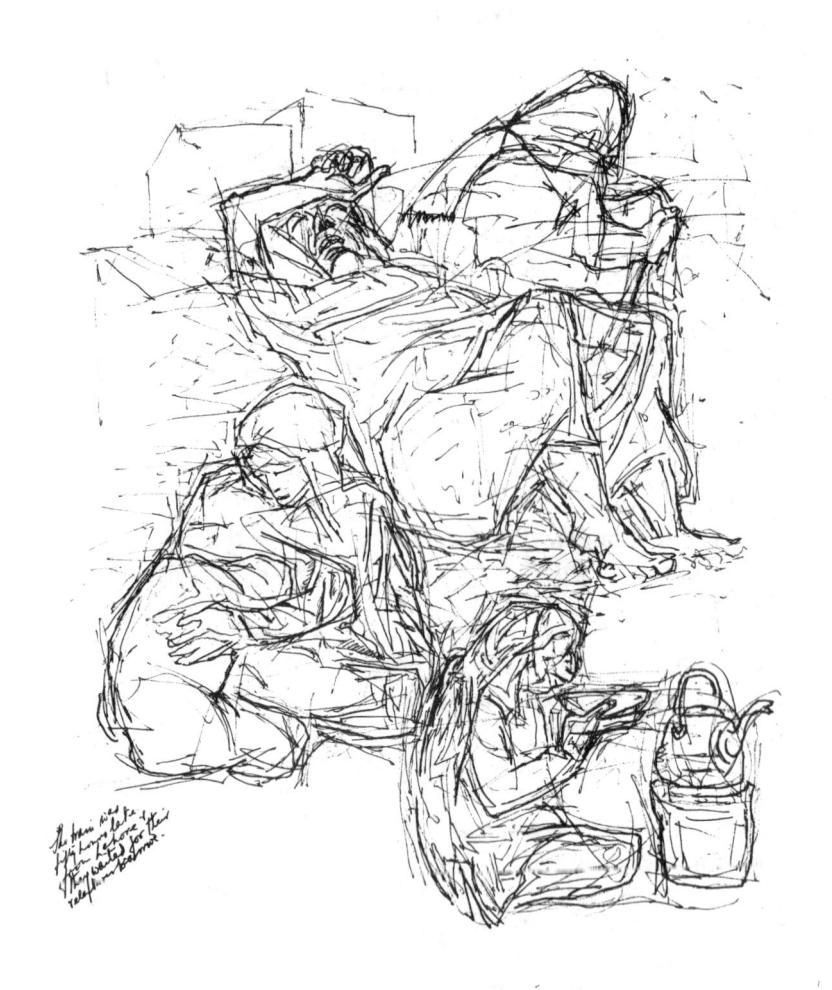

—1948, Krishen Khanna

How Much is the Difference?
HUMAYUN AKHTAR

This pamphlet by Humayun Akhtar, managing director of the Orient Gold Industries on 45 Dharamtalla Street in Calcutta, was published by the Bengal Provincial League and widely read. The Bengal Provincial League published 50,000 copies.

Orthodox Islam	*Orthodox Hinduism*
Salutation: As-*Salam*mo-alaikum	Ram Ram
Acclamation: Allah-o-Akbar	Banda Mataram
Religious Book: Quran Majeed	Vedas, Puranas, Upanishads, Bhagavad Gita, etc.
Belief in the Unity of God. Islam stands for unity and brotherhood.	Belief in numerous inanimate and animate representations of God incarnating on earth.
Islam stands for fraternity and universal brotherhood.	Hinduism perpetuates social distinctions and upholds the caste system.
Muslims: Abolishers of Idolatory.	Hindus build and worship idols.
Discrimination between truth and falsehood considered the prime object of creation.	Belief in the doctrine of 'Ram-Lila'; i.e., all things were created by God for sport.
Man responsible and accountable for all his actions and deeds in this world.	Man's actions in this world considered to be designed and prompted by God.
In Islam any Muslim can qualify to become a religious leader.	In Hinduism only a Brahman is eligible.

Muslim law of Inheritance provides for an equitable distribution of the deceased property to the heirs and successors.	By the Hindu Law of Succession, property is inherited by the sons only, mostly by the eldest son.
Circumcision: an initiatory rite among Muslims.	Not approved.
Tattooing or colour-marking the body not permissible.	Religious symbols are marked on forehead and pig-tails kept.
Lusty music and dancing prohibited among Muslims.	Distinctive cultural virtue.
Obscenity in art explicitly prohibited.	Cave-idols representing nude bodies and phallic symbols considered as relics [*sic*] of praise and charm.
Fishes and all sea animals considered the normal creation of God.	Evolved by the sperm emitted by their God.
Growth of trees are of no religious significance in Islam.	'Pipal', 'Tulsi' and the 'Plantain' considered sacred.
Snake considered a venomous reptile, thus generally killed.	Considered a divine creature.
Muslims believe eclipse to be a geographical phenomenon.	Hindus observe the moment as an evil-ridden occasion.
Muslim bury the corpse.	Hindus cremate the dead.
Muslims purify by ablution.	Hindus consider cow's urine to be a sanctifying fluid.
Muslims eat beef.	Majority worship cow.
Majority are meat-eaters.	Majority vegetarian.
Muslims generally dine in company in common dishes.	Hindus commonly dine on leaves.
General dress: *Pyjama* and *Teh-mad*.	General dress: *Saree* and *dhoti*.

Urdu script (Arabic character).	Hindi script (Devanagri character).
Muslims perform the *Haj* at the Kaaba.	Hindus go for their *tirath* to Banaras, Gaya and Mathura.
Muslims have no belief in palmistry, magic and superstitions.	Most Hindus harbour such beliefs.
Muslims believe in the existence of Paradise and Hell.	Hindus believe in life after death, and that human soul, after achieving *mukti*, will be absorbed into their God.

The Divine Law

HARI CHARAN LAL

The following is an English translation of a Hindi poem by Hari Charan Lal, a resident of Patna. The first edition of the poem and the pamphlet entitled 'The Divine Law', priced at three paise, was published in 1939. The poem reproduced here in full (without editorial changes) is drawn from file number 272(1939) from the Bihar State Archives in Patna.

Aum

The knowledge which all wise men ask for,
Give me also the same knowledge O God.
Always do good acts so that (you) may again get the
    body of a man,
Fortunate you are O dear that you have got this
    auspicious occasion.
Let all Hindu Arya unite now; the time has come
To sacrifice body, wealth and mind for the sake of the nation.
Let you organise yourselves soon, when you have owned the
    untouchables.
Let you all become Kshatriyas at present, when you have
    arms.
Prepare yourselves, save (your) religion, the (problem of) Hyderabad
    has cropped up.
Everywhere parties of Muslims are ready to fight.
It there is disunity even now, the Hindus will be effaced from the
    world.
Dayanand (Saraswati) was sent to you by God for instructing you.
Always do good acts so that (you) may again get the body of a man.
In the margin
In every house, women will have to be instructed
To kill those who enter the house.
If they be afraid they shall have to lose not only their wealth but
    their honour also.
Losing their chastity they shall have to weep, without wealth.

It's Voting Day: Let's March . . . *Mukhiaji*

The following Urdu poems, written mostly in 1945-46, illustrate the nature of the Muslim League mobilization campaign and help to understand the extraordinary buildup to the Pakistan movement. It is clear that these poets, along with many others, endowed the new nation with a historic destiny and projected the Pakistan idea as a crusade for an Islamic State. They catalogued the social and cultural divide between the Hindus and Muslims, described at length their unique and distinctive features, boasted of their glorious past through the vicissitudes of history and took pride in pan-Islamism and in being part of the Islamic culture and civilization. They idolized Jinnah, described him as the custodian (*pasbaan*) of the community, its leader (*Mir-i Karawaan*) and the symbol of Islam (*Nishan-i Islam*).

These poems by Mehboob Ludhianvi, Muzaffar *Sahib*, Mahir-ul Qadri, along with the excerpts from Rahi Masoom Reza's *Aadha Gaon*, shed light on an important aspect of the Pakistan movement which is generally not covered in most historical accounts. Drawn from various collections at the Quaid-e Azam Academy in Karachi, the poems are rendered into English by Kedarnath Komal and Rukmani Bhaya Nair.

IT'S VOTING DAY: LET'S MARCH, LET'S MARCH IN STEP, MUKHIAJI!

The land and the nation are our bread and butter
But ploughing the nation yields the best crop
Come to the League, overwhelm all others
Your people are in anguish.

It's voting day: let's march, let's march in step, Mukhiaji!

There is only one God, one flag, all else is fraud
The flag of the League is our flag
That flag of the other will throttle you
Those others are just slaves to wealth.

It's voting day: let's march, let's march in step, Mukhiaji!

Talk of the division will utterly destroy us
Reciting the *Kalima* has united us
What sense does caste make to us?
Ploughman or grasscutter, each is dear to us.

It's voting day: let's march, let's march in step, Mukhiaji!

If you want power, join the League
The League puts us straight on the righteous path
Whosoever has deserted the flag of the League has been trapped
It's our country, our rule, the claims of the other are false.

It's voting day: let's march, let's march in step, Mukhiaji!

O *Mukhia*, ruler of the village
Such a storm will come, will destroy your roof
Your fields will be trampled to a pulp
When this storm breaks, only the League can save you.

It's voting day: let's march, let's march in step, Mukhiaji!

Do you remember the *Dilli-wallahs*?
They lived in the Red Fort once
You were kings then, you carrot-eating wretches, but
Only those who wield a stick can protect their sisters.

It's voting day: let's march, let's march in step, Mukhiaji!
. . . .
What can I say?
You've lost your kingdom
Now even your fields will be snatched from you
You'll be bullied, laid low by spears hurled at you.

It's voting day: let's march, let's march in step, Mukhiaji!

Even as they hug you, they will not let you draw breath
Their honeyed words mean only that they wean you away
Daggers in their pockets, *mantras* in their mouths
And prayer-beads in their hands.

It's voting day: let's march, let's march in step, Mukhiaji!

O brother, such is the law
That the vote will count for everything

The vote will be the mark of strength, will prove supreme
Like the power of the shepherd over his flock.

It's voting day: let's march, let's march in step, Mukhiaji!

The others number more, and there is fear
Fear of their voices, of their tricks, of their money-power
In every cranny, corner, in every remote jungle
Have they spread their far-flung net.

It's voting day: let's march, let's march in step, Mukhiaji!

Your destiny and your religion depend upon this country
Wake up, O sleeping wayfarer
If you set your own house on fire
Whose house can you shelter in?

It's voting day: let's march, let's march in step, Mukhiaji!

NEITHER FISH NOR FOWL

If you can't be a man and knock down your enemy
Join those goddesses, spin yarn in their company!

Go swell the ranks, add to idol-worshipping queues
Don't delay! Abandon the Muslims, join the Hindus!

Get busy kneeling and praying to the gods of Hindustan
Fragment the unity of the faithful down to the last man!

Praise Gandhi, Nehru and Moonje to the fullest extent
And call Jinnah names to your heart's content!

Lakshmi'll come home and shower you with wealth untold
And you'll find yourself wallowing in heaps of gold!

Those creatures you see in the Congress trap
Are not real but only paper-tigers in a flap!

Though Muslims in name, in action they are Hindus
Call them half fish, half fowl—if you choose!

How can anyone, Mehboob, have faith in those
Who the Mussalmans of Hindustans trick and expose?

THE LEAGUE DURBAR

The League is the pride of Islam
Its glory touches the sky

Fertile is the garden of the League
Its flowers bloom; its thorns glisten

How does a Muslim affirm his faith?
By dedicating his heart, his hearth to the League

The Muslim League is the sole defender of Islam
To recognize this is the sign of faith.

ADDRESS TO THE MUSLIMS

Let stars scintillate under the dust of your feet
When the infidel threatens you, do not retreat

Rustling pages from Islam's history will inspire you
Listen! and face up to the battles before you

Emulate the probity, the character of Ibrahim
It will the desert into an oasis redesign

Live for Islam, die for Islam
No sacrifice is too small for Islam.

Aadha Gaon
RAHI MASOOM REZA

Rahi Masoom Reza (1927-92) was born in a Shia family of Ghazipur district in Uttar Pradesh. In his own words: 'The Jana Sangh says that Muslims are outsiders. How can I presume to say they're lying? But I must say that I belong to Ghazipur. My bonds with Gangauli are unbreakable. It's not just a village, it's my home. . . .' Rahi was educated at the Aligarh Muslim University, where he also taught Urdu for many years. He later moved to Bombay and became a successful screenplay writer. Author of quite a few novels in Hindi, the most celebrated amongst them being *Aadha Gaon*, he also scripted B. R. Chopra's *Mahabharata*, a popular television version of the epic.

Aadha Gaon is a tale about the passing time in village Gangauli, about the dreams and aspirations of young and old people. 'This is a tale of those ruins which were once houses, and it is a tale of those houses which have been built upon those ruins. . . .' *Aadha Gaon* is, in parts, also a political commentary with insights into the massive mobilization campaign conducted under the aegis of the Muslim League. Rahi unfolds the political panorama from 1937-52, captures the anguish and dilemma of the people who were torn between conflicting loyalties, and sensitively assesses the impact of partition on their daily lives.

'*Adaab, Chacha!*' Anwarul Hasan's son Farooq greeted Phunnan Miyan.

'*Eh, bhaiya*, how is your Pakistan doing?'

'It's being made.'

'Of course it is, *bhaiya*! You said it would be so it must be. But will Gangauli go to Pakistan or stay in Hindustan?'

'It'll stay in Hindustan. Pakistan will be made up of the Frontier

---

From *The Feuding Families of Village Gangauli*, trans. from Hindi by Gillian Wright (New Delhi: Viking, 1994), pp. 149-50; 237-51; 255-6; 273-6; 283-5; 292-5. The Urdu and Hindi words are mostly not italicised in the translation by Gillian Wright. I have changed the spelling of Qaid-e-Azam to Quaid-i-Azam and dropped one 'a' from *bhaiyaa* to be read as *bhaiya*.

Province, Punjab, Sind and Bengal. And we're trying to get the Aligarh Muslim University in Pakistan too.'

'You're not trying for Gangauli?'

'There's no question of trying for Gangauli.'

'If there's no question, then what is it to me if Pakistan is made or not.'

'There'll be an Islamic government.'

'Is there true Islam anywhere that you can have an Islamic government? *Eh, bhai,* our forefathers' graves are here, our *tazia* platforms are here, our fields and homes are here. I'm not an idiot to be taken in by your "Long live Pakistan!" '

'When the British go, the Hindus will rule here!'

'Yes, yes, so you say. You're talking as if all the Hindus were murderers waiting to slaughter us. *Arre,* Thakur Kunwarpal Singh was a Hindu. Jhinguriya is a Hindu. *Eh, bhai,* and isn't that Parusaram-*va* a Hindu? When the Sunnis in the town started doing *haramzadgi,* saying that we won't let the bier of Hazrat Ali be carried in procession because the Shias curse our Caliphs, didn't Parusaram-*va* come and raise such hell that the bier was carried. Your Jinnah *Sahib* didn't come to help us lift our bier!'

Farooq laughed.

'In reality the "sincerity" of the Hindus is a deception,' he said using an English word.

'Their what is deception?'

'"Sincerity" . . . I mean that . . . *Arre, sahib,* that is to say . . .'

'What is it, *bhai*? Have you forgotten the language of your forefathers?'

Farooq began to scratch his head.

'So, Mir *Sahib,* I'll take my leave,' said Samiuddin Khan.

'I forgot about you with all this talk of that *susar* Pakistan. Where are you off to?'

'*Salaamalaikum!*'

He (Kammo) was startled at this greeting. Two unfamiliar young men in black *shervani* coats were standing outside.

'*Valaikumassalaam!*' he returned their greeting, 'Please come in, take a seat.'

They did come in, both of them! Fiddu laid out a bamboo bedstead for them to sit on.

'We hail from Aligarh,' said one of the young men in the correct Urdu of an educated city-dweller.

'*Eh, sahib,* are there holidays there nowadays?'

'No, there are not,' said the second young man, also in Urdu. 'We are not on vacation but you must have heard that elections are at hand.'

'That I have.'

'Your respected mother and father are also voters.'

This sentence intoxicated Kammo. For the first time he had heard his mother called 'respected mother', otherwise she was called neither mother nor wife. She was just Rahman-*bo*. He smiled.

'*Acchu,* tell me this—will Aligarh go to Pakistan or stay here?'

'It is our endeavour that Aligarh be incorporated into Pakistan as it is a beacon of Islamic culture.'

'Beacon?' repeated Kammo in amazement. '*Eh, sahib,* I'd heard there was a university there, and you're saying that it's a beacon.'

The young men smiled. They said, 'Please try to see, the reality of the situation is. . . .'

'*Eh, sahib,* listen here, what I say is simply this,' interrupted Kammo, 'if Aligarh is to go to Pakistan then say so straight out. Because if it is then my respected mother and father cannot give you their votes!'

'I beg your pardon!' exclaimed one of the young men.

'If Pakistan is not created the eighty million Muslims here will be made, and made to remain, untouchables,' said the other.

'*Eh, bhai,* it looks to me as if it's been a waste of time educating you. What else? If you people don't even know that *Bhangis* and *Chamars* are the untouchables. What sort of *Bhangis* and *Chamars* do you think we are? And how can anyone who's not an untouchable be turned into one, *sahib*? Go on, tell me! I'm listening.'

One of the young men proceeded to deliver a complete speech which Kammo didn't understand in the least because the young man was mentioning matters not one of which had any connection with him or with Gangauli.

'I can't believe all that, *sahib*!' said Kammo after listening to the whole speech. Why should this Gaya *Ahir,* this Chikuriya or Lakhna *Chamar* or this Hariya *Barhai* become our enemies, for no reason, after Hindustan gets free? Is that what you people learn over there?'

'At this moment you may not be able to comprehend this fact, but that is indeed what is going to happen. Cows will be tethered in our mosques.'

'*Eh, sahib*, if all the Muslims go to Pakistan, what difference does it make if horses are tied in them or cows? It's not as if Hindus are going to say prayers there. It's a fine old bit of nonsense that we all go to Pakistan and then expect the Hindus to look after our mosques.'

At first the young men tried to persuade the peasant in front of them, but then gradually they became angry—and rightfully so. After all there's a limit to everything. One of them said hotly, 'Very well, but don't you complain when the Hindus come and carry off your mother and sisters.'

'Which *behenchod* can carry off my mother and sisters?' Kammo began to tremble with rage. 'If you people weren't my guests, I wouldn't rest till I'd torn the legs off you!'

A *Chamar* was heading towards them, a bottle of kerosene hanging from one hand. He stopped when he heard Kammo's voice.

'Did you hear that?' Kammo asked him.

'What is it, *Miyan*?' asked the Chamar.

'These people have come from Aligarh to tell me that when Hindustan gets free, you people are going to carry off our mother and sisters,' Kammo explained.

'*Arre*, Ram-Ram!' said the *Chamar*, quite unnerved. He turned to the boys from Aligarh, 'You people know reading-writing and all that. Just ask yourselves whether any man can even look at the sisters and mothers of the *Miyans* as long as we are alive!'

'Better than you people is this *Chamar* of ours,' said Kammo, 'who says "Ram-Ram!" just at hearing someone talk about carrying off our womenfolk.'

'I apologize,' said one of the young men, 'that was most certainly not what we intended. We merely wished to express the fact that Hindus cannot be relied upon.'

'But why not, *sahib*?'

'Now how can I convince you?'

'You expect me to tell you?' said Kammo with a smile. 'Would you like some tea?'

'No, thank you.'

Both the young men stepped down from Kammo's house into the lane. Kammo irritably took down the cloth-bag from its peg. The young men walked on. They unfolded a list of voters.

'We've dealt with Fussu *Miyan*, and seen Javad *Miyan*'s home too. Abbu *Miyan*'s gone to Ghazipur. So if we just deal with Hammad *Miyan* we'll have finished off Dakkhin Patti. As for the *Miyans* of Uttar Patti, their vote is in our pocket.'

'But these weavers?'

'Maulana Azad Subhani and Maulana Abdul Baqi are coming to deal with them tomorrow. I can't bring myself to speak to weavers and Biharis. They're all *saala* mother-borne cunts.'

'*Assalaamalaikum*, sir!' the other young man loudly greeted the weaver, Haji Ghafoor Ansari, seeing him appear from a nearby house.

'*Valaikumassalaam, bhaiya,*' replied the Haji *Sahib*, 'have you people come from Aligarh?'

'Yes, we have!'

'I guessed as much as soon as I saw you,' said the Haji *Sahib* stroking his beard, and so pleased with his power of recognition that he smiled and asked, 'Will you people be speaking today?'

'No,' one of them replied. 'The public meeting will be tomorrow. Maulana Azad Subhani and Maulana Abdul Baqi will grace the occasion with their presence.'

'But why are they bringing their gracious presence here?' asked the Haji *Sahib* in the same coin [*sic*]. 'We people belong to the Weavers' Association. We can't vote for any *Aslim*-Muslim League.'

'It is our duty to request you to consider it.'

'It's your duty to say your prayers and keep the fast, *bhaiya*.'

'Pakistan is necessary to safeguard those very prayers,' chipped in one of the black *shervanis*.

'No, *Miyan*,' said the Haji *Sahib*, 'I'm an illiterate peasant. But I think that there's not the slightest need to make Pakistan-*Akistan* for the sake of our prayers. Lord God Almighty said quite clearly, "*Eh*, my Prophet, tell these people that I am with people of the Faith." And someone was saying that this Jinnah of yours doesn't say his prayers.'

'False allegations were made even against the prophets, sir!' one young man replied heatedly.

'But the prophets used to do some miracle-aracle to show who was right!'

'Jinnah *Sahib*'s miracle is Pakistan.'

'Well, bless me! I didn't know that Jinnah *Sahib* had become a prophet.'

The young men stammered and inwardly began to reel off curses against the Haji *Sahib*. One of them said, 'God forbid! What are you suggesting, sir! That was just a manner of speech. How can there be any question of there being a further prophet after the Seal of the Prophets, Saiydna and Maulana, Hazrat Muhammad-e-Mustafa, peace be upon him!'

'You people raised the question!' smiled the Haji *Sahib*. Finally he had defeated two University boys. '*Accha bhaiya, Assalaamalaikum!*'

He walked off quickly. Then both the young men remembered that it was Friday and almost time for Friday prayers. They hurried off too.

But when they slipped into the mosque the congregation was already on its feet. They quickly joined in the rearmost row. One of them joined his hands across his stomach, the other dropped his by his sides. His companion nudged him with his elbow and he too hastily joined hands.

After the prayers were over one of them stood up.

'Brothers in Islam! *Assalaamalaikum!*'

'*Valaikumassalaam!*' replied the brothers in Islam in chorus.

'You must all be aware that at the present time, throughout the country, the Muslims are engaged in a life and death struggle for existence,' began the speech. 'We live in a country where our position is no more than equivalent to that of salt in *dal*. Once the protective shadow of the British is removed, these Hindus will devour us. That is the reason that Indian Muslims require a place where they will be able to live with honour. I am not suggesting that the descendants of Caliph Khalid-bin-Walid and Muhammad-bin-Qasim, conqueror of Sind, fear Hindus. However. . . .'

It was a very rousing speech. The brothers in Islam even interrupted from time to time to cry out *Allah-o-Akbar*! As a result, a large section of the traders and weavers decided that they should vote for the League as a religious duty. Haji Ghafoor tried to speak several times but the young men wouldn't allow him the opportunity.

'So you people go ahead and fuck your mothers!' he fumed. In his rage he even forgot that he was in a mosque. The visitors from Aligarh took full advantage of this foul language. Even the men who were wavering became absolutely solid in their conviction.

The Haji *Sahib* stormed out of the mosque. The speech had been quite beyond his comprehension. He didn't even understand why all of a sudden Muslims needed a place of refuge. And where was the protective shadow of the British that those boys had made such a song and dance about? No Englishman had ever been seen in Gangauli. And why then hadn't the Hindus killed the Muslims before the British came to India? And what about the fundamental question—was life and death in the hands of God or the British and Jinnah *Sahib*?

'And we'll still be just weavers. Will Saiyids start marrying their children to weavers in Pakistan?'

'What are you talking about, *Chacha*?' asked Chikuriya, seeing him muttering furiously to himself. At that moment Chikuriya was sitting at Phunnan *Miyan*'s door chatting to Dullan. Pammo was playing with his moustache, and Sultan Fatima, or Fatto, was telling him about her doll's marriage and complaining that Kaniz Fatima, or Kuddan, had been very miserly with the wedding gifts. Kuddan was sitting on her haunches in the kitchen eating *dal* and rice.

Kuddan had grown up to be a very beautiful nine-year-old. She had inherited all the charm of her mother Razia. Her features were similar too. Big, deep eyes, the same wheat-coloured, oval face and shining white teeth. She had the same well-shaped body. Kulsum never looked at her to her heart's content, and if she ever chanced to, she would glance down at her heels immediately to ward off the evil eye. And if Maghfiya ever scolded Kuddan, Kulsum berated her. As a result, Kuddan would start laughing and Maghfiya would start crying. So Kuddan thought no end of herself, and when she heard that Fatto was talking against her she shrieked, 'That *matimili* is a complete liar! Don't you believe a word she says. And just you ask her what she brought herself. She couldn't even put together two fistfuls of sugar and then she goes and calls me mean!'

'And I suppose the sweet rice was cooked with sugar you brought!' exclaimed Fatto warmly.

This left Kuddan speechless.

'So who are you going to vote for, *re*?' Kulsum called out to Chikuriya from where she lay.

'We've decided that we should vote for Gandhiji,' said Chikuriya, watching the muttering Haji Ghafoor, who was walking along repeatedly straightening his shouldercloth. 'Who are you going to vote for?' he asked. 'We've heard that the *Miyans* are voting for the Muslim League.'

'We would never on our lives vote for that *matimili* Muslim League!' replied Kulsum with feeling. 'I'm going to give my vote to my son Muntaz. Both those Aligarh boys came to our house. I told them straight out.'

'*Eh, Bibi,* where is this Pakistan being made?' said Chikuriya, asking a question which had been bothering him for some time.

'Who knows where the *matimili* thing is being made?'

'If it's made in Ghazipur then I can go and see it!' said Chikuriya, taking out some raw tobacco leaf from a fold in his *dhoti*. 'I'm thinking that this Pakistan must be some mosque or other.' He was about to rub the tobacco in the palm of his left hand with the thumb of his right, when he noticed Tannu heading towards him. He stood up. '*Salam,* Mir *Sahib*!'

Tannu smiled, 'What are you doing, *beh*?'

'I was asking the *Bibi* if Pakistan was some mosque or other.' Tannu laughed. He had no answer to Chikuriya's eminently sensible enquiry and so, walking inside laughing, he greeted Kulsum and lay down on a *charpoy*. At the foot of the *charpoy* Maghfiya was sitting chopping spinach.

'*Eh, beta,* I've heard that you've refused to marry Sallo?' asked Kulsum, handing him a *paan*.

'But when did I ever consent, *Dadi*?' asked Tannu.

'But, *eh beta,* didn't your father make a last wish?'

'Could he only find Fussu-*cha* to make his last wish to?' said Tannu, asking the question to which no one in Gangauli had an answer, and which all the inhabitants of the Saiyid homes were considering. There was not a single person in the entire village who could be certain that Shabbu *Miyan* had made this wish. But not one of them could look Fussu *Miyan* in the eye and say that the story of Shabbu *Miyan*'s last wish was an invention. The fact was that even when Javad *Miyan* was reprimanding Tannu he had been sure that Shabbu *Miyan* had never made any such wish. Now when there was no one in any Saiyid home who could answer this question, how could Kulsum? So she could only say, 'Forget about the wish. But just think, son, what a bad name it brings.'

'Tell me, Maghfiya, *bhai*,' Tannu addressed Maghfiya, 'is Mohammad-*cha* sending you rupees-*upees* regularly or not?'

'And why wouldn't he, *beta*?' replied Kulsum, 'He definitely sends money, the poor man. But you know that ever since your *dada* went to jail there's been not one *paisa* of income. There's only Imtiyaz's salary, and the Aziz *dulha*'s rupees to somehow provide us a little food.'

Aziz *dulha*—dear bridegroom! This title struck Tannu. What women these mothers-in-law were! What names they gave their sons-in-law. Dear bridegroom. Delicate bridegroom. Handsome bridegroom . . . and no one ever asked the bride, 'Tell me, what's your opinion?' He looked at Maghfiya. She was busy cutting spinach just as before.

'Shall I tell you a story?' asked Fatto, sitting down at the head of his *charpoy*.

'Tell me.'

'Once there was a king. . .'

'Look, Nanna. . .' shrieked Kuddan from the kitchen, 'the *matimili's* telling stories in the daytime. *Arre*, Imtiyaz-*mamun* will forget his way home.'

'Yes *beta*!' said Kulsum, 'Imtiyaz is a wayfarer. He'll forget his way.'

'*Eh*, Tannu-*bhai*, what's a wayfarer?' asked Fatto.

'A wayfarer? A wayfarer is a man who . . .' he halted in the middle of his answer.

Maghfiya burst into laughter.

'Get on with you, Tannu-*bhai*,' she managed to say, 'you don't even know a little thing like that.'

'Very well then, you explain,' said Tannu, looking into Maghfiya's eyes. She looked away in embarrassment. Her whole body began to sing. She didn't know the language of the eyes, because Mohammad Husain had never spoken to her in it. Perhaps he didn't know it himself. But at that moment she had immediately understood the language of Tannu's eyes. It seemed to her as if she had known that language for ever and ever, just like the language of her home, and she could speak it fast and fluently. She looked back at Tannu from underneath her long, long eyelashes, but he had already turned towards Fatto.

'We're going to take —Pakistan!' 'Long live—the Revolution!'

Dullan came into the house swinging his schoolbag and shouting slogans.

'I'm hungry!' he shouted after throwing a greeting in the direction of Tannu.

'What are you going to do with Pakistan once you've taken it?' asked Tannu.

'What do I know?' said Dullan. 'But all the boys were shouting it (*sic*) so I did.'

'And you want a revolution as well as Pakistan?' Tannu put a second question. 'Are you a Congress supporter or a League supporter?'

'I'm a Muslim!' said Dullan, thumping his chest.

'You've become a Muslim and you've not even been circumcized,' said Maghfiya.

Dullan was thrown into confusion at the mention of circumcision. Taking advantage of this, Fatto piped up with the words barbers used to distract a boy's attention while they cut his 'foreskin,' 'See the golden bird fluttering and flying away.'

'Quiet, you shameless girl!' Kuddan scolded her from the kitchen.' 'Are you watching her, Nanna?'

'What is there to be ashamed of in that?' asked Fatto, '*Eh*, Tannu-*bhai*, what is there to be ashamed at circumcisions? You had it done, didn't you?'

Tannu was lost for words, and Maghfiya went into another fit of laughter. Kulsum turned her face away to smile, and then gave Fatto a slap, '*Matimili*, shameless girl!'

'*Accha, Dadi*, I'll be going now,' Tannu said, getting to his feet. 'Sit down please!' said Maghfiya, fighting to control her mirth, 'No one's going to ask you any more questions.'

'No, I'll be off. I'm thinking of going to Ghazipur.'

'Weren't you just saying that you'd be staying a few days more?' asked Kulsum.

'Yes, but . . .' he fell silent.

'*Eh, beta*, be strong and do the right thing,' said Kulsum, 'or it'll bring a very bad name.'

'How many people will you make to be strong and get married?' asked Maghfiya, 'It's a very fine sort of thing to force people to get married whether they want to or not. All out of fear of getting a bad name!'

Tannu was startled by her outburst, and turned to look at her.

'Very well, *Dadi*!' he said to Kulsum, 'What is it to me! And there are several other girls in Fussu-*cha*'s house besides Sallo. In the end I have to marry someone or the other, so why shouldn't it be Sallo? Isn't that so?'

He didn't wait for Kulsum's reply. When he left the house he was pursued by thoughts of Saiyda. Saiyda! Why am I so much older than you? And why aren't relations between our families good? Why aren't they? . . . He grew irritated. He should at least have told Saiyda how much he liked her. But then, what if she had laughed at him? That is the one thing wrong with these girls of the family. They exist to show affection to everybody. Now how can anyone tell the difference between just a show of affection and real affection?

Gaya Ahir was sitting on his haunches at Hammad *Miyan*'s doorway smoking a *beedi*. Chikuriya had already left. Mighdad was standing opposite the gate of the *zenana imambara* playing with his little daughter, whom he had named Nikhat, but whom he called Nakko out of affection. Perhaps long names cannot be spoken by those who love.

In front of the Great Gate some weaver boys were playing with a spinning top and swearing at one another. And at Balli Sain's corner a procession of boys was shouting 'Long live the Muslim League!', 'Long live the Quaid-i-Azam!' and 'Long live the Revolution!', and two women peeping out of two doorways were perhaps laughing at this procession.

Tannu saw that there was no hurricane blowing through Gangauli. Life was just as it had been. Weavers were untangling thread. Women were complaining and arguing and laughing and chatting. Boys were spinning tops and playing hopscotch. Mighdad was kissing his little girl. Gaya Ahir was squatting smoking a *beedi*. The Hakim *Sahib* must have been feeling his patients' pulses and swearing at young boys. He smiled at the thought of the Hakim and asked himself why he should bring a hurricane into Gangauli's life which was flowing happily like the Ganga. Heaven only knew how many Tannus had loved how many Saiyads in these village families! Respectable people didn't reveal their love. If you were to rake the ashes of any wife's heart who was to say what spark of love for which *Miyan* would appear. So what was so special about Tannu's love? It's not as if it'd been touched by the wings of the *surkhab* bird*. And who was to say that his father hadn't made a last wish? Yes, who knew? Sallo may not have been as sinuous as a Hindi film song, but she was simple and innocent like a folk-song from home. And then was it necessary that. . . .

---

*Brahminy duck—pairs said to enshrine the souls of dead lovers doomed to remain in sight and hearing but separated by a flowing stream.

Tannu was startled to find himself face to face with the Hakim *Sahib*. He saw that he was standing at the Hakim's gate, and hastily greeted him. He recognized the black-*shervanied* young men from Aligarh. All the men of Uttar Patti were present. One black *shervani*, a cigarette pressed between his fingers, was waving his arm around and explaining in Urdu to the *Miyans* where in the Quran Allah *Miyan* had given instructions to vote for the Muslim League.

'. . . and the most important thing is that the map of the world will be marked with the colour of one more Islamic government. And neither is it impossible that the green standard of Islam may be seen fluttering once more on the Red Fort of Delhi. If Pakistan is not created. . . .'

Tannu had no interest in whether Pakistan was created or not. He sat down on the foot of a *charpoy*, began watching the two young men and started to think . . . but the thread of his thought was tangled. He was thinking of everything at once—Saiyda, Sallo, Gangauli, Pakistan, Kulsum and Mighdad.

'We've heard that Jinnah's a Shia!' some unidentified person called out.

'He's a Muslim,' replied the black *shervani*.

'You must have heard this verse of Iqbal's,' began the second *shervani*:

> For thousands of years the yellow-eyed
> narcissus laments its sightlessness!
> 'Tis hard indeed in the garden
> to be born with discerning eyes!

Tannu began to observe the smoke issuing from the young man's nostrils and mouth.

'Recite the poetry of Anis to us, *Miyan*!' said Husain Ali *Miyan*. '*Ya Ali*!' he put his hands on his knees, stood up and left without waiting to listen to any verse of Anis.

'If the line of Prophets and Caliphs was not complete, then I would say . . .'

'What is that to you Sunnis?' the Hakim *Sahib* interrupted the black *shervani*. 'Make yourself another Caliph!'

'Look here, sir!' said the black *shervani*, 'This is no occasion to remember petty sectarian disputes. Hold strongly to the rope of Allah. Today that rope's name is Mohammad Ali Jinnah. He is the strength of Allah. Rise up and proclaim that you want to create

Pakistan. Just look at your leader, and then at those Congress-wallahs. Whether it's Gandhi or Nehru, they roam around in every back alley. And then there is one man, our Quaid-i-Azam, who is so difficult to meet that even the Viceroy himself has to take an appointment.'

'So if he doesn't meet anyone, then. . . .'

'Yes, quite right!' Hakim *Sahib* interrupted Ubbad, 'When he doesn't meet anyone then, heaven forbid, he's become Allah *Miyan*.'

'What are you insinuating?' asked the black *shervani*.

'I'm not insinuating-*vinsinuating* anything,' said the Hakim *Sahib*. 'We people are in any case going to vote for the League, but we're not going to stop from asking one thing. When Jinnah *Sahib* doesn't meet anyone and neither does Allah *Miyan*, then why don't we vote for Allah *Miyan*?'

Tannu burst out laughing.

'You gentlemen can have no reply to this rustic logic', said Tannu in pure Urdu. 'So why are you delivering speeches to no purpose? This Patti of loyal government Muslims can't vote for anyone but the League. But you will not be able to take the vote of *musammat* Kulsum. She will vote for her "Muntaz". She is a totally illiterate woman. She cannot call her son by his correct name, but mispronounces Mumtaz as "Muntaz". He was a very noble young man. How would you know him! He was shot dead at the Qasimabad police station. I was not here at that time but I have heard that he died very bravely. That is to say that when he was sure that he was dying he did not cry for fear of death. They say that he caught hold of the hem of the shirt of a man running away and said, "*Eh, Bhaiya*, if you go to Gangauli, tell my mother I'm dead. These *darad behenchods* have killed me." Perhaps you will not have understood his language, because you gentlemen have made the Urdu tongue Muslim. But I swear by God that the language I am speaking now is not my mother tongue. My mother tongue is the one in which Mumtaz sent that message to his mother. Because of his speaking Urdu, Hammad-*da* is looked down upon by the whole village. After Pakistan is created will you leave this Urdu here or take it with you?'

'Look, I'm no politician. But I have seen the field of war. Those who die in battle die a very helpless death. Those who kill become very ugly too, because to save their lives they are forced to regard those before them as enemies and to hate them. It's possible that if any one of those enemies were to meet me here, in Gangauli, I would give him a cigarette to smoke and sugarcane juice to drink, invite him to swim in my tank, and then at night, spread out soft and warm bedding on a *charpoy* strung as tight as a drum, and talk to him about his country . . . and tell him about mine. But there I killed him. Because if I hadn't he would have killed me. That's why I am afraid. You gentlemen are making people fear for their lives, but it's we people here who will have to cut the harvest of this fear. This is why I am so afraid.'

'You, descendent of Muhammad-bin-Qasim. . . .'

'I am not a voter!' Tannu interrupted the black *shervani*, 'I am a Muslim. But I love this village because I myself am this village. I love the indigo godown, this tank and these mud lanes because they are different forms of myself. On the battlefield, when death came very near, I certainly remembered Allah, but instead of Mecca or Karbala, I remembered Gangauli. And I used to be upset and cry at the thought that I may never again be able to chew sugarcane at the indigo godown, and that I may never again taste the *halva* of the eighth of Moharram. Allah is omnipresent. Then what is the difference between Gangauli and Mecca, and the indigo godown and the Ka'aba and our pond and the spring of paradise?'

'People like you are selling out the Indian Muslims to the Hindu!' said the black *shervani* angrily. 'Have you no shame? Are you comparing the Noble Ka'aba with this miserable village?'

'Yes, that's just what I am doing!' replied Tannu. 'And neither am I ashamed to do so. Why should I be? Gangauli is my village. Mecca is not my city. This is my home and the Ka'aba is Allah *Miyan*'s. If God loves His home then won't He be able to understand that we too can love our home as much as He loves His?'

'*Eh, beta*, you're talking like a *kafir*,' said the Hakim *Sahib*, in the same breath shouting out, 'what are you doing, you *haramzade*!' and making a boy about to spit into the tank run off in fear. 'The Ka'aba's after all the Ka'aba, son.'

'When did I say that it wasn't? But Lahore is not the Ka'aba, is it?' asked Tannu. 'Look, *Chacha*, you have not seen all that I have, and so you cannot see what I can. Anything constructed on a foundation of hate and fear cannot be auspicious. Even after the creation of Pakistan, Gangauli will remain in India, and Gangauli is after all Gangauli. Then when Gaya *Ahir*, Lakhna *Chamar* and Chikuriya *Bhar* ask you why, when they have never shown you any enmity, you voted for Pakistan, what answer will you give?'

'So then should we vote for the Congress, which is sitting there with its eyes on our lands?' asked Ubbad *Miyan*.

'Whether you vote or not, it's the Congress which is going to rule in Gangauli.'

'What sort of justice is that?' said the Hakim *Sahib*.

'And you can take it for granted that the days of *zamindari* are over too.'

'What else!' said the Hakim *Sahib* heatedly, 'The *zamindaris* belong to that Gandhiya's father, don't they, so he can break them up the moment he arrives!'

'Don't you listen to him, revered sir!' the black *shervani* said. 'The Congress will certainly try to break the *zamindari* system, because most of the zamindars are Muslims. But it won't be so easy for them to do so. If they try then the Islamic army of Pakistan will launch an attack on Delhi!'

'You can talk about attacking Delhi because you have never seen war,' said Tannu. His tone became bitter. 'By all means create a Pakistan!' he said as he got up, 'but from time to time send us a letter from there to let us know that all is well'.

Touching the empty *tazia* platforms he walked out of the Great Gate and into the lane. He was very angry with himself—what need had there been to make a speech? But he really was scared of where this hatred would end. Did Indian Muslims really not belong to this land? Surely the Rajput Muslims of Dildarnagar and Gahmar were formed of this earth. So why were they going to vote for the Muslim League? Why did they feel the need for a homeland? Why were Muslims who had kissed the sandals of Lord Rama, accepting them as footprints of the Prophet, making Pakistan?[*] And did they really want to create Pakistan? Did all of them, who were going to vote for the Muslim League, know what Pakistan would be, and what it would be like? Pakistan was no God that it could be accepted unseen! It takes several generations for the name of a new country to come easily to the tongue. So what would happen to the generations in between? What would become of these generations suspended in midair? The black *shervanis* had no interest in these

---

[*]One theory of Indian Muslim thought is that there have been 1,24,000 messengers of God, of whom only a few are known. Therefore all sages and prophets can be considered messengers of God and respected as such— including for example Rama and Mahavir.

questions. They weren't even prepared to consider the fact that man cannot live by hate, suspicion and fear alone.... Tannu was trapped in the crowd of his own questions. He began to feel stifled and asked himself, 'What should I do now?'

Kulsum *Dadi* wants to vote for her Muntaz. Hakim Ali Kabir for the Muslim League. Which of them is right?

'Oh, dammit!'— he suddenly returned to army language— 'Bastards!' He kicked a dog which ran off yelping.

'... We're going to take—Pakistan!' shouted Dullan, as he came into the house.

'You and whose army?' Phunnan *Miyan* shot back at him. Dullan was astounded.

'Won't you greet your grandfather?' said Kulsum.

'*Adaab*!' said Dullan, offering his salaams.

'Who are you going to take Pakistan with?' Phunnan *Miyan* repeated his question.

'With the men from Aligarh!' replied Dullan, after some consideration.

'Where did you come across these men from Aligarh?'

'Two of them came here to ask for votes!' said Kulsum, 'They told us to vote for the Muslim League. What are these wretched votes?'

'So what did you say?'

'I said that I'm going to vote for my Muntaz. But when I went to vote, Muntaz's name wasn't there, so I brought the papers home. Did you get any news of Imtiyaz in jail or not?'

'Do you think I opened a post office in jail?' said Phunnan *Miyan*, 'But I think that Imtiyaz must be gone.'

'*Eh*, God forbid!' said the boy's mother, writhing inwardly, 'How could you say such a thing!'

'All the army *wallahs* have come back,' said Phunnan *Miyan*. 'A lot of them have ended up in jail. Someone came back and immediately got involved in a fight, someone else carried off somebody's wife. One man pulled off a theft and another a dacoity. If Imtiyaz had been alive he would have come back by now. The joy of children is not written in our fate. We had just two sons. Both have been killed. Girls can't shoulder our biers. Who's going to lift our corpses?'

'You go and have a bath,' said Kulsum. 'What sort of things are you saying!'

'I met one prisoner in jail. Some Singh or other!' said Phunnan *Miyan*. 'He was a Communist. He said that God-*vod*, everything was a lie. I didn't believe what he said. One day when he began squealing a lot I gave it to the *saala* with both hands. But it is something to think about. Hammad has stolen everyone's rights and that's why he's enjoying life. If Allah *Miyan* did exist, Hammad's bow couldn't have been strung like this.'

He walked out of the house with the *lungi* over his shoulder. Kulsum noticed that his broad shoulders were drooping. And it also seemed to her that the sparkle was missing from his eyes. Her heart became full. Her big, big eyes filled with tears.

Phunnan *Miyan*'s glance fell upon Hammad, who was in his high porch explaining something to Gaya *Ahir*. Phunnan *Miyan* immediately cleared his throat loudly, stroked his moustache and walked past.

'*Salam*, Mir *Sahib*!' said Haji Ghafoor.

'How are you, *bhai*?' said Phunnan *Miyan*, 'And, *eh bhai*, the couple of black hairs left in your beard are still there just as they ever were.'

'The things you say,' said Haji Ghafoor, heaving a sigh. 'I've not grown old but I've been buggered by rising prices!'

At Balli Sain's corner a procession of boys suddenly began shouting slogans:

'*Nara-e-takbir*!'
'*Allah-o-Akbar*!'
'Long live . . .'
'The Quaid-i-Azam!'
'Long live . . .'
'The Muslim League!'

'Have all these boys gone mad or what?' asked Phunnan *Miyan*.

'The amazing thing is, Mir *Sahib*, that the people who are shouting and screaming are the ones who aren't voters. I'm a voter and no one asks what I think. But whoever you see will be making a speech. And they're all looking for Pakistan to be made. This Jinnah *Sahib*, now, where's he from?'

'Who knows who he is and where he comes from. I've heard that he was a lawyer in London.'

'So have the British tutored him in all this and sent him here?'

'To hell with all of them!' said Phunnan *Miyan*. 'If Pakistan's made, it'll be a long way from Gangauli. You go and look after your spinning wheel, and keep your warp straight. Pakistan-*Akistan* is just a game for filling stomachs.'

Phunnan *Miyan* went on.

Barikhpur was full of activity. And amidst this activity the three or four Muslim families there were standing in amazement wondering what on earth was about to happen.

A few Muslims went and sat in the mango grove to hear stories from the holy man. They were instantly recognized.

'. . . then Lord Krishna said, "Oh, Arjun! I am Myself, and there is nothing else but Me." Today that Divine Flute-Player is calling to every Hindu of India, saying, "Arise, and remove these unclean Muslim aliens from the holy banks of the Ganga and Yamuna. . ."' The holy man was not delivering a religious discourse!

'If we're removed from here then where will we have to go?' one middle-aged Muslim asked a Hindu. They had both played together as children. They were close friends.

'That's what I'm thinking too,' came the reply. 'But if it's the order of God, then you'll surely have to go. They're making Pakistan, go there.'

'You tell me to go there. Say somehow I manage to get together the money for my fare, still how can I take my fields to Pakistan? I ask you, haven't my ancestors and your ancestors always gone together with the ancestors of the Thakur *Sahib* to attack Salimpur? So why isn't anyone today asking us to come with them to attack the fort?'

'Look at this, people!' said a young Hindu from another village, 'This *behenchod Miyan* is squealing right here!'

'Are you insulting us, Bafati-*chacha*?' asked a young *Chamar* angrily.

'No, *bhaiya*!' said Bafati, trying to prevent a fight, 'I was just asking where we would have to go.'

'Go to Pakistan, you *behenchod*!'

'I've spent my whole life here. Now, when I've not long in this world, should I go to Pakistan? I won't go!'

'Swearing at your elders and betters!' said the middle-aged Hindu, 'Don't you have any shame?'

'. . . the faith is in danger. Raise Ganga water and vow to wash clean the pure land of India with Muslim blood!' The holy man had worked himself up to a climax,' See, how these unclean Turks have insulted our mothers in Calcutta, Lahore and Noakhali. . . .'

'Say—Victory to . . .' came a lone voice.

'*Bajrangbali*!' resounded the whole village.

Then the crowd rose to its feet. The holy man went off in the darkness to another village, and once he was gone the crowd was forced to think for itself. It thought that Muslims are Muslims and the only difference between the Muslims of Salimpur and Barikhpur was that the Salimpur Muslims were rather far away and those of Barikhpur were nearby. Therefore, raising the slogan of 'Victory to *Bajrangbali*!' the crowd set off towards Barikhpur.

When this news reached Thakur Prithvipal Singh he was unnerved. It was one thing to launch an offensive against the Khan *Sahib* of Salimpur and another to murder the barbers, weavers and one or two Pathans of Barikhpur. What harm had they ever done? They had always lived and died with the other people of Barikhpur.

'Save us, *mai-baap*!' said Bafati, as he collapsed in the Thakur's courtyard. Hindus from some other village were chasing after him. They stopped when they saw the Thakur *Sahib*. One of them lit a *beedi*.

Thakur Prithvipal Singh recognized Bafati. How could he not recognize his Bafati, the vegetable-seller?

'Victory to *Bajrangbali*!' came a shout from somewhere nearby.

'Who beat you?' Prithvipal Singh asked Bafati. His body was shaking with rage.

'I didn't recognize those people, *sarkar*!'

The flames of torches were setting fire to the night. It was ablaze.

'And now they're all going off to burn our houses. They were saying, "Go to Pakistan." I said we won't go. Then they just went mad.'

The Thakur *Sahib* rushed over and picked up his *lathi*. No one in the Thakur's household asked a single question. Every *lathi* was silently raised.

And when that crowd, coming to announce its dark decree in torchlight, reached those few Muslim homes it halted in amazement.

'Why have you people stopped, *bhaiya*?' asked Prithvipal Singh, 'Come on with you!'

The crowd could not comprehend why the Thakur *Sahib* wanted to save Muslims. The holy man had said that the *puris* cooked in the mango grove had been provided by the Thakur *Sahib*. And didn't the Thakur *Sahib* know what treatment the Muslims had meted out to Hindu women and children? Therefore, one of them said, 'These are all Muslims, *sahib*!'

'You think you know more than I do?' asked the Thakur *Sahib*. 'The best thing for you people is to go back! Did Bafatiya, and Dildar-*va* and Kalua rape the Hindu women of Noakhali? If you people are so brave and so worried about the honour of the Hindus you should go to Calcutta and Lahore! What is there here that you should attack these people?'

'We've come here to burn down their houses!'

'Yes, yes! Why not! Come and try it! Just let me see which mother has given birth to a son with strength enough!' Prithvipal Singh turned to the men of his house. 'See what's going on! Beat the *behenchods* and make them run!'

Seeing the *lathis* raised in the hands of the Thakurs the crowd split like an old sheet and tore apart. Later the few Muslims in the village came to the Thakur Sahib's house. Bafati said, 'If you allow us, we'll go to Bahadurganj or Mau Mubarakpur!'

'I'll fuck the mother of anyone who mentions leaving this village. Look at these *bhonsriwalas*! They want to go to Mau Mubarakpur to get buggered!'

By morning the story of the events of the previous night had travelled all over the surrounding countryside. The simple, straightforward farming community couldn't understand, even after tours by several holy men, why Bafati of Barikhpur, Ghurau of Alavalpur, Ghasita of Hundarh—in short, their own Muslims, should be punished for the sins of the Muslims of Calcutta. How and why should they rape Muslim girls who as infants had pissed in their laps? Neither could they understand why and how they should set fire to the houses of Muslims whom they had been living with for centuries. How could anyone kill the *Mullah* who, after saying his prayers in the mosque, would come out and blow over the heads of all the children, Hindu and Muslim, to ward off evil. . . . The farmers could understand that the crops of disputed land should be looted. A couple of murders over land was nothing to worry about. But to murder someone or burn his house down simply for the crime of being a Muslim was beyond their comprehension.

In all directions such great cities were ablaze that Bacchaniya and Saghir Fatima fell into that fire like straw and were immediately consumed. Delhi, Lahore, Amritsar, Calcutta, Dacca, Chittagong, Saidpur, Rawalpindi, the Red Fort, the Juma Masjid, the Golden Temple, Jallianwalla Bagh, Hall *Bazar*, Urdu *Bazar*, Anar Kali. . . . Anar Kali—the Lahore *bazar* named after the Mughal Prince Salim's beloved, who died cruelly and tragically on the orders of the Emperor. Now Anar Kali was named Saghir Fatima, or Rajni Kaur, or Nalini Banerjee—Anar Kali's corpse was in the fields, on the streets, in mosques and temples, and on her naked body were the marks of nails and teeth. And men carefully collected strips of blood-soaked skirts, *shalwars* and *saris* and put them away in boxes of memorabilia as keepsakes.

> Four-year-old Sakina was petrified with fear,
> The sweet child cried out and held her mother near,
> "I am close to death, someone call the Great King here!
> Oh, listen people, someone call my father here!
> Oh, listen people, where's my brother Ali Akbar to be found?
> Where's my aunt's beloved nephew? Who will bring him safe and sound?
> His bride is being robbed, where is Qasim, Hasan's kin?
> Where's now the brave Abbas? I am sacrificed for him."
>
> Sajjad lay all alone unconscious on his bed,
> Half beyond her wits, Sakina to the hero fled,
> With her tiny little hands she shook his arm and said,
> "My mother's veil's been seized, rise up, brother, from your bed!
> I am very, very scared, hold me close against your breast!
> Don't let them take my pearls, hide me close against your breast!"

The listeners began to weep out loud.

Wazir *Miyan* lay the book of *marsias* down upon the pulpit. Then he himself put his handkerchief over his eyes and began to cry. He stepped down from the pulpit. Everyone stood up.

The *nauha* began to the rhythm of the cries, 'Husain! Husain!'

"Sughra, Medina's been despoiled!"

Screamed Zainab and beat her head,
"Sughra, Medina's been despoiled!"
Medina was Delhi. Medina was Lahore. Medina was Hindustan. Medina was Pakistan—and Medina was being looted and despoiled.

The Saiyids began to cry more and more loudly. The chandeliers and lotus-shaped candleshades began to tremble to the rhythm of the *matam*. The petromax lamp hanging in the doorway of the hall watched silently and its gas hissed out in long breaths.

'I had a letter from Tannu today,' Fussu *Miyan* told Phunnan *Miyan* when Javad *Miyan* began to distribute the blessed sweets after the *matam*.

'What does he say? Is he all right?'

'Yes. And here's something strange—after going to Pakistan, Safir-*va*'s suddenly become Saiyid Safirul Hasan Zaidi!'

'*Eh, bhai*, what fault is it of Safir-*va*'s? After all here Hammad became Saiyid Hammad Husain Zaidi.'

'Safir-*va* didn't have your name put down as his father, did he?' asked Ali Mehdi *Miyan*, laughing.

'Leave jokes until after Moharram!' Javad *Miyan* reprimanded Ali Mehdi *Miyan*, 'Here, take your share.'

'Do you get letters from Saddan?' Fussu *Miyan* asked the Hakim *Sahib*.

'What need does he have to write to me? replied the Hakim *Sahib*.

'He shouldn't have gone,' said Shabbar *Miyan*, 'I tried hard to persuade *Miyan* Tannu too.'

'You wasted your time!' said the Hakim *Sahib*. 'We're no longer the fathers of our sons, now our sons all think they're fathers to us. I told Saddan countless times, "Son, what need have you to go to Pakistan?" And he would say that the roads for the progress of Muslims were closed here. Now if he would only take his wife and children too I could rest content. *Eh*, Bashir! This Pakistan was made to separate Hindus from Muslims. But as far as I can see it's separated husband from wife, father from son and brother from sister. Saddan's gone there and so he's a Muslim. I'm still here—does that make me, heaven forbid, a Hindu?'

'*Accha*, now let's be off to the *majlis*!' said Javad *Miyan*, 'It looks like this Pakistan is doing Imam Husain's work, making people grieve.'

'Answer that, *Miyan* Abbas!' said Shabbar *Miyan*.

'He's got no answer, poor man,' said Abbu *Miyan*. 'His Jinnah *Sahib* has washed his hands and gone, leaving the Muslims here to go, God forbid, to hell. All very fine, I must say. The Muslims here give their votes for Pakistan, and when Pakistan is made Jinnah says they can be sent to the devil.'

'And your Aligarh is still in India, hero Abbas!'

No one in the whole village knew how happy Kammo was that Aligarh was still in India. And no one knew why Tannu had gone to Pakistan—not even Saiyda. And without Tannu this Moharram seemed very strange to her. The war was different—men return from war. But no one came back from Pakistan. Did that make it a land of the dead?

'*Eh sahib*, if all the Hindus had voted for Pakistan, what would Jinnah *Sahib* have done then?' Kammo asked Shabbar *Miyan*.

'What a world of loneliness lies upon Husain this day!' Husain Ali *Miyan* had only recited the first line when the whole *majlis* dissolved into tears. Even Hakim Ali Kabir, who never wept, was crying. Phunnan *Miyan*'s white moustache was wet with tears. Fussu *Miyan* wept so loudly that Shahida, asleep in his lap, woke up with a start, and seeing her grandfather crying, began to cry herself. Besides Hammad *Miyan* and Haqdar *Miyan*, everyone was weeping, because the cut umbilical chord of Pakistan was around their necks like a noose, and they were all suffocating. Now they knew what 'a world of loneliness' meant! For the Hakim *Sahib* it meant his only son being in Pakistan, and himself being in India with his daughter-in-law and grandchildren, leaving him clucking like a chicken which has been stopped from laying and lost its feathers. But the Hakim *Sahib* didn't have much opportunity to think because Kammo's medical practice had become such a runaway success that most of his time was taken up with cursing him, and mocking homoeopathy. Sallo's loneliness had bitten deep into Fussu *Miyan*, and Phunnan *Miyan* had felt himself completely isolated from the day of the inauguration of the martyrs' memorial at Qasimabad. When he had told the gathering that his son too had been martyred there, he had himself been startled by the loneliness of his voice. That one moment had produced a boundless emptiness . . . the universe began to echo, as if there was no one else but himself for a vast distance. . . . In short with independence several kinds of loneliness had been born, from the loneliness of the bed, to the loneliness of the heart. Every individual in the Uttar and Dakkhin Pattis had found himself suddenly alone. Old age, youth and childhood, wedded life and widowhood, friendship, enmity and inter-Patti rivalry—all these conditions of man were alone too. Every emotion was alone. The relationship between day and night and night and day had been broken. The days could be got through much as they used to be—the same curses and abuses, the same disputes between the Pattis . . . the same tingling sensations of touch . . . the same shadows of meaningless smiles, the same fields . . . the same threshing floors . . . But the nights became intolerable. There was a desire to dream, but what was there safe to dream about? What could Nakko dream? Or Mighdad? Or Hakim Ali Kabir? Or Phunnan *Miyan*? It was possible to go alone to the mosque inhabited by jinn, or the burning *ghat*, but no one could tread alone the crooked pathways of dreams. And the atmosphere was such that the blood of one's veins was wandering hopelessly in Pakistan, and the relationships and mutual affections and friendship upon which society was based were breaking, and in place of confidence, a fear and deep suspicion was growing in people's hearts. They say that the amarbel creeper sucks dry even the greatest tree. . . . The splendid great tree of the gatherings at the Saiyids' gates was withering day by day. Several new centres of power were being established in Gangauli. It was obvious that people would gather where a *hookah* was passed round, where *paan* was distributed, and tea made; but, as long as they just heard that their *zamindaris* were going to be taken from them, the *Miyans* kept laughing and making fun of whoever suggested such a thing. How on earth could *zamindari* ever be abolished? This was not a concept they could grasp. Neither could the men who tilled their lands, the old farmers in the village, believe that *zamindari* could come to an end. They used to enjoy listening to what Parusaram had to say, but the fear that had been sitting in their hearts for centuries held them back. *Zamindari* was as strong as religion. Their personalities were in its grasp. They wanted *zamindari* to be abolished so that they could own the land they tilled, but they didn't have the courage to make this wish consciously. Therefore, when one night at midnight a drum beat out and it was announced that *zamindari* was no more, the old farmers, like the *zamindars*, couldn't accept it. The *zamindars* collected funds and held meetings. The meetings passed 'resolutions'. The *Miyans* opposed Parusaram tooth and nail. Only Hammad *Miyan* supported him openly, while Phunnan *Miyan* repaid him for his friendship. Parusaram became an MLA, and was accorded a splendid welcome procession in Gangauli. He came to the Gate of the *Miyans* to offer his respects. That day Hakim Ali Kabir, Abbu *Miyan*, Sibtu *Miyan*, Fussu *Miyan* and Husain Ali *Miyan*—in short all those living in the Saiyid households—realized once and for all that *zamindari* had been abolished. Orchards and fields spreading over huge distances—that great universe—contracted and was contained in a few documents. Documents are, after all, only paper. No society can be based on them. The land which the *zamindars* traditionally cultivated themselves, but had given out to sharecroppers, was taken from them too. Apart from Hammad *Miyan* no *zamindar* had land left equivalent even to the hub of the great wheels which had been their *zamindaris*.

In a few moments all the *zamindars* collapsed like the tomb of Nuruddin the Martyr.

Moharram was celebrated with great zeal. '*Zamindari* bonds' were sold at forty rupees each. *Halva* was distributed at the *majlis* of the eighth. The pulpit was filled with sweets offered by Saiyid ladies for prayers granted. The *majlises* (*sic*) where bread was distributed were held. Respected and elderly ladies prayed with all their hearts for the British to return. At every *namaz* ill-wishes were heaped on the Congress party.

'*Arre*, may leprosy strike those *matimile* Congressmen! May their last rites never be performed. . . .'

But neither the Saiyids' prayers nor their ill-wishes were granted. The *Miyans*, who for centuries had made Gangauli their home and had lived and died there, realized that they no longer had any links with the village they had called and believed to be their own. Whether to create Pakistan or not had been of no meaning to them, but the abolition of *zamindari* shook the very foundations of their souls. They left their homes, and when their homes were lost, what difference was there between Ghazipur and Karachi?

'At least there's an Islamic government in Karachi.' Ashrafullah Khan *Sahib* at first stood firm at Salimpur. One year he even held the *majlis* where bread was distributed with the same old munificence; but the very next year he denounced the custom of preparing *tazias*, the platforms on which they were placed, his mansion and the beautiful mosque built in its courtyard, and went to Pakistan. But for the Saiyid gentlefolk of Gangauli it was not easy to go to Pakistan. It was their fate always to be in a minority. Pakistan belonged to the Sunni Muslims, and what hope could Shias have of Sunnis? And so they stood firm in Gangauli, holding to their breasts whatever land belonged to their wives and to the widows of the family.

But the amount of blessed food distributed after each *majlis* declined. The covers of the *tazias* became old and began to split. The paper *tazias* offered for fulfilment of prayers were no longer so tall. The Orphan's share was no longer auctioned. The Gates of the Saiyids began to look deserted. All thought of lifting the Great *Tazia* on the tenth of Moharram was given up. Neither were there any bearers willing to carry it, nor spare money for repairs. Only Hammad *Miyan*'s *tazia*, decked out in gold and silver thread, was taken out in procession like a bride. It was a modest, but very beautiful *tazia*, with a black velvet covering very finely embroidered with gold and silver thread.

After returning from its procession around the village on the fifth night, the *tazia* was taken into the *shahnashin* and the smoke of fragrant incense wafted all around it like temple dancers.

'I'm not staying here!' said Maulvi Bedar, perhaps to Hammad Miyan's *tazia*, but it didn't take the slightest notice. The standards too stood there just as disinterested as before. The white flag next to the bathroom fluttered once, but no one paid it any attention as they were all looking at Maulvi Bedar.

'Well, I'll be . . . !' said Phunnan *Miyan*, 'We people with wives and children aren't going, so what need is there for you to go? If you die here you can be near your ancestors, and if you die there who knows what *susar* will be buried next to you!'

'No, I'm not staying!' said the Maulvi, 'The Sikhs have taken control over Delhi's *imambara*!'

'All the mosques in Amritsar and Jalandhar have been turned into temples, *bhai*!' someone said.

'*Arre*, so what's so dreadful in that?' said someone else. The fact was that the petromax light had run out of fuel some time ago, flared up and died. The hall was in pitch darkness, but the Maulvi's words had so shocked people that they no longer noticed.

'How can you say there's nothing dreadful about it?' spoke out Maulvi Bedar, recognizing his own voice.

'Muslim emperors demolished temples to build mosques and used the idols of gods and goddesses to make their toilets. . . .'

India, My India!

SHAMIM KARHANI

Portions from an Urdu poem by Shamim Karhani, one of the premier progressive poets of India, rendered into English with omissions by S. M. A. Husaini. This poem was published in the front page of the first issue of *Qaumi Awaaz*, the nationalist Urdu daily, and acclaimed all over India as the best poem on Pakistan among all that have been written for or against this subject.

Proudly we hail from Ind.
That is our motherland:
Land of Ind! Land of Ind!
Where we were born,
And our forefathers,
And their forefathers,
Through centuries and centuries vivid, unforgettable spans of time,
They were born and they were nourished, and they flourished.
And then mingled their dust with her dust, the dust of Ind.
They were made one with her, ingrained in her soil;
The soil contains our graves.
Our mothers and sisters, our fathers it holds,
And those whom we loved,
And those whom they loved,
Every sod is full of our stars and our moons.
Beautiful and slim minarets of mosques
Are planted on this sacred soil.
Through the dim stars of the morn,
Amidst peacefully sleeping temple spires,

The Guardian, Madras, 17 January 1946. Reprinted in M.S. Vairanapillai, *Nationalities in Indian Politics* (Lahore: Forman College, 1946), pp. 243-5.

INDIA, MY INDIA!

Sails forth our *Azan*; The *Muezzin* calls, and the Faithful flock
and the word of God is raised;
The outpours of the Faithfuls' hearts
Multiply and sally forth with the temples' blast of conches
And the air resounds, and the echoes rebound, with prayers.

We are rulers no more, but the memory of our reign
Is hallowed and enshrined in forty million hearts,
It shines as the Taj!
Which in the moonlit night, with its breathtaking beauty
Makes our hearts ache with love and with pride.
We are rulers no more but slaves;
And yet we owe allegiance only to the land
Where our gardens bloom in laps of countless tracts
Of velvet grass.
And sweet smelling mango groves thrive,
And pearly lakes, by lovely countryside,
Gleam palely under the shade of glimmering stars,
And sleeping corn and drooping buds and flowers
Are swayed and tossed and rocked by winter winds,
And childhood's favourite nooks and lanes
Beckon with trusting love: where we live
As one great family, and our neighbours
Rejoice in our rejoicings and console us in our griefs,
And cherish us throughout our lives.

Impossible to desert such a land!
Impossible to sever the ties of heart rooted so deep!
Say what is Pakistan? Where are we asked to live?
What do they mean by it?
Do we live in an unconsecrated land?
The pillars of our faith, do they rest on polluted soil?
Scorpion spare! The heart of Chishti bleeds!
Is the ground of Ajmer profane? By the soul of
Waris
Is the earth of Dewa unsanctified?
The mausoleums of Imams, situated in Lucknow,
Are they, God forbid, on unblessed ground?
Why dost thou build mosques on accursed sites?
And lay down thy forehead on earth abhorred?

Forbear for God's sake from shouting Pakistan,
Forbear from insulting thy forefathers:
Forbear from cutting a heart in two;
The nation will die, and the English will rule,
Look at Europe, piece by piece it has become divided.
And not one piece can call its soul its own.
Look at Arabia, tiny satellites
All paying tribute to the white-faced English King.
We Muslims of India, hundred million strong,
We will not lick the English boot!
We are the sons of unity!
Hearken the *Muezzin's* call.
We will not bow before the trinity!
We will not break the nation's head!
United we stand, divided we fall!

The Land of Moon and Stars
MAKHDOOM MOHIUDDIN

Makhdoom Mohiuddin (1908-69) represented the best traditions of the Progressive Writers' Movement, combining his literary pursuits with political activism. He resigned his teaching position in Hyderabad to join the Communist Party in 1943 and was founder-president of the All Hyderabad Trade Union Congress. Active in reviving the *ghazal*, a genre which had been set aside by the early adherents of the Progressive Movement, he has several poetry collections including *Surkh Savera* and *Gul-e-Tar*. For *Bisat-e-Raqs* he received the Sahitya Akademi Award (posthumously). A biography of Makhdoom, written by a Russian scholar, has been translated into Urdu.

Two of his poems are presented here. The first reflects the sentiments current, before and after Independence.

> Our martyred bodies burned like wax,
> The candle of our nation's dawn
> Flickered through the night.
> The land of moon and stars kept glowing.
> Still thirst was not slaked
> But even thirsty we were drunk.
> Bearing the empty cups of thirsty eyes
> Men and women waited.
> Their revelry, merry-making and wantonness ceased.
> Those bodies which glowed in the night:
> In the morning became a wailing wall,
> Became a thicket dense with thorns of grief.
> The pulsing artery of night
> Flowed out a river of blood.

Translated by Baidar Bakht in *An Anthology of Modern Urdu Poetry*, eds. Baidar Bakht and Kathleen Grant Jager (Delhi: Educational Book House, 1984), vol. 1, pp. 10-12.

Some wily leaders,
Serpent-tongued,
With hearts black with hate,
Leapt forth from ambush,
And drank the blood of morning's light.

The sky shows streaks of light,
But darkness too.
Friends,
Let us join our hands
And walk towards our goal
Past milestones of our love,
Past milestones of their gallows,
Through streets of the beloved,
Carrying our crosses on our shoulders.

INDEPENDENCE*

Victory to India! Hail India!
Sworn by the blood that has brought the garden
To fullness of colour,
Sworn by the blood of peasants and the blood
Of martyrs!

It is possible that the world's oceans should go dry,
It is possible that rivers should tire and sleep,

That hell's fires should stop burning is possible,
It is possible that lightning should lose speed—

This sacred land will not any more stand
Profanity,
This country's light of freedom will never be
Snuffed!

Victory to India! Hail India!

*'Azadi' from *Zabt Shuda Nazmen*, eds., Khaleeq Anjum and Mujtaba Husain, (Delhi, 1975), pp. 253-4.

Those young Indians who bore the flag of Independence,
Those defenders of the land who are
The bright and sharp sword of Independence,

That holy spark washed in lightning, that ember
In which life reigns,

That torch of life nourished by storms, that boat
Which the hurricanes have themselves protected, that
Impact which shakes the world, that stream which carries
the vessel of action!—

Hidden, silent sighs issue as the resonance
Of Resurrection,
Smothered flames have leapt to the glory of the sun's
Brightness!

India's youth has tempered the inevitability
Of prisons,
The warriors of Independence looked and broke
The chains of imprisonments!

Victory to India! Hail India!

Translated from Urdu by Rakshit Puri

The Morning of Freedom
August 1947
FAIZ AHMAD FAIZ

If ink and pen are snatched away from me, shall I
Who have dipped my finger in my heart's blood complain—
Or if they seal my tongue, when I have made
A mouth of every round link of my chain?

Next to Mohammad Iqbal, Faiz Ahmad Faiz (1912-85) was probably the greatest Urdu poet of the twentieth century. He was a leading figure in the Progressive Writers' Association, founded by Sajjad Zaheer and Mulk Raj Anand. From February 1947 to March 1951 he edited simultaneously two progressive daily papers, the English-language *Pakistan Times* and the Urdu *Imroze*. He was identified with the trade union movement and became vice-president of the Pakistan Trade Union Federation (1951). In March 1951, he was arrested and charged with taking part in a conspiracy to overthrow the Pakistan government. He was released in April and acquitted in September 1958.

Eight collections of his verse were published in his lifetime, the first *Naqsh-i Faryadi* in 1941, and *Dast-i Saba*, the second one in 1952. *Poems by Faiz*, with parallel verse translations by V.G. Kiernan, was published in 1971.

'Freedom's Dawn', along with 'To a Political Leader' and 'Speak', are eloquent commentaries on the August 1947 settlement, on the disappointment with the 'much stained radiance' and the 'night-bitten' morning. For Faiz, as for Jawaharlal Nehru in his tryst with destiny speech, freedom's dawn represented a moment of unfulfilled expectations, a time of anguish.

This daybreak, pockmarked—
this morning, night-bitten.

'Subha-i-Azadi' from *Dast-i Saba* (1952); *Journal of South Asian Literature*, vol. XXV, no. 2, p. 128.

THE MORNING OF FREEDOM

Surely it is not the morning we'd longed for
in whose eager quest all comrades
had set out, hoping that somewhere
in the wilderness of the sky
would appear the ultimate destination of stars.
Somewhere the wave of the slow night will meet the shore
and somewhere will anchor the boat of the heart's grief.

As our friends set out on the mysterious highways
of young blood, how many hands caught them by the sleeve.
From the dreamlands of beauty's pleasure-houses
kept beckoning to them, impatiently, seductive arms and bodies.
But we yearned only for the morning's face,
even though within easy reach was the hem of the radiant beauties.
Delicate was our longing and faint our sense of exhaustion.

It's heard that light and darkness have parted—
also, that there's now union between quest and goal
that the lot of the afflicted is now changed
that granted is the pleasure of union
and banished is the torment of separation.

Fire in the bosom, longing in the eyes, and the heart-burn—
nothing can solve the problem of separation.
Where did the sweet breeze come from and where did it vanish—
the street lamp has no news yet.
Even the night's heaviness is just the same;
still the moment of salvation has not arrived
for the heart and the eye.
So let's press on as the destination is still far away.

Black Margins
SAADAT HASAN MANTO

Saadat Hasan Manto (1912-55) belonged to a middle class Kashmiri family of Amritsar. Educated in Amritsar and briefly at the Aligarh Muslim University, he arrived in Bombay in 1936 to edit a film weekly, joined the All India Radio at Delhi in 1941 and returned to Bombay in 1943 to work with a group of friends at the famous Bombay Talkies. In January 1948 he moved to Karachi, the capital of the newly-created State of Pakistan. Virtually drinking himself to death at the age of forty-three (forty-two according to Ralph Russell), he wrote his own epitaph on 18 August 1954, a year before his death:

> Here Saadat Hasan Manto lies buried—and buried in his breast are all the secrets of the art of story writing. Even now, lying under tons of earth he is wondering whether he or God is the greater short story writer.

In all, Manto wrote over 200 stories and scores of plays and essays, the first story collection coming in 1940. Some were received well, but most were ignored or condemned for their alleged obsession with sex and the seamy side of life.

On two occasions, once in the early forties and the second time in 1948, Manto was prosecuted for obscenity. His stories about 1947 were denounced and he was accused of cynicism and sensationalizing a tragedy. A critic even went so far as to say that Manto had desecrated the dead and robbed them of their personal possessions to build a collection. Manto was angry not because the critic had done him an injustice, but because he had allowed himself to be led by the nose at the instance of a movement which was 'morbid' and 'sterile'. 'He questioned my sincerity because such were his instructions. These men moved in line with external political *diktat*. I had been judged and condemned because in their book what was not red was not acceptable.'

'Siyah Hashye' from *Atish Pare Aur Siyah Hashye* (Delhi, Urdu *Bazar*, 1984 edn.), pp. 142-85.

Manto was reacting to the criticism levelled by some of the leading lights of the Progressive Writers' Movement to *Siyah Hashye*. His own defence was:
> For a long time I refused to accept the consequences of the revolution, which was set off by the partition of the country. I still feel the same way; but I suppose, in the end, I came to accept this nightmarish reality without self-pity or despair. In the process I tried to retrieve from this man-made sea of blood, pearls of a rare hue, by writing about the single-minded dedication with which men had killed men, about the remorse felt by some of them, about the tears shed by murderers who could not understand why they still had some human feelings left. All this and more, I put in my book, *Siyah Hashye*.

Dedicated to the man who, in the course of narrating his bloody exploits, conceded: 'When I killed an old woman only then did I feel that I had committed murder.'

SWEET MOMENT
Sa'at-i-Shireen

It is learnt that sweets were distributed at several places in Amritsar, Gwalior and Bombay to rejoice the death of Mahatma Gandhi. (A.P.)

WAGES OF LABOUR
Mazdoori

Looting and plundering was rampant. More so following the inflamed communal passions.

A man was singing gleefully to his harmonium: *Jab tum hi gaye pardes laga kar thes; O pritam piyara duniya me kaun hamara.* Now that you too have abandoned me, living in a land far removed; whom can I call my own, O beloved.

An urchin scurried past with a packet of *papads*. He stumbled. The *papads* were strewn on the floor.

'Son, why bother to pick up the *papads*. They will turn to a crisp because the surface of the road is so hot,' admonished a man carrying an obviously stolen sewing-machine.

A heavy gunny bag landed right in the middle of the road with a thud. A man surged ahead and pierced his dagger into it expecting perhaps to find a bleeding fugitive. Instead out came crystal white sugar. People filled up their shirt fronts with the spilled sugar. One man in the crowd had no shirt on. He promptly took off his *tehmad*, spread it on the floor and filled it with sugar from his cupped hands.

'Make way! Make way!,' a *tonga* sped past loaded with almirahs with a fresh coat of paint.

Out came a bale of muslin from a high-rise building overlooking the street. It caught fire on its way down. The muslin was reduced to ashes before it hit the ground.

'*Po, Po,*' the loud honk of a car mingled with the screams of two women.

Ten or fifteen persons managed to haul the big iron safe out of the house. They tried to break it open with *lathis*.

Another man rushed out of a shop carrying a load of 'Cow and Gate' milk tins, his chin resting on them. He drifted towards the *bazar* lackadaisically.

A cry rent the air, 'Lemonade! Come, come, quench your thirst. It is summertime.'

A man with a car tyre hung around his neck came forward, picked up two bottles of lemonade and made off without a word of thanks.

Another frantic cry filled the air. 'Fire! My goods have caught fire. Please send for the fire brigade!' Nobody took notice.

Looting and pillage was still on. The fire was blazing and had spread. Then came the rattling sound of gunfire.

The police found a deserted *bazar*. But far away they spotted a hazy figure through the dense smoke. They too dashed in that direction.

The smoke cleared. They saw a Kashmiri labourer weighed down by a heavy load on his back. A heavy gunny bag indeed it was. The man kept running furiously. He did not stop, as if he was carrying an empty sack.

The men in uniform were breathless. One of them fired the first shot in exasperation. The bullet pierced through the Kashmiri labourer's calf. He could not hold on to the gunny bag. Yet he kept running. He looked at his bleeding calf, turned in anguish towards the policemen in hot pursuit, promptly lifted his gunny bag and started running again.

'Let him go to hell,' the policemen thought.

The Kashmiri stumbled, fell heavily on the ground trapped under the weight of the bag.

He was arrested and taken to the police station with the bag. On way to the police station, he pleaded innocence. '*Hazrat* Sir, why have you arrested me? I'm poor. I carried only a bag of rice. I'll cook some at home. You have needlessly fired at me.'

The Kashmiri labourer said a great deal more in the *thana*.

'*Hazrat*, other tall poppies are busy looting and plundering bigger things. Why me? I've merely taken a bag of rice. *Hazrat*, I'm very poor. I eat rice everyday.'

Ultimately, the Kashmiri gave up. He was worn out. He took out his dirty skullcap, wiped the sweat from his forehead. He eyed the rice bag—the final look. With his outstretched hands, he said to the *thanedar*, 'Okay, *hazrat*, you keep the rice. I demand my wages. Four *annas*!'

SHARING THE LOOT
Ta'awun

Forty-fifty *lathi*-wielding men headed towards a large house to loot and plunder.

Just then a middle-aged person appeared in the melee. He turned around and exhorted the rioters: 'Brothers, this house is full of wealth, priceless objects. Come, let us take over and share the booty.'

Several *lathis* were raised. Fists clenched. And loud and excited cries rent the sky.

The group of forty-fifty *lathi*-wielding characters, led by a frail-looking middle-aged man, speedily moved towards the house with precious objects.

The slim man spoke once more at the entrance.

'Comrades, everything here belongs to you. Make sure there are no clashes over who secures what. Come, this way. Avoid friction.'

'But the door is locked,' somebody shouted.

'Let us break in,' said someone else.

'Yes, yes, let's break in.'

Several *lathis* were raised. Fists clenched. And loud and excited cries rent the sky.

The frail man prevented the door from being broken down. 'Comrades, please wait. Let me open the lock with a key,' he said smiling.

He selected a key from his key-bunch and let open the *shisham* door.

Pandemonium prevailed. The crowd entered the house frantically.

The frail man tried to soothe tempers. 'Patience please, patience. Whatever is in here belongs to you. So, why this chaos?'

The crowd was pacified. One by one people began entering the house. But they became disorderly soon after. Without scruple they laid their hands on precious objects.

The frail man witnessed this disorderly scene.

'Comrades, take it easy. There is no need to quarrel or exchange blows. This is a large house. Find something precious for yourself. Don't take offence if somebody finds something invaluable. Don't act like savages. Vandalism is not on. It will hurt you more than anybody else,' he said in an anguished tone.

The rioters paid heed to his advice. Order was restored. Slowly the house was denuded of its precious belongings.

From time to time the frail man kept on repeating his directives. . . . 'See *bhaiya*, this is a radio. Handle it gently. Make sure it doesn't break. Take the cord along, too.'

'Fold it up, *bhai*, fold it up. It's a walnut table inlaid with ivory work. It's very delicate, very fragile. Well, it's alright now.'

'No, no, don't have a swig here. You will get tipsy. Take the bottle home.'

'Wait, wait, let me turn off the main switch. I don't want you to be electrocuted.'

In the meanwhile there was a scuffle in one corner of the room. Four rioters were embroiled in a dispute over a rolled length of silk.

The frail man rushed towards them. He chided them. 'You are so naive. This cloth will be torn to shreds. And it's so expensive. Find a tape-measure (*gaz*). Measure the cloth and share it equally.'

Just then, a dog barked—woof, woof, woof. Like a flash of lightning the big Alsatian made his way and mercilessly pounced on three or four intruders.

'Tiger! Tiger!' the frail man cried out.

Tiger had the end of a rioter's shirt in his mouth. He wagged his tail, lowered his head and moved towards the frail man.

The intruders had vanished. Only one person—the one attacked by Tiger—remained. 'Who are you?'

'The owner of the house. Beware! The crystal vase is slipping out of you fingers.'

FIFTY-FIFTY
Taqseem

One of them fancied a large wooden box. It was heavy. He could not move it an inch.

The other, having failed to find anything useful, extended a helping hand. 'May I help?'

'Yes,' came the answer.

The man who was unable to lay his hands on any worthwhile object moved the box with his strong hands and placed it on his back with one mighty heave.

Both stepped out.

The box was indeed very heavy. The man carrying it was weighed down. His legs caved in. But the prospect of reward kept him going despite the physical strain.

The man who had spotted the box was, in comparison, weak. He placed his hand firmly on the box, assuring himself that it was his.

When the two reached a safe destination, the man carrying the box placed it on the floor. 'So, what is my share?' he asked.

'One-fourth.'

'This is too little.'

'I don't think so. I think it is too much. I was the one who found the box.'

'Right. But who has carried this heavy load all the way?'

'Do you agree to fifty-fifty?'

'Very well. Open.'

The box was opened. Out came a man with a sword in his hand. He cut the two claimants into four.

LEGITIMATE USE
Jaiz Istemaal

The Pathan was fortified after firing forty rounds and injuring three men.

There was pandemonium all round. People were at one another's throats. They were running helter-skelter. There were violent skirmishes as well.

The Pathan jumped into the fray with his gun. He wrestled with the crowd for an hour before making good with a thermos.

Nobody was around when the police came. Not even the Pathan. A bullet grazed past his right ear. He took no notice. He held on to the red-coloured thermos firmly; his grip on it tightened.

To friends he displayed his prized trophy with pride. 'What have you brought?' he was asked by one of them with a smile.

The Khan *Saheb* gave an approving look at the shimmering lid of the flask. 'Why?'

'Well, don't you know? This flask keeps warm things warm and cold things cold.'

Khan *Saheb* tucked the flask in his big pocket. 'Fine, I'll keep my snuff. It will stay warm during summer and cold in winter.'

USE OF IGNORANCE
Bekhabri ka Faida

The trigger was pressed; the bullet shot out of the barrel.

A man looking through his window collapsed on the spot.

The trigger was pressed a second time. Another shot fired.

The water carrier's water-bag burst. He too collapsed. His blood mixed with water started flowing on the road.

The third shot. But this time it was off target. The bullet simply went through a damp wall.

The fourth bullet hit the back of an elderly woman. She died instantly—without a scream.

Nobody was killed. Nobody was injured. That was the fifth and sixth bullet.

The man was enraged. Suddenly he spotted a child sprinting across the road. He turned his pistol in his direction.

'What are you doing?' his companion said.

'Why?'

'You have no rounds to fire.'

'You keep quiet! How would that little child know?'

APPROPRIATE ACTION
Munasib Karawai

When the *mohalla* was attacked, some members of the minority community were killed. The survivors fled. A couple however sought refuge in the cellar of their own house.

For two days and nights they waited in vain for the assailants.

Two more days passed. They were much less afraid of death. They longed for food and water.

Four more days went by. By then the couple were no longer concerned with life or death.

They came out of hiding.

The husband tried to draw the people's attention. 'Please kill us. We've come to surrender,' he said in a feeble voice.

'Killing is a sin in our religion.'

They were Jains. Had a powwow. And handed over the couple to the people of another *mohalla* for 'appropriate action'.

MIRACLES
Karamaat

The police conducted raids to recover stolen goods.

Out of fear, people got rid of stolen goods under the cover of darkness. Some even put away their own possessions to avoid the police.

One man who was greatly troubled had looted two bags of sugar from the local grocer's shop. Somehow he dumped one into the nearby well. While doing the same with the other bag he fell into the well.

People heard the noise. They gathered at the well. Ropes were lowered. Two sturdy men hauled up the man. But he died a few hours later.

Water drawn from the well the next day tasted sweet.

Candles were lit at the man's grave that night.

CORRECTION
Islaah

'Who are you?'

'But, who are you?'

'Har Har Mahadev! Har Har Mahadev!'

'Har Har Mahadev!'

'What's the proof?'

'Proof? My name is Dharamchand.'

'This is no proof.'

'I'm well-versed in the four Vedas. Ask me about them.'

'We don't know the Vedas. We demand proof.'

'What?'

'Loosen your *pyjamas*.'
A cry went up when the *pyjama* was lowered. 'Kill him! Kill him!'
'Wait, wait I'm one of you. I swear I'm your brother.'
'Then what's all this?'
'The locality I live in is full of enemies. So I was forced to do it—only to save my life. This is my only mistake. For the rest I'm fine.'
'Chop off his mistake!'
The mistake was chopped off. So was Dharamchand.

AN ENTERPRISE
Dawat-i Amal

Fire gutted the entire *mohalla*. The hoarding on the shop that escaped the flames read:

'A complete range of building and construction materials sold here.'

PATHANISTAN

'*Khu*, speak out immediately. Who are you?'
'I . . . I. . . .'
'Son of Satan, speak, speak, speak! Are you an Indu [Hindu] or a *Muslimeen* [Muslim]?'
'*Muslimeen*.'
'*Khu*, who is your Prophet?'
'Mohammad Khan.'
'That's right, go.'

A WARNING
Khabardaar

The rioters wrestled hard with the landlord to drag him out of the house. He stood up, brushed his clothes and told them: 'Kill me for all I care. But I warn you not to touch my money—not a *paisa*.'

A RAW DEAL
Ghate ka Sauda

There were ten or twenty girls. Two friends paid forty-two rupees to buy off one of them.
'What is your name?' asked one of them.
The man was furious when the girl disclosed her name.

'We were told that you belonged to the other community!'
'He pulled a fast one on you,' the girl replied.
The man rushed to his friend's house.
'That bastard has cheated us. He palmed off to us a girl from our own community. Come, let's pack her off.'

BEASTLY TALE
Haiwaniyat

The couple managed to save some household possessions. But their young daughter was missing. The other baby girl clung to her mother.

The rioters took away their brown buffalo. The cow escaped their notice though not the calf.

Everyone went into hiding—the husband, the wife, the child and the cow.

It was dark. The fear-stricken girl started crying. In the stillness of the night it sounded like the beating of drums.

The mother panicked. She did not want the enemies to know the hiding place. She put her hand on the child's mouth. The father placed a thick sheet to cover her up.

Just then a calf mooed in the distance. The cow was alerted. It stood up and started running around from here to there excitedly. Efforts to quieten her down were in vain.

Having heard the noise the enemies surfaced with burning torches.

'Why bring this wretched beast along,' the wife chided her husband angrily.

HOSPITALITY DELAYED
Kasre-Nafsi

Rioters brought the running train to a halt. People belonging to the other community were pulled out and slaughtered with swords and bullets.

The remaining passengers were treated to *halwa*, fruits and milk.

The chief organizer said, 'Brothers and sisters, news of this train's arrival was delayed. That is why we've not been able to entertain you lavishly—the way we wanted to.'

CONVICTION
Istaqlal

'I refuse to be converted to Sikhism. Please return to me my razor.'

SUPERVISION
Nigrani Me

By declaring B as his co-religionist A travelled in a military truck to a certain destination.

En route B asked: 'Well *Janab*, has an untoward incident taken place around this area?'

'Nothing in particular. Of course, a dog was killed in that *mohalla*.'

'Any further news?' an anguished B asked.

'Nothing in particular. Just a few dead bitches were found floating in the nearby canal.'

Sensing the fear in B's mind, A said: 'Is the army not making arrangements?'

'Sure, everything is done under military supervision.'

MOURNING THE DEAD
Juta

The mob turned to its next target—Sir Ganga Ram's statue. They rained *lathi* blows on it, hurled bricks and stones. One of them disfigured the statue with coal tar. Somebody else collected old shoes to make a garland out of them. He proceeded towards the statue.

The police appeared and opened fire.

The man holding the garland of shoes was hit by a bullet. He was sent for first-aid to the Sir Ganga Ram Hospital.

INITIATIVE
Pesh-bandi

The first untoward incident occurred near the crossing of the hotel. Immediately a policeman was posted.

The very next day another incident took place in the evening in front of the store. The cop posted at the earlier spot was brought to the place where the second incident occurred.

The third incident happened at midnight around the laundrette.

When the inspector commanded the sepoy to move to the fresh

area of tension, he thought for a while and said 'Have me stationed at a place where a fresh skirmish is likely to occur.'

'A MISHTAKE'
Sorry

The knife slid down his groin. His *pyjama* cord was cut into two. '*Chi, chi, chi, chi,* I've made a *mishtake*,' the assassin said with a sense of remorse.

A RESPITE NEEDED
Aaram ki Zaroorat

'He isn't dead yet. See, see, he is still gasping for breath.'
'Let it go, *yaar*. I am already exhausted.'

JELLY

At six in the morning, the man selling ice from a pushcart next to the petrol pump was stabbed to death. His body lay on the road until seven, while water kept falling on it in steady driblets from the melting ice.

At a quarter past seven, the police took his body away. The ice and blood stayed on the road.

A *tonga* rode past. The child noticed the coagulated blood on the road, pulled at his mother's sleeve and said, 'Look mummy, jelly.'

VACATION FOREVER
Hamesha ki Chutti

Pakar lo, pakar lo! 'Catch hold of him, catch hold of him, don't let him get away!'

After a brief chase, the quarry was overtaken. He was about to be lanced to death when he said in a frightful voice, 'Please don't kill me, please don't . . . you see I'm going home on vacation.'

WHAT'S THE DIFFERENCE
Halal aur Jhatka

'I placed my knife across his windpipe and, slowly, very slowly, I slaughtered him.'
'What have you done?'

'Why?'
'Why kill him like that?'
'I love it that way.'
'You idiot, you should have hacked his neck off with a single blow. Like this.'
And the kosher-killer's neck was chopped off accordingly.

A CONCESSION
Riyayat

'Don't kill my young daughter right before my eyes.'
'All right, let's agree. Take off her clothes and throw her in with the rest.'

PROPRIETY
Safai-pasandi

The train was stationary.

Three gunmen appeared and looked into the [railway] compartment. 'Any turkey in there?' they enquired.

One of the passengers was about to say something but the other said 'no'.

After a while four men holding lances looked into the compartment windows. 'Any turkey in there?' they asked.

The man who was quiet before, spoke. 'I don't know. Come in and check out the lavatory.'

The men stepped in, broke down the lavatory door and emerged with a turkey.

'*Kar do halal*', said one of them holding the lance.

'No, not here', his other friend announced. 'The carriage will be spoilt. Let's move to the platform.'

PRAISE BE TO THE LORD
Sadqe us ke

The *mujra* [dancing session] was over. The clients went away. This is when *Ustadji* said, 'Having lost everything [during the country's partition] we came to this city. Praise be to Allah *Miyan* for having showered us with these riches in just a few days.

SOCIALISM
Ishtirakyat

He loaded his own belongings in a truck and started driving out of town. That is when he was stopped by some people. Eyeing the goods greedily, one person said to the other, 'Just look how conveniently he is decamping with so much of booty.'

The owner smiled. *Janab*, these are my personal belongings.

Two or three persons laughed [sarcastically]. 'Yes, we know everything.'

Somebody yelled. '*Loot lo*, he is a rich man—a robber using a truck.'

FERTILITY
Khaad

Commenting on a friend's suicide, his friend said: 'He was a fool. I kept arguing with him that if his beard was forcibly shaved off and his long hair scissored, it did not mean that he had forsaken his religion.' 'Use yoghurt everyday', I advised him, 'and by the *Guruji's* benediction your hair will grow again in a year and you will be just the same.'

DOUBLE CROSS [Title as translated by Khalid Hasan]
Ulhana

Look *yaar* [buddy], you sold me petrol at black-market prices and not a single shop could be set on fire.

ILL-LUCK
Qismat

'Well friend, despite all the hard work I could lay my hands on just this case. And do you know what I found? Pork.'

BLIND TO REALITY
Aankhon par Charbi

'How ungrateful are my co-religionists. I took great pains to find 50 pigs and slaughtered them in this mosque. But nobody at this end is buying pork. On the other hand, people out there [in the Hindu locality] are buying beef in temples.'

Translated from Urdu by Mushirul Hasan

The Book of Divine Knowledge
FIKR TAUNSVI

'With the passing of Fikr Taunsvi (1918-87),' commented Ali Jawad Zaidi, historian of Urdu literature, 'the subcontinent is deprived of a giant among historians.' He began as a journalist in Lahore and served on the editorial staff of *Savera* and *Adab-i Lateef*. He returned to India and wrote some excellent stories, 'Chatta Darya' and 'Satwan Asman' being the most well-known, on the havoc caused by partition. A noted columnist, his 'Pyaz ke Chilke' appeared in *Naya Zamana* and *Milan* with unfailing regularity for 25 years. From the time *Awadh Punch* was published in Lucknow, humour and satire occupied a prominent place in Urdu literature. Fikr Taunsvi enriched this tradition. He was a gifted writer with acute sensitivity to human tragedies. Three of his stories included in this collection, which have not found a place in any other anthology, illustrate how 'the natural flow in his humour knits puzzling images of fun and frolic, of sarcasm and exposure.'

Bequeathed simultaneously to the
Refugees of India and Pakistan.

THE GENESIS

In the beginning Lord God created the Englishman and his politics. The Englishman was clever and cruel. Politics was in his blood and the spirit of God was with him.

The Englishman said, 'Part!' So the partition took place. God blessed the partition. And then God divided the Muslim from the Hindu and called this division Pakistan. Pakistan was thus created.

'Aasmani Kitab' from *Satvan Shastra* (Delhi: Burki Press, 1950), pp. 67-86.

THE BOOK OF DIVINE KNOWLEDGE

And then God said, 'Let there be Hindu refugees in India!' And so it happened. The refugee was angered with fire in his eyes. And then God sanctified that fire and turned it into pure light. Let every free person be pure like that.

And then Lord God also created the Muslim refugee. It was necessary that the Hindu and the Muslim refugee be the same. His eyes like that of the Hindu refugee were also fired. Once again the Lord God sanctified that fire.

And then the Hindus and the Muslims fell apart; proof that they had once been one. The Lord God decreed, 'Let my earth be drenched with so much blood that it becomes crimson, and the whole land be filled with daggers, swords, spears! May the fire rage and consume the neighbourhoods where you live and enjoy the pleasures of life, the places you sow your desires, the fields where you grow golden ears of corn! Be cut into pieces, and lose your humanity and become devil's incarnate, barbarians. Let your women know the secret of nudity and learn to recognize its pleasures! May your tender children wail and cry hanging from the barrels of bayonets!'

And this is what happened. The sons of Adam became Hindu refugees and Muslim refugees, because they revelled in raising slogans and desired to make common hatred and barbarity. *La-ilaha*, *Sat Siri Akal* and *Bajrangbali* dominated the minds of the refugees. They, in turn, were dominated by their guardians, their new rulers who had inherited the kingdom from the king, namely their leaders, who were popular and loved. They possessed vast and enormous industries. They, the privileged sons of God, laid claim to the earth. So when the king handed over the kingdom to them and withdrew, he declared that it was disgraceful to dominate over free human beings. It was the duty of the free people to concede the right of domination to whomsoever they wanted. The Englishman had said that, and his laws were designed to fight fraud and injustice. The free human beings had thus capitulated and debased and degraded themselves. Such was the law of God—to give power and privilege to those who owned the vast earth. . .

The sons of Adam now saw that their daggers dripped with blood and their swords had become crimson; they saw their fields deserted and devastated. Gripped by depravity they began to wage a war. . . . The spirits of these slaves, who simply obeyed orders and did not deserve to be called freemen, fell upon one another. Everything appeared meaningless to them before the one passion that surged in their minds, the passion to defend their endangered religion. As they did so, the sons of God cheered them on, glorified their exploits. From slaves to freemen, from freemen to devils and from devils they turned to being Hindus and Muslims, and indulged in strife, murder and killing.

And the sons of God were pleased that their orders were obeyed. But the spate of killings and endless strife caused sorrow and grief; the future seemed bleak and startled them. They feared that the fruits of freedom might be frittered away. They commanded the people, 'Oh you! Why do you behave like animals? Have you no shame? Don't you know that God has placed you in our care? Doubtless, our country is free. All this endless strife, loot and plunder is dangerous. Don't you trust us to take care of you? Learn to live peacefully. Not like animals and ignorant fools: for that is what religion teaches us. Pay heed to the call of religion. Here we are! We desire to rule you. And you are bent on robbing us of our leisure and pleasure. Preserve the veil of shame and modesty! Look at this vast ocean stretched before you and jump into it. After all, the sovereignty over the sky, the earth, and over each and every particle of this universe has been bestowed upon us by Lord God Himself. And the burden of your life and security is on our heads.'

The people of India and Pakistan were ashamed and bowed their heads penitently. They realized that the sons of Lord God spoke the truth and that their orders were not to be flouted.

They commanded the people, 'You go to the country of the Hindus and you to that of the Muslims. It is only fit that you behave like sheeps. We will drive you!' So those sheeps came to be called refugees. They followed the orders of God, fled from their homes and became refugees.

II

THE MARCH OF THE CARAVAN

Hereafter begins the account of the caravan.

When the refugees left their homes they were to cross an endless plain—silent, frightening and full of horrors. But God's command was the same for everyone. They had found favour with His sons. So they were obliged to be on the move.

They longed for their homes where their souls dwelt, grieved for the bonds which gave meaning to their lives, pined over lasting memories, their link with their past. Now that bond was broken. The wealth amassed during centuries of toil was looted and plundered Confused and bewildered, they wept. Mothers abandoned their children and wives were separated from husbands. Nobody was left to take care of the old and the aged. Young and attractive beauties, possible victims of lust, were stripped, as if by choice.

And then the phantoms came out of their caves holding torches. They waved their spears, flashed their swords, their daggers. And then those hallowed figures scattered over the land where the river of lust was already in spate. . . .

And then the sons of God blew their bugles to celebrate freedom. They declared, 'Oh people! Organize yourselves into caravans.' The refugees replied, 'Oh hallowed and beloved sons of Lord God! You deprived us of everything. Now who will protect us?'

'But the Lord God will send the army.'

And then the army appeared and the refugees marched on. These caravans looked like a swarm of locusts. Afraid of the phantoms, the caravans marched on and on with their carts, oxen, horses, donkeys, cycles, their sisters, their wives, their mothers. They kept awake at night and travelled during the day. And they wept, tears welling up in their eyes. Cold sighs brought some relief.

And then the special bands of men, the agents of God's sons, attacked them with bombs and guns and thundered *La-ilaha* and *Sat Sri Akal.* Then the army appeared and showered bullets. Drinking the wine of martyrdom the refugees shouted to their God, 'Thy will is our will.' The women disappeared with these special agents, the children became a part of the piles of corpses. Their belongings, their gold and silver jewelry was plundered. They were thus relieved of their burden. They set out on the journey once again. God's command was being fulfilled.

And then the caravan started moving by special trains. The refugees were not allowed to come out to quench their thirst. Stations and jungles sped past. At times the train came to a sudden halt, not moving for as long as eight or ten hours. The refugees quarrelled with one another, which God claimed they were prone to doing. Then the phantoms descended on them beating drums, holding spears, daggers, guns. And then the refugees put their children before them, surrendered their wives and offered their unlawful belongings. Since they had disobeyed, their possessions were plundered, they were blinded and given a taste of death. And then darkness descended. The plains and the trains were littered with corpses—the place was a pool of blood. ... And the caravan moved on. That is what the Lord God had ordained.

At last the refugees reached the border where the flags fluttered—the border sanctified by the sons of Lord God. The Lord God announced, 'From now on this land is yours.' But the refugees replied that their land had been left behind. God was angered by their insolence. And then the refugees raised slogans to wish the sons of Lord God a long and happy life. The sons of God, too, realized the value of the refugees' loyalty. 'Look, we will control every refugee who has come on foot, by train or car, whose women have disappeared, whose children are dead and who lives on the earth under the sky. We will pick the fruit from your trees because we are your Lord God, and because the burden of your protection had been placed on our shoulders—he, whose leg has been cut, and he who has lost his eyesight, and all the others.' The refugees were consoled. 'Long live our religion! May our religion flourish till eternity, and may our enemies be crushed forever!' And then the earth shuddered just once, for God's command was binding on it as well.

III

THE REFUGEE CAMPS

An account follows of the camps, that handiwork of God, which He created for the refugees. Here they lived in adversity, their bodies scorched, and in search of a home. So the sons of Lord God raised the tents.

Now the refugees settled in tents made of cloth. In each tent lived more than ten families. 'Be thankful to God for this gift,' the sons of God tom-tomed. And then God commanded that the tents be exposed to the winter, lashed by rains and scorched by the sun. But the bond of love and loyalty to the guardians of this country was not to be broken. 'For that is what we expect from you. You shall have no cause to fear.' But the refugees could not overcome their fear. To mollify them God's sons provided them with wheat flour, roasted gram and clothes. But the refugees' stomachs ached with the gram. And the sons of Lord God assured them it was due to their obedience and their spirit of self-sacrifice. The refugees' failed to understand the logic. This angered the sons of God. But the refugees were also infuriated. They did not have sufficient clothes to cover themselves, the flour was full of stones, gravel, sand particles. The sons of God were perturbed. They admonished them to improve their behaviour. 'It is in their nature to be perturbed and gloomy,' added the sons of God.

The tents pitched in a huge desert gave the impression of being haunted. The refugees' faces were pale, their clothes had gaping holes in them. Broken pots and pans lay about. Bewilderment and expectation peeped from the refugees' eyes and half-open lips; an expectation of burnt *rotis*, *dal* and rice. And the women with silken bodies, who had never stepped out of their homes, were clad in rags.

God's sons seemed to have developed a compassionate feeling. But the refugees thought that they were being deceived. So they took the cotton out of their quilts and used the covers as clothes. And then the Lord God said, 'Oh! People! I mean refugees. Learn to be patient!' So the refugees learnt to be patient, hungry, clotheless. Then the Lord God added, 'If you have any home on this earth, then this is it. Just be quiet! The sons of God will protect you and look after you.' So, the sons of God looked after them. And then the dirt and stink in the camp spread all around them. The refugees begged, 'Do not kill us with cholera.' The Lord God admonished them, 'Oh! People! Learn to be clean. Have a bath everyday!' But the refugees did not learn to have a bath. They learnt to sell their jewelry, their daughters and preferred to die in their tents. The beloved sons of God were disgusted.

After that the Lord God sent his angels to their tents to distribute alms, flour, clothes, and give birth to corruption. The angels did not think it worth their while to provide the first three and concentrated on the last. And the refugees pleaded with God not to ridicule them but to tell them how to improve their lot. But having sent them the angels, God totally ignored them and was lost in His own dreams. The angels asserted, 'Your complaint is not justified. You'd better stop creating trouble for your country, for it is written in the holy book that silence is the sign of profound wisdom and insight.'

And so six months passed. The refugees concluded that they lived like savages. The angels of God agreed and chided them for being so good. 'Your limbs have become atrophied and you are a burden. Take your wives and get out of here! The whole world, over which I rule, is open to you: go anywhere! You have become a nuisance for the whole country! Have you no shame left in you! Fed on doled out gram, your limbs have become paralyzed!'

The refugees did not understand: they did not refrain from creating trouble. On the contrary, they confronted the angels, 'Actually it's you who have lost all sense of shame. We certainly want to work. You show us the way. We grope in the dark.' The angels added, 'You are blind. That is why you see nothing.'

The refugees' life hung in a balance. Their shelters stank. Their food was still full of stones and gravel. The clothes still had gaping holes in them. Nowhere was work to be found. They concluded that their efforts had been in vain; instead they were humiliated and disgraced. Their souls still dwelt in their former homes; only their bodies were in the tents.

At this point they called out, 'God! Your dream is right in its own place, but pay heed to our clamour. Take away your tents! Give us the security of our own home. Give us enough food to fill our bellies. Is this how you fulfill the promise to look after....?'

This awakened the Lord God and His privileged sons, and they commanded, 'Scatter over this vast land under our rule. Your noise makes us doubt our achievements. If you don't desist, we will teach you a lesson you will remember all your lives!'

And then the refugees learnt their lesson. The tents were removed. And the sons of Lord God ordered the angels to disperse the people. The angels bowed and carried out the Lord's decision, for they were, from the beginning, the most obedient servants of the Lord.

IV

THE REHABILITATION

This account of rehabilitation unfolds how the Lord God eventually solved the refugee problem.

It is considered 'most exalted' for all the sons of God to find a place in it. The kingdom belongs to them, the entire universe is suspended between their jaws. Their word is law, so they could perform the miracle of refugee rehabilitation. On the other hand the wretched and insignificant children of Adam could only be refugees.

Consequently the refugees and their children who were not destined to die in the tents, their women who constantly coughed because they had high fever and lung congestion, their old and aged who suffered from palsy, were made to march from their camps. Marching made the blood run faster in the veins and gave vigour to their limbs. So said the hallowed sons of God.

And then the sons of God established a new department—rehabilitation. The refugees hoped that this department would be different. But their expectations were belied. The sons of God asserted, 'Oh, people! This department is at your service. Let everyone, high or low, benefit from it.' But soon limits were laid down. God's chosen angels descended to take charge, as no one else was wise and able to accomplish the task that lay ahead. Having done so, the people were divided into different categories. This method proved useful and made the task of writing the fates of people easier. The established order was such that even the angels could not change it. And then they looked around. Their eyes fell on the villages and cities proclaimed by the Lord God as his kingdom.

The land lay devastated and barren. Not a grain grew on it, as if it had been cursed. Homes lay broken, battered. The abandoned homes were destroyed with a vengeance. The angels of God brought the refugees to these villages and said, 'All this vast expanse of land belongs to the Lord God. Cast a glance, and be thrilled that God—the Lord of us all—owns this land which resembles gold.' The refugees desired to share land between themselves. 'But this would create harmony and fellowship between you people,' the angels of God said. So the refugees pleaded with folded hands, and turned indifferent. They did not produce a single grain from the land. They were angered. They wanted to commit the folly of living in fellowship and harmony with one another. But this was not in conformity with God's command. To do so was a sacrilege. Neither the kingdom of India nor Pakistan were willing to tolerate this. 'Is this how you are going to destroy all that differentiates you from them?' the sons of God asked indignantly.

So the Lord God picked up some prominent refugees and gave them the large estates that they had left behind in their villages. This angered the refugees. They sent delegations, and protested, 'Lord God! Why ignore us? And what about your promise to take care of us? It is we who gave you your crown.' And God replied as always, 'Angels and Gods have been a part of this land for ages. Their beloved landlords deserve to be respected by us. This is our sacred duty. Their knowledge, status and possessions give them immense power. So, people! Be thankful to us that we have restored the old order and bestowed upon you the same distinguished position that you have always enjoyed as slaves. Rise, and yoke your oxen to the plough and sow the seed so that the land produces gold! Work hard—work is an essential mark of man's freedom! Grow sweet and juicy fruits so that your Lord God, His angels and His sons and all his beloveds, who live in magnificent palaces, may enjoy themselves and feel happy! Are you angry? Why? After all you are tenants. Labour is your birthright and helplessness comes naturally to you. Why lament? To do so is a sin in the eyes of God. Expression of resentment will incur the wrath of God, as it did during the time of Noah.'

The refugees began to sigh and cry, betraying their helplessness, sorrow and subjection. Before them sprawled the land, the angels' command hung over their heads, and the power of the landlords loomed large over them. Want and hunger hovered around them like vultures.

And then it thundered and rained. The land was soaked. They lifted the ploughs on their shoulders. The cattle went into motion. They sweated and ears of corn sprouted. And then the sons of God expressed their joy. The refugees gathered the grain and filled the granaries of the landlords to the brim. Then suddenly the grain disappeared from the granaries. They called it 'black market'. The angels of God declared famine in the country. The refugees had no idea how that famine had come about. Someone suggested they'd better ask the Lord God, for the ploughs had ploughed the land, sweat and labour had been poured into the land, heaps of grain had been produced. Then why this famine? But questioning God was a folly. It was not done in God's world. The hallowed sons of God knew perfectly well why the famine had come about, but the poor refugees—the product of hate—were the only ones who knew nothing about this, the famine in reality being man-made.

And then, as ordained by God's law, the landlords demarcated the land to become its masters. The landlords were also refugees, but had refugees as tenants. So the refugees who ploughed the land, sowed the seeds, grew the ears of corn, faced hunger and thirst. They helplessly observed the events around them and tried to find out why their fellow-refugees were dying around them. Soon, they realized that they belonged to a different category of refugees. Like the land, the houses too were divided into categories. Big houses and small houses; lofty houses and low houses; grand houses and dilapidated houses. And then the categories of refugees were fitted to the categories of houses. That is how they were forced to live in houses which were not even fit for animals. The Lord God was greatly troubled and pained that this was so. But then God does not keep his wealth to himself. To whomsoever he gives his wealth, he gives in plenty. Those who he chooses not to give, receive nothing. The angels of God made this known loud and clear, but the refugees considered it as plain nonsense and attributed it to God's vanity. The Lord God knew the truth but considered the refugees as treacherous.

What follows is a description of the cities which had grand mansions, huge bungalows and industries, and where there was much business activity. Along with them were huts and burnt houses left behind by the refugees. There too the angels were appointed to take up rehabilitation.

And then a new class of people surfaced, resembling the sons of Lord God. They had white cloth caps on and assumed the responsibility of rehabilitating the city. A committee was formed by these people, in red and white cloth caps. The houses, industries and shops were their chessboard and they played a game which the refugees did not comprehend. Pawn after pawn was being beaten and thrown out. New pawns were introduced to take their place. They too met the same fate. And the sons of Lord God approved of the game because in this way the refugees were being eliminated systematically.

And then a word descended from the heavens which was called 'allot' by the sons of God, but the refugees mistakenly called it 'cut'. For them it meant that the white-capped ones first allotted and then had their cut. And whatever little was left between 'allot' and 'cut' was considered by the refugees as a sleight of God's hand. But the Lord God affirmed, 'This does not, in anyway, fall into the category of sleight of hand or jugglery. Try to see it in terms of rehabilitation. Do not point out any mistakes. Leave all that to us. We have kept all this under our control because we do not want it to be used as an instrument that would destroy our peace.'

This went on for many days. The vast and spacious bungalows, the gardens full of sweet and juicy fruit, the industries and their enormous production, and the trucks loaded with wealth, were distributed among the respectable, dignified and the white-capped. They were refugees, though of a superior kind. And then came the turn of those who made so much noise about 'allotment' and had faith in the law of God. They did not find favour and were humiliated. Their condition was pathetic. They occupied a house for a day. The next day they were on the roadside with their belongings. Another house was allotted to them the third day. But that allotment too was provisional. God's law was in the process of being implemented, hence on-the-spot cancellations. So the refugees spent every third evening on the roadside. 'That is all that we can do for you,' the angels of God told the refugees. The department of rehabilitation was saved from closing down because of allotments and cancellations. The refugees said to the sons of Lord God, 'If you think that all that is going on is right, you are wrong. It is certainly not so.' 'How dare you say that?' The refugees were put down, because the sons of Lord God had prisons, the police and the army at their command, which were completely subservient to them. The refugees must remain a harassed lot. So decreed the sons of God.

The revelations about loans and employment were no different. The refugees belonging to the superior category benefited greatly, and though small in number, wielded great influence.

And then the sons of God attained an exalted position. The world was told with great flourish about their accomplishments. As a result, they earned honour and respect. 'May God protect them till eternity and may they retain the power of interfering in the affairs of His Kingdom,' prayed the angels of God.

And the refugees repeated their insults and humiliation. Even though they lost their land, their children, their women, yet they loved their new country (even before its birth). And what did they gain? So they turned insolent. And according to God's law book, His sons had every right to punish them for that reason.

This book of divine knowledge bequeathed to the refugees is considered by the sons of God as unlawful and an instrument for instigating violence. The refugees must accept this truth. Lord God will make them suffer in perpetuity. Amen.

Translated from Urdu by A.S.Judge*

---

*This is not a literal translation, though every effort has been made to reflect the theme of the story as well as Fikr Taunsvi's anger and anguish at the partition of the country.

We Have Arrived in Amritsar
BHISHAM SAHNI

Bhisham Sahni (b. 1915), a product of Lahore's Government College, took the last train to India, settled in Delhi and lectured in the Delhi University. He has published five novels, eight collections of short stories, three full-length plays and a biography of his extremely talented actor brother, Balraj Sahni. He is a recipient of numerous awards, including the Sahitya Akademi Award for his novel *Tamas* (Darkness), in 1975, on which a highly acclaimed television serial was based. The Bombay High Court and the Supreme Court of India, rejecting the petition for suspending its telecast in 1988, held: '*Tamas* takes us to a historical past—unpleasant times, when a human tragedy of great dimension took place in this subcontinent. . . . Naked truth in all times will not be beneficial but truth in its proper light indicating the evils and the consequences of those evils is constructive and that message is there in *Tamas*.'

There were not many passengers in the compartment. The Sardarji, sitting opposite me, had been telling me about his experiences in the war. He had fought on the Burmese front, and every time he spoke about the British soldiers, he had a hearty laugh at their expense. There were three Pathan traders too, and one of them, wearing a green *salwar-kameez*, lay stretched on one of the upper berths. He was a talkative kind of a person and had kept up a stream of jokes with a frail-looking *babu* who was sitting next to me. The *babu*, it seemed, came from Peshawar, because off and on they would begin to converse with each other in Pushto. In a corner, under the Pathan's berth, sat an old woman telling beads on her rosary, with her head and shoulders covered by a shawl. These were

'Amritsar Aa Gaya Hai' from *The Penguin Book of Modern Indian Short Stories,* eds. Stephen Alter and Wimal Dissanayake (Delhi: Penguin Books, 1989), pp. 180-192.

the only passengers that I can recollect being in the compartment. There might have been others too, but I can't remember them now. The train moved slowly and the passengers chatted away. Outside the breeze made gentle ripples across the ripening wheat. I was happy because I was on my way to Delhi to see the Independence Day celebrations.

Thinking about those days it seems to me that we had lived in a kind of mist. It may be that as time goes by all the activities of the past begin to float in a mist, which seems to grow thicker and thicker as we move away further into the future.

The decision about the creation of Pakistan had just been announced and people were indulging in all kinds of surmises about the pattern of life that would emerge. But no one's imagination could go very far. The Sardarji sitting in front of me repeatedly asked me whether I thought Mr Jinnah would continue to live in Bombay after the creation of Pakistan or whether he would resettle in Pakistan. Each time my answer would be the same, 'why should he leave Bombay? I think he'll continue to live in Bombay and keep visiting Pakistan.' Similar guesses were being made about the towns of Lahore and Gurdaspur too, and no one knew which town would fall to the share of India and which to Pakistan. People gossiped and laughed in much the same way as before. Some were abandoning their homes for good, while others made fun of them. No one knew which step would prove to be the right one. Some people deplored the creation of Pakistan, others rejoiced over the achievement of independence. Some places were being torn apart by riots, others were busy preparing to celebrate Independence. Somehow we all thought that the troubles would cease automatically with the achievement of freedom. In that hazy mist there came the sweet taste of freedom and yet the darkness of uncertainty seemed continuously to be with us. Only occasionally through this darkness did one catch glimpses of what the future meant for us.

We had left behind the city of Jhelum when the Pathan sitting on the upper berth untied a small bundle, took out chunks of boiled meat and some bread, and began distributing it among his companions. In his usual jovial manner he offered some of it to the *babu* next to me.

'Eat it, eat it. It will give you strength. You will become like us. Your wife too will be happy with you. You are weak because you eat *dal* all the time. Eat it, *dalkhor.*'

There was laughter in the compartment. The *babu* said something in Pushto but kept smiling and shaking his head.

The other Pathan taunted him further.

'O *zalim*, if you don't want to take it from our hands, pick it up yourself with your own hand. I swear to God that it is only goat's meat and not of any other animal.'

The third Pathan joined in: 'O son of a swine, who is looking at you here? We won't tell your wife about it. You share our meat and we shall share your *dal* with you.'

There was a burst of laughter. But the emaciated clerk continued to smile and shake his head.

'Does it look nice that we should eat and you should merely look on?' The Pathans were in good humour.

The fat Sardarji joined in and said, 'He doesn't accept it because you haven't washed your hands,' and burst out laughing at his own joke. He was reclining on the seat with half his belly hanging over it. 'You just woke up and immediately started to eat. That's the reason *babuji* won't accept food from your hands. There isn't any other reason.' As he said this he gave me a wink and guffawed again.

'If you don't want to eat meat, you should go and sit in a ladies' compartment. What business have you to be here?'

Again the whole compartment had a good laugh. All the passengers had been together since the beginning of the journey, a kind of informality had developed amongst them.

'Come and sit by me. Come, rascal, we shall sit and chat about *kissakhani*.'

*

The train stopped at a wayside station and new passengers barged into the compartment. Many of them forced their way in.

'What is this place?' someone asked.

'Looks like Wazirabad to me,' I replied, peering out of the window.

The train only stopped for a short time, but during the stop a minor incident occurred. A man got down from a neighbouring compartment and went to the tap on the platform for water. He had hardly filled his glass with water when suddenly he turned round and started running back towards his compartment. As he ran the water spilled out of the glass. The whole manner of his dash was revealing to me. I had seen people running like this before and knew immediately what it meant. Two or three other passengers, who were queuing at the tap also began running towards their compartments. Within seconds the whole platform was deserted. Inside our compartment, however, people were still chatting and laughing as before.

Beside me the *babu* muttered: 'Something bad is happening.'

Something really had happened but none of us could figure it out. I had seen quite a number of communal riots and had learnt to detect the slightest change in the atmosphere; people running, doors shutting, men and women standing on housetops, an uncanny silence all round—these were signs of riots.

Suddenly the sound of a scuffle was heard from the back-entrance to the compartment. Some passenger was trying to get into the compartment.

'No, you can't come in here,' someone shouted. 'There is no place here. Can't you see? No, no. Go away.'

'Shut the door,' someone else remarked. 'People just walk in as though it was their uncle's residence.'

Several voices were heard, speaking simultaneously.

As long as a passenger is outside a compartment and is trying desperately to get in, he faces strong opposition from those inside. But once he succeeds in entering, the opposition subsides and he is soon accepted as a fellow traveller, so much so that at the next stop, he too begins to shout at the new passengers trying to get in.

The commotion increased. A man in soiled, dirty clothes and with drooping moustache forced his way into the compartment. From his dirty clothes he appeared to be a sweet-vendor. He paid no attention to the shouts of protest of the passengers. He squeezed himself inside and turned around to try and haul in his enormous black trunk.

'Come in, come in, you too climb,' he shouted, addressing someone behind him. A frail, thin woman entered the door followed by a young dark girl of sixteen or seventeen. People were still shouting at them. The Sardarji had got up on his haunches.

Everyone seemed to be shouting at the same time: 'Shut the door. Why don't you?' People just come barging in.' 'Don't let anyone in.' 'What are you doing?' 'Just push him out, somebody. . . .'

The man continued hauling in his trunk, while his wife and daughter shrank back and stood against the door of the toilet, looking anxious and frightened.

'Can't you go to some other compartment? You have brought womenfolk with you too. Can't you see this is a men's compartment?.

The man was breathless and his clothes were drenched with perspiration. Having pulled in the trunk, he was now busy collecting the other sundry items of his baggage.

'I am a ticket holder. I am not travelling without tickets. There was no choice. A riot has broken out in the city. It was an awful job, reaching the railway station....'

All the passengers fell silent except the Pathan who was sitting on the upper berth. He leaned forward and shouted, 'Get out of here! Can't you see there is no room here?'

Suddenly he swung out his leg and kicked the man. Instead of hitting the man, his foot landed squarely on the wife's chest. She screamed with pain, and collapsed on the door.

There was no time for argument. The sweet-vendor continued to assemble his baggage into the compartment. Everybody was struck silent. After pulling in the heavy bundle he was struggling with the bars of a dismantled *charpoy*. The Pathan lost all patience.

'Turn him out, who is he anyway? he shouted.

One of the Pathans sitting on the lower berth got up and pushed the man's trunk out of the compartment.

In that silence only the old woman could be heard. Sitting in the corner, she muttered abstractedly, 'Good folk, let them come in. Come, child, come and sit with me. We shall manage to pass the time somehow. Listen to me. Don't be so cruel....'

The train began to move.

'Oh, the luggage! What shall I do about my luggage!' the man shouted, bewildered and nervous.

'*Pitaji* [father], half our luggage is still outside! What shall we do?' the girl cried out, trembling.

'Get down. Let's get down. There is no time,' the man shouted nervously, and throwing the big bundle out of the door, he caught hold of the door-handle, and hurried down. He was followed by his trembling daughter and his wife who still clutched at her chest and moaned with pain.

'You are bad people!' the old woman shouted. 'You have done

a very bad thing. All human feeling has died in your hearts. He had his young daughter with him. There is no pity in your hearts....'

The train left the deserted platform and steamed ahead. There was an uneasy silence in the compartment. Even the old woman had stopped muttering. No one had the courage to defy the Pathans.

Just then the *babu* sitting next to me touched my arm and whispered agitatedly, 'Fire! Look! There is a fire out there!'

By now the platform had been left far behind and all we could see was clouds of smoke rising from the leaping flames.

'A riot has started! That's why the people were running about on the platform. Somewhere a riot has broken out!'

The whole city was aflame. When the passengers realized what was happening, they all rushed to the windows to get a better view of the inferno.

*

There was an oppressive silence in the compartment. I withdrew my head from the window and looked about. The feeble-looking *babu* had turned deathly pale, the sweat on his forehead was making it glisten in the light. The passengers were looking at each other nervously. A new tension could now be felt between them. Perhaps a similar tension had arisen in each compartment of the train. The Sardarji got up from his seat and came over and sat down next to me. The two Pathans sitting on the lower berth climbed up to the upper berth where their compatriot was sitting. Perhaps the same process was on in other compartments also. All dialogue ceased. The three Pathans, perched side by side on the upper berth, looked quietly down. The eyes of each passenger were wide with apprehension.

'Which railway station was that? asked someone.

'That was Wazirabad.'

The answer was followed by another reaction. 'The Pathans looked perceptibly relieved. But the Hindu and Sikh passengers grew more tense. One of the Pathans took a small snuffbox out of his waistcoat and sniffed it. The other Pathans followed suit. The old woman went on with her beads but now and then a hoarse whisper could be heard coming from her direction.

A deserted railway platform faced us when the train stopped at the next station. Not even a bird anywhere. A water carrier, his water-bag on his back, came over to the train. He crossed the platform and began serving the passengers with water.

'Many people killed. Massacre, massacre,' he said. It seemed as though in the midst of all that carnage he alone had come out to perform a good deed.

As the train moved out again people suddenly began pulling down the shutters over the windows of the carriage. Mingled with the rattle of wheels, the clatter of closing shutters must have been heard over a long distance.

The *babu* suddenly got up from his seat and lay down on the floor. His face was still deathly pale. One of the Pathans perched above the others said mockingly: 'What a thing to do! Are you a man or a woman? You are a disgrace to the very name of man!' The others laughed and said something in Pushto. The *babu* kept silent. All the other passengers too were silent. The air was heavy with fear.

'We won't let such an effeminate fellow sit in our compartment,' the Pathan said. 'Hey *babu*, why don't you get down at the next station and squeeze into a ladies' compartment?'

The *babu* stammered something in reply, and fell silent. But after a little while he quietly got up from the floor, and dusting his clothes went and sat down on his seat. His whole action was completely puzzling. Perhaps he was afraid that there might soon be stones pelting the train or firing. Perhaps that was the reason why the shutters had been pulled down in all the compartments.

Nothing could be said with any sense of certainty. It may be that some passengers, for some reason or the other, had pulled down a shutter and that others had followed suit without thinking.

*

The journey continued in an atmosphere of uncertainty. Night fell. The passengers sat silent and nervous. Now and then the speed of the train would suddenly slacken, and the passengers would look at one another with wide-open eyes. Sometimes it would come to a halt, and the silence in the compartment would deepen. Only the Pathans sat as before, unruffled and relaxed. They too, however, had stopped chatting because there was no one to take part in their conversation.

Gradually the Pathans began to doze off while the other

passengers sat staring into space. The old woman, her head and face covered in the folds of her shawl, her legs pulled up on the seat, dozed off too. On the upper berth, one of the Pathans awoke, took a rosary out of his pocket and started counting the beads.

Outside, the light of the moon gave the countryside an eerie look of mystery. Sometimes one could see the glow of fire on the horizon. A city burning. Then the train would increase its speed and clatter through expanses of silent country, or slow down to an exhausted pace.

Suddenly the feeble-looking *babu* peeped out of the window and shouted, 'we have passed Harbanspura!' There was intense agitation in his voice. The passengers were all taken aback by this outburst and turned round to stare at him.

'*Eh, babu*, why are you shouting?' the Pathan with the rosary said, surprised. 'Do you want to get down here? Shall I pull the chain?' He laughed jeeringly. It was obvious that he knew nothing about the significance of Harbanspura. The location and the name of the town conveyed nothing to the Pathan.

The *babu* made no attempt to explain anything. He just continued to shake his head as he looked out of the window.

Silence descended on the passengers of the compartment once again. The engine sounded its whistle and slowed its pace immediately. A little later, a loud clicking sound was heard; perhaps the train had changed tracks. The *babu* peeping out of the window looked towards the direction in which the train was advancing.

'We are nearing some town,' he shouted. 'It is Amritsar.' He yelled at the top of his voice and suddenly stood up and, addressing the Pathan sitting on the upper berth, shouted, 'You son of a bitch, come down!'

The *babu* started yelling and swearing at the Pathan, using the foulest language. The Pathan turned around and asked, 'What is it, *babu*? Did you say something to me?'

Seeing the *babu* in such an agitated state of mind, the other passengers too pricked up their ears.

'Come down, *haramzade*. You dared kick a Hindu woman, you son of a ....'

'*Hey*, control your tongue, *babu*! You swine, don't swear or I'll pull out your tongue!'

'You dare call me a swine!' the *babu* shouted and jumped on to his seat. He was trembling from head to foot.

'No, no, no quarrelling here', the Sardarji intervened, trying to pacify them. 'This is not the place to fight. There isn't much of the journey left. Let it pass quietly.'

'I'll break your head,' the *babu* shouted, shaking his fist at the Pathan. 'Does the train belong to your father?'

'I didn't say anything. Everyone was pushing them out. I also did the same. This fellow here is abusing me. I shall pull out his tongue.'

The old woman again spoke beseechingly, 'Sit quietly, good folk. Have some sense. Think of what you are doing.'

Her lips were fluttering like those of a spectre, and only indistinct, hoarse whispers could be heard from her mouth.

The *babu* was still shouting, 'You son of a bitch, did you think you would get away with it?'

The train steamed into Amritsar railway station. The platform was crowded with people. As soon as the train stopped they rushed towards the compartments.

'How are things there? Where did the riot take place?' they asked anxiously.

This was the only topic they talked about. Everyone wanted to know where the riot had taken place. There were two or three hawkers, selling *puris* on the platform. The passengers crowded round them. Everyone had suddenly realized that they were very very hungry and thirsty. Meanwhile two Pathans appeared outside our compartment and called out for their companions. A conversation in Pushto followed. I turned around to look at the *babu*, but he was nowhere to be seen. Where had he gone? What was he up to? The Pathans rolled up their beddings and left the compartment. Presumably they were going to sit in some other compartment. The division among the passengers that had earlier taken place inside the compartments was not taking place at the level of the entire train.

The passengers who had crowded round the hawkers began to disperse to return to their respective compartments. Just then my eyes fell on the *babu*. He was threading his way through the crowd towards the compartment. His face was still very pale and on his forehead a tuft of hair was hanging loose. As he came near I noticed that he was carrying an iron rod in one of his hands. Where had he got that from? As he entered the compartment he furtively hid the rod behind his back, and as he sat down, he quickly pushed it under the seat. He then looked up towards the upper berth and not finding the Pathans there grew agitated and began looking around.

'They have run away, the bastards! Sons of bitches!'

He got up angrily and began shouting at the passengers: 'Why did you let them go? You are all cowards! Impotent people!' But the compartment was crowded with passengers and no one paid any attention to him.

The train lurched forward. The old passengers of the compartment had stuffed themselves with *puris* and had drunk enormous quantities of water; they looked contented because the train was now passing through an area where there was no danger to their life and property. The new entrants into the compartment were chatting noisily. Gradually the train settled down to an even pace and people began to doze. The *babu*, wide awake, kept staring into space. Once or twice he asked me about the direction in which the Pathans had gone. He was still beside himself with anger.

In the rhythmical jolting of the train I too was overpowered by sleep. There wasn't enough room in the compartment to lie down. In the reclining posture in which I sat my head would fall, now to one side, now to the other. Sometimes I would wake up with a start and hear the loud snoring of the Sardarji who had gone back to his old seat and had stretched himself full length on it. All the passengers were lying or reclining in such grotesque postures that one had the impression that the compartment was full of corpses. The *babu* however sat erect, and now and then I found him peeping out of the window.

Every time the train stopped at a wayside station, the noise from the wheels would suddenly cease and a sort of desolate silence descend over everything falling on the platform or of a passenger getting down from a compartment, and I would sit up with a start.

*

Once when my sleep was broken, I vaguely noticed that the train was moving at a very slow pace. I peeped out of the window. Far away, to the rear of the train, the red lights of a railway signal were visible. Apparently the train had left some railway station but had not yet picked up speed.

Some stray, indistinct sounds fell on my ears. At some distance

I noticed a dark shape. My sleep-laden eyes rested on it for some time but I made no effort to make out what it was. Inside the compartment it was dark, the light had been put out some time during the night. Outside the day seemed to be breaking.

I heard another sound, as if someone scraping the door of the compartment. I turned around. The door was closed. The sound was repeated. This time it was more distinct. Someone was knocking at the door with a stick. I looked out of the window. There was a man there; he had climbed up the two steps and was standing on the footboard and knocking away at the door with a stick. He wore drab, colourless clothes, and had a bundle hanging from his shoulder. I also noticed his thick, black beard and the turban on his head. At some distance, a woman was running alongside the train. She was barefooted and had two bundles hanging from her shoulders. Due to the heavy load she was carrying, she was not able to run fast. The man on the footboard was again and again turning towards her and saying in a breathless voice: 'Come on, come up, you too come up here!'

Once again there was the sound of knocking on the door.

'Open the door, please. For the sake of Allah, open the door.'

The man was breathless.

'There is a woman with me. Open the door or we shall miss the train....'

Suddenly I saw the *babu* get up from his seat and rush to the door.

'Who is it? What do you want? There is no room here. Go away.'

The man outside again spoke imploringly: 'For the sake of Allah, open the door, or we shall miss the train.'

And putting his hand through the window, he began fumbling for the latch.

'There's no room here. Can't you hear? Get down, I am telling you,' the *babu* shouted, and the next instant flung open the door.

'*Ya* Allah! the man exclaimed, heaving a deep sigh of relief.

At that very instant I saw the iron rod flash in the *babu*'s hand. He gave a stunning blow to the man's head. I was aghast at seeing this; my legs trembled. It appeared to me as though the blow with the iron rod had no effect on the man, for both his hands were still clutching the door-handle. The bundle hanging from his shoulder had, however, slipped down to his elbow.

Then suddenly two or three tiny streams of blood burst forth and flowed down his face from under his turban. In the faint light of the dawn I noticed his open mouth and his glistening teeth. His eyes looked at the *babu*, half-open eyes which were slowly closing, as though they were trying to make out who his assailant was and for what offence had he taken such a revenge. Meanwhile the darkness had lifted further. The man's lips fluttered once again and between them his teeth glistened. He seemed to have smiled. But in reality his lips had only curled in terror.

The woman running along the railway track was grumbling and cursing. She did not know what had happened. She was still under the impression that the weight of the bundle was preventing her husband from getting into the compartment, from standing firmly on the footboard. Running alongside the train, despite her own two bundles, she tried to help her husband by stretching her hand to press his foot to the board.

Then, abruptly, the man's grip loosened on the door-handle and he fell headlong to the ground, like a slashed tree. No sooner had he fallen than the woman stopped running, as though their journey had come to an end.

The *babu* stood like a statue, near the open door of the compartment. He still held the iron rod in his hand. It looked as though he wanted to throw away but did not have the strength to do so. He was not able to lift his hand, as it were. I was breathing hard; I was afraid and I continued staring at him from the dark corner near the window where I sat.

Then he stirred. Under some inexplicable impulse he took a short step forward and looked towards the rear of the train. The train had gathered speed. Far away, by the side of the railway track, a dark heap lay huddled on the ground.

The *babu*'s body came into motion. With one jerk of the hand he flung out the rod, turned round and surveyed the compartment. All the passengers were sleeping. His eyes did not fall on me.

For a little while he stood in the doorway undecided. Then he shut the door. He looked intently at his clothes, examined his hands carefully to see if there was any blood on them, then smelled them. Walking on tiptoe he came and sat down on his seat next to me.

The day broke. Clear, bright light shone on all sides. No one had pulled the chain to stop the train. The man's body lay miles behind. Outside, the morning breeze made gentle ripples across the ripening wheat.

The Sardarji sat up scratching his belly. The *babu*, his hands behind his head, was gazing in front of him. Seeing the *babu* facing him, the Sardarji giggled and said, 'You are a man with guts, I must say. You don't look strong, but you have real courage. The Pathans got scared and ran away from here. Had they continued sitting here you would certainly have smashed the head of one of them....'

The *babu* smiled—a horrifying smile—and stared at the Sardarji's face for a long time.

Translated from Hindi by the author

My Native Land
VISHNU PRABHAKAR

Vishnu Prabhakar (b. 1912), a Gandhian, is known for his short stories, radio plays, journalism and social work. Concerned with the everyday life of an ordinary citizen who suffers structured injustices, he communicates his situation in simple, poignant prose. He has authored several books and received the Sahitya Akademi Award for his novel *Ardhnarishwar*.

As on any other day, he had a *tehmad* and a *fez* cap on. He walked on and on, his feet moving mechanically. But sometimes, his heart gave a sudden jolt, like a brake on a moving cycle. Yet he didn't let the exhaustion affect his stride. The bystanders considered him decrepit, disabled and slightly touched, grotesque enough to be ridiculed, even with choice swear words. But then he would raise his head. The far-off, lost look in his eyes made them withdraw into their shells. Their laughter now subsided, like effervescence from an aerated drink. Once again, the gaze that kept his heart smouldering like a live coal, was lowered.

'A tragic figure!' a man remarked. 'They must have ransacked his house and killed his kith and kin.'

'The *kuffar* must have done this to him,' another onlooker said. 'They could be up to anything. They could have thrown his children into the raging fire or impaled a child on a spear to hear him squeak like the little one of a sparrow between the claws of a cat.'

'And he must have watched the ghastly scene in awe.'

'What else could he do? The same fear is seen in his eyes and congealed in his blood.'

'Fear? Who says it's fear?' another bystander said. 'It's death

'Mera Vatan' from *Kitne Toba Tek Singh* ed. Bhisham Sahni (New Delhi: People's Publishing House, 1987), pp. 24-32.

lurking in his eyes. Death which takes stock of mayhem, murder, bloodshed and the gallows.'

A passerby, deeply touched by the sight of the man, asked a shopkeeper who he was.

'A man in distress, *janab*, as you can see,' the shopkeeper replied.

'He lived in Amritsar. The *kuffar* ransacked his house and threw his wife and children into the fire.'

'Alive?'

The shopkeeper laughed. 'Where do you live *janab*?' he asked. 'Gone are the days when they burnt dead bodies. Now the same fire consumes living persons.'

The passerby abused the *kuffar* in the vilest terms. The shopkeeper beamed with joy. 'Please come and sit down.'

The passerby sat down for a moment and then got up.

'It seems he was a big shot.'

'Yes, he was a lawyer,' the shopkeeper replied. 'A prominent lawyer of the city. He practised in the High Court and owned property worth lakhs.'

'Really!'

'*Janab*, a man does not become a lunatic so easily. It's only when he gets a big jolt that his heart is torn into pieces. And once that happens, there is no way to mend it. It's the same story everywhere. I had no house of my own, but my shop was so choked with stocks that I could buy three houses if I wanted to.'

'Oh, yes,' the passerby said sympathetically. 'You're right. But I hope you got away safely and in good time with your family.'

'Oh, yes. May God be praised! I had sent off my wife and children in advance. Don't ask me what happened to those left behind. The very thought brings tears to my eyes. May God destroy Hindustan, root and branch.'

The passerby rose. 'Mark my words,' he said with an air of finality. 'One day that country is sure to be wiped out from the face of the earth. Though God's mill grinds slow, it grinds fine.'

The passerby walked away. But the maimed person's antics continued. He tore through the crowd in the *bazar*, muttering and jostling. Sometimes his eyes would rest at one of the shops. They would remain fixed there, like a magnet. As he resumed walking, some shops which had been razed to the ground and now looked more like ancient ruins held his attention, as if they were trying to enter his very being. He stood still for a while. Perhaps he was ruminating over his past in an effort to resurrect old memories. As they came back to him with the force of a gale he was jolted. It was as if a sharp knife had pierced his heart. Though completely shaken, he wanted to live with these memories. That is why he had refused to die. Tearlessly and wordlessly, he sighed and wept.

Suddenly he saw his own house hovering in sight. His father was born in an upper room of this house built by his grandfather. He too was born there. His own children had seen the light of day here. The story of his life was all there. He got so absorbed recalling these episodes that he became totally oblivious of his surroundings. . . . He found himself climbing the stairs and, as usual, his fingers automatically went to the calling bell. The bell, hitherto lifeless, suddenly came alive and rang through the house breaking his slumber. He looked around the room. It was like a phantasmagoria. The men here did not look alike. Nor did they speak the same language. Yet there was that 'something' in them that gave them a common identity, merging them into 'one'. He found himself completely out of place. He tried to edge past them. Just then he saw a man, clad in loose *kurta-pyjama* coming down the stairs. 'How are you *janab*?' he asked.

The man faltered and mumbled.

'Are you looking for something? Want to meet someone, *janab*?'

'I just wanted to know if there is a house here on rent?'

The man in loose clothes gave him a hard look, as if he were a thief. 'Make yourself scarce before! . . .' he said harshly.

Not waiting to hear any further, he ran away, deeply upset by the experience. When he regained himself, he found he had traversed the entire distance from Anarkali *bazar* up to the Mall, a long distance indeed. His body was shaking violently. Pain shot through it as if a carpenter were spinning it on a screwdriver. He found himself standing before the magnificent High Court building on the Mall. He could not take his eyes off it. He recalled his niche in this building and the clothes he wore while attending court. His hand went to his head. Swiftly he withdrew it, as if he had touched a snake. But the glow of his dreams was undiminished. He was steeped in the world of variegated colour that the world outside seemed unreal. He looked intently at the soil beneath his feet and his past flitted by swiftly like the reel of a film. It was a very different, very beautiful world. This was the soil on which he had walked, where people saluted him right and left, bowed before him and came to his house in droves to seek legal advice. Members of the law fraternity held him in high esteem and warmly shook hands with him. . . .

Then, with one long leap, like Hanuman jumping across the sea to Lanka, his thoughts landed with the High Court judge. As he argued his case, people heard him in pin-drop silence. His voice would resound in the judge's chamber to the exclusion of everything else. He frequently punctuated his speech with 'Milord' and the 'Milord' would put down his pen and pay him full attention.

Hanuman took another leap, this time landing in the Bar Association room. Guffaws of laughter, animated discussions on politics, commemorative functions in honour of martyrs, fake melodramas of welcome and farewell—he played a leading role in all.

He thought of his chair in the room he permanently occupied and of the doormat outside the room. Trifling, inconsequential details, but what great mental relief they provided! Effacing everything else from his mind, he moved on with complete abandon. Then he squirmed as if something had scratched him. He saw the luscious green lawn disappearing, halting his onward march. He saw an array of soldiers with terrifying looks, wearing steel helmets and holding rifles ready to shoot down anybody who tried making a move. Homeguards in green uniforms were a familiar sight as also the gun-toting Pathans who shot people at will. For them a gun was nothing more than a baton and the sanctity of life depended on whether the bullet found its mark or not. At that time he too did not attach any value to the sanctity of life. He did not shed tears at the sight of ruins. He had seen the blazing fury of leaping flames, now reflected in his own eyes. He thought of the ruins upon which was laid the foundation of a prosperous Indraprastha, the edifice which triggered off the *Mahabharata*, ending forever the intoxicating valour which had gone to the people's head. Was the same story repeating itself?

One day he said to his elder son, 'Life can play all sorts of tricks. It is many-faceted, changing its face like a clown. It does not take long to create a new world. That is why God in His wisdom has created the earth—for man to extract gold from it.'

The son was a true heir. Leaving his family behind in a small town, he ventured forth into the world. Having gone to rack and ruin, he was determined to make good in a new world. Just then he received a telegram from his younger brother, 'Father disappeared. Whereabouts not known.'

The elder brother read the telegram with deep concern. He returned home immediately to set out in search of his father. He wrote to friends, had the news announced over the radio and put out advertisements in newspapers. He did everything to trace his father. But he could not understand why his father disappeared. He did not know his whereabouts. He thought over the matter day and night, when one day to his great surprise, he saw his father heading towards his house, looking serene and unconcerned.

'Where have you been?'

'Lahore.'

'Lahore?' his son shook his head in disbelief. 'You mean you were in Lahore?'

'Yes.'

'But how did you get there?'

'By train. And I returned the same way.'

'But what took you there?'

'Why did I go? Just to visit the place.'

Unwilling to dwell on the point, he got up and went away. He was in no mood to answer his son's searching questions. They noticed a change in his demeanour but could not comprehend why it was so. True to form, the father did not change his daily routine. But whenever their conversation veered round to Punjab, he would sigh and say, 'Gone! It's gone. Punjab does not exist any more.'

They were all engrossed in their work, the father lending a hand to improve the family's condition. In between he visited Lahore quietly, but returned before his children got wind of it.

'What's the matter?' his wife asked him.

'Nothing.'

'No, there's something. Why do you go to Lahore repeatedly?'

He was silent for a few moments and then said in a low voice, 'So you want to know why I go there? It's because it's my country. I was born there. The secret of my life lies hidden in its soil. The story of my life is inscribed in the breeze of that place.'

His wife's eyes overbrimmed. 'What of that?' she said. 'We have lost everything. It's all over and gone.'

'Yes, everything is gone,' he replied. 'I know I'm helpless. But something happens to me when I remember those days. Then I forget everything else, even myself. I am drawn to my country like a magnet.'

His wife gave him a strange look as if she was seeing him for the first time. For a moment or two she sat dazed. Then she said, 'You must not let your mind dwell on it. You must keep your imagination on leash. I know what you've lost will torment you for the rest of your life. Things were fated to happen that way. So why jump into the fire knowingly? What will you get out of it?'

'Yes, I agree,' he said. 'As you say we must preserve what little we have and push the cart along to where it must go.'

As if turning over a new leaf, he once again donned his lawyer's robe and started practising law in earnest. As before, his name was announced in the Bar Association. He did his best to leave his past behind and was so engrossed in work that people wondered.

'These refugees have guts,' they said. 'Their families struggled for centuries to carve out a place for themselves,' people commented. 'In the twinkling of an eye their properties were reduced to ashes. But without shedding a tear, they set about creating a new world for themselves. These people have guts.'

It was not surprising that people held this opinion about them. To begin with, any place was good enough for these deprived persons. They lived in tents along the roadside, in ruins haunted by ghosts, and in deserted villages. They did not give up. They were determined like the atheist friend of the Christian padre to change hell into heaven. The earth was boundless; there was no question of accepting defeat.

On the day his eldest son was to perform the inauguration ceremony of his new shop, he received a telegram from his younger brother: 'Father missing for the last five days.'

Infuriated, the son tore up the telegram and threw it away. 'If he is not prepared to mend his ways, let him suffer. I bet he must have gone to Lahore.'

His guess was right. At the time when his children were worrying, a decrepit and maimed man wearing a *tehmad* and a *fez* cap perched on his head, was wandering around the *bazars* of Lahore. He looked dazed. A shopkeeper called out, 'Sheikh *Saheb*, are you listening? I haven't seen you for a long time. Where were you all this while?'

The broken man replied in a listless voice, 'I was in Amritsar.'

'What? Amritsar?'

'Yes, I had gone to Amritsar. It's my country.'

'I know there were three and a half lakh Muslims living in Amritsar. But not one has survived.'

'Yes, the *kuffar* drove them away. But we also paid them back in the same coin. Not a single Hindu or Sikh is to be found in Lahore. And there will be none in future.'

He laughed. His eyes lit up. He kept laughing, on and on. . . . 'One's country, earth, love—what small, inconsequential things these are. The most important thing is religion, one's faith, one's faith in God. The earth on which God's human creation lives, the earth on which they chant God's name. That is my country, my earth, my love—love for God and man.'

The shopkeeper whispered to his companion, 'When a man is unbalanced, he comes out with the truth.'

His companion remarked, 'It's God speaking through this man.'

'Of course, of course,' the shopkeeper agreed. Then he turned to the broken man, 'Sheikh *Saheb*, have you located your house?'

'All these are my houses.'

'Sheikh *Saheb*, won't you sit down. Well, were you recognized in Amritsar?'

The man roared with laughter. 'I've been in jail for three months,' he said. 'That's where I come from.'

'Really!'

'Of course.' He blinked.

'You are a bold man indeed.'

Pleased, the shopkeeper sent for *rotis* and *kebabs*. Carelessly wrapping the food in his apron, the man moved on, took a bite and chewed the *roti* slowly.

The shopkeeper said to his companion, 'A strange man indeed. He was a millionaire once and now he craves for crumbs.'

'God always tests his chosen ones.'

'It's such people who find a place in heaven.'

'Yes, he is courageous. He jumped into the fire knowingly.'

'It's love for one's country,' the shopkeeper's companion said. 'Even now when I think of Delhi, I get nostalgic. I'm moved to tears.'

Empathy is rarer than sympathy. Sometimes it is not possible to feel for the sufferings of the other man. But suffering, whatever its intensity, is suffering.

The man walked on. There were more people on the Mall and more cars drove past. As always there were more of English, Anglo-

Indian and Christian women. Even so it was not the same Mall he had known so well. The body was the same but the soul seemed to have departed. Maybe his eyes were to blame. In any case the pedestrians were seemingly indifferent to their souls.

He turned round. There was no need to ask for directions. Even bullocks do not stray from their path. The grand University building appeared. He glanced at the festive crowd and then skirting the statue of Dr. Woolner, the Vice-Chancellor of the University, he entered the campus.

Nobody stopped him from entering through the main gate. Making a detour, he stopped in front of the Law College. He was struck by a pang of nostalgia. He had studied in this college. . . .

It sent a tremor through his body. Later, he had taught at this college. . . .

Tearful, he looked away. He reached the crossing leading to the Dayanand College.

A crowd passed by him. They were all refugees—uprooted, homeless. But his heart did not melt at their sight. Instead, he wanted to hurl abuses at them. Suddenly, two passersby stopped abruptly. One of them bent forward and gave him a close look. Their eyes met. He was petrified. It was getting cold. He was scantily clad and quickened his pace, anxious to make it to the college campus as soon as he could. The man who had recognized him said to the other, 'I know him.'

'Who's he?'

'A Hindu.'

'You mean a Hindu?' His companion gave him a quizzical look.

'Yes, a Hindu—a prominent lawyer of Lahore! . . .'

Hardly finishing his sentence he took out a pistol from his overcoat pocket and advanced. 'I'm sure he has come to spy on us,' he said.

He fired. A slight commotion, a faint stirring. A person faltered and fell. . . . The police turned a blind eye to what was happening. But one of those who had bent over him out of curiosity recognized him. Taken aback, he cried, 'Puri, you here!'

Puri opened his eyes. His face had turned pale. The shadow of death hovered over it. As he turned his gaze on his interlocutor, he recognized him. 'Hasan,' he said in a feeble voice.

Their eyes met. The bewildered Hasan turned to a policeman. 'Hurry up. Hail a taxi. We must take him to the Mayo Hospital. Immediately!'

The crowd swelled. The military, the police and the homeguards gathered. Hasan had studied with him at the Law College and later been his partner in fighting cases. He was now looking at him with dazed eyes. Bending over him, he said, 'Puri what made you come here? In this condition, under such circumstances?'

Puri opened his eyes with some effort and mumbled, 'Hasan, so you ask why I came here? I never went from here. I just can't. This is my country, my native land.'

And then, it was over.

Translated from Hindi by Jai Ratan

The Last Wish
BADIUZZAMAN

Syed Mohammad Khwaja Badiuzzaman (1928-1986), novelist, short story writer and translator, wrote in Urdu under the pen name of Badi Mashhadi. By 1960, he took to writing in Hindi and authored several important novels and short stories, including *Ek Chuhe ki Maut*, *Chhako ki Wapsi* (novels), *Pul Tuttathe Hue* and *Chautha Brahman* (short story collections). *Ek Chuhe ki Maut* received the Madhya Pradesh Sahitya Parishad Award, while *Pul Tuttathe Hue* was honoured by the UP Government. In *Ek Chuhe ki Maut* he employs fantasy to represent contemporary reality in a Kafkaesque mould. Restraint and understatement characterize his style. Badiuzzaman was closely associated with the Progressive Writers' Movement until the 1950s and was a member of the Communist Party of India before joining government service.

I retired to the outer room after lunch and lay down on the *takhtposh* for my siesta. I slept fitfully, each time waking up no sooner had I slid into sleep—once I woke up at the barking of a dog and the second time with the noise of children in the lane. But I was not going to give up so easily and tried to snatch some sleep. My eyelids were sleep-laden. A good sign that sleep might at last get the better of me. The room was tranquil, except for the gentle ticking of the wall clock. It did not sound unpleasant. But before sleep could fully overpower me, I heard someone weeping out in the lane. But I was not to be distracted. Let them cry for all I care. How was I concerned anyway? The sound of weeping kept drumming against my ears. I could not exorcize it from my mind.

The wailing rose to a higher and higher pitch. There were many voices, many people weeping, perhaps at somebody's death.

'Antim Ichcha' from *Chautha Brahmin* (New Delhi: Praveen Prakashan, 1982), pp. 118-128.

It was impossible to ignore the sound of mourning from the neighbourhood. Who could it be? Was it Sapati Raj's son who had been ailing for a long time? The doctor had come to examine him that morning. His condition was not so bad. No, it was not Sapati Raj's house. Was it from *Chhoti Amma*'s house? But why? I had visited her just the other day. Nothing was wrong in her family. I was sure the noise came from somewhere else. I felt a bit relieved and tried to sleep again. But it was in vain. The wailing reached a crescendo, spreading gloom. The shadows of death hovered around me.

Suddenly *Amma* entered my room; she looked agitated. 'Just go and find out what's the matter. They are mourning in *Chhoti Amma*'s house. May God have mercy on them! Go, hurry up.'

I ran to *Chhoti Amma*'s house which was in mourning. *Chhoti Amma* was wailing loudly. Now and then she would bang her head against the wall.

'Pakistan has jolted our family. It has taken away my gem of a son,' she wailed.

The entire family wailed loudly. The calamity came like a bolt from the blue. The news was so sudden, so unexpected. Unable to get the full hang of what was going on, I stood there confused. I did not dare ask for details. The telegram from Karachi brought news of Kamal *bhai*'s death. But how did it happen? He wrote just a week ago. If he was ill he would have at least mentioned in passing. This was not so. True, he was unwell for a long time. When he had come on a visit two years ago, he was a changed man, hard to recognize. The firm, muscular body was gone. He looked weak and had lost his good looks and his fair complexion. His face had turned sallow and his eyes had sunk into their sockets. One could not believe that it was the same Kamal *bhai*. He found Karachi's climate uncongenial and complained of loss of appetite and frequent indigestion.

I vividly remember that when Kamal *bhai* was leaving for Pakistan, the members of his family had tried to dissuade him from going. *Chhote Abba* was alive at that time. Kamal *bhai* did not listen to him. *Chhote Abba* had said in a huff, 'I knew he would spurn my advice. He was like that from the beginning. He does not care much for his parents.'

Kamal *bhai* was very wilful. *Chhote Abba* and *Chhoti Amma* despaired but he was unmoved. On the other hand he had the audacity to say, 'You also come along. Otherwise, you'll regret.'

In reply, *Chhoti Amma* had said, 'We will be the last to do so. How can we leave our home to live in a country of which we know so little?'

Kamal was married for just six months. He went to Pakistan accompanied by his new bride.

It was very unexpected, very sudden. Our mind was boggled by the turn of events.

The night advanced. An oppressive silence filled the atmosphere. But *Chhoti Amma*'s wailing kept breaking through it. Sometimes a dog barked, his growl ending in a groan. I felt distraught. As soon as I closed my eyes, Kamal *bhai*'s face would loom large before me, making me restless. Memories of him crowded my mind, but were unfocused. Tumbling one upon another, they were like a cavalcade rushing forward hurriedly.

Amma lay on an adjoining cot, restless. Sleep had deserted her also. She was also thinking of Kamal *bhai*.

'Death overtook Kamal when he was still so young and that too in a foreign land,' I heard *Amma* saying. I made no comment.

Many faces of Kamal *bhai* haunted me—the boy's face at the age of twelve or so, naughty and full of gumption; the youthful face in his teens, that of an eloquent speaker and good singer. Defying any logical sequence the memories came pell-mell, in disarray.

Kamal *bhai* was four or five years older than me. I was very scared of him, not daring to take liberties with him or rub him up the wrong way. Secretly I was also jealous of his fair complexion, his big eyes, tall and sinewy, his charismatic personality. I was a weakling in comparison. He lost no opportunity of thrashing me, coming down upon me once in a while. I used to seethe with anger but I could never have my way with him. If I complained to *Amma* she would keep quiet. She would not even mention anything to *Abba*. She knew *Abba*'s affection for Kamal *bhai*. He was not prepared to hear anything against him. *Amma* was upset but would not join issue with *Abba*. Sometimes, she would unburden her mind to me. 'May *Allah* do justice. I keep mum because Allah is a witness to all this. Look at the viciousness of Salim's spouse! Her tongue is like a sharp shooter. It's our ill luck that she is married into our family. Like mother, like son.'

Amma and *Chhoti Amma* had a running feud. Left to themselves they would have devoured each other like raw meat. Knowing *Abba*'s temper, *Amma* generally kept her thoughts to herself. *Abba* was given to throwing tantrums. Nobody could offend him. His presence in the house was intimidating. But it was the other way round with *Chhoti Amma*. She dominated *Chhote Abba*. *Amma* used to say: 'Kamal's maternal grandparents have cast a spell on Salim (*Chhote Abba*). He dare not defy his wife.'

Amma was also jealous of Kamal *bhai*, though she did not make it evident. Once, when he failed in his examination and I passed, *Amma* had remarked: 'Allah serves the proud right. Those who humiliate others are humiliated by Allah.'

To tell the truth, I was equally pleased that he had failed—more pleased at his failure than at my own success. The episode had made me more jealous.

Chhoti Amma's house that day was gloomy. Kamal *bhai* did not show up for many days. It also made *Abba* very unhappy. He did not show much happiness at my success. How could he when his favourite nephew had failed?

Amma's barbed comment pleased me. Kamal *bhai*'s behaviour towards me aroused my ire—more so because he was being pampered a lot. *Abba* liked Kamal more than me. This thought drove me mad.

These long-forgotten things were revived in my subconscious mind. How very important they were at the time! Not anymore. Still, I was surprised that I had attached such importance to such inconsequential things.

When *Abba* died *Amma* could not control her emotional outburst to. 'So now you are satisfied,' she had said.

Chhoti Amma was taken aback. She was dumbfounded. She could not say a word in reply.

When *Chhote Abba*'s bier was being carried out, *Chhoti Amma* repeated the same words to *Amma*. *Amma* had a stunned look, she did not say a word.

The same happened today. *Chhoti Amma* exploded: 'So now your mind is at peace,' she said. 'My precious son was like a thorn in your flesh, and now he is no more.' *Amma* heard her in stunned silence.

Kamal *bhai* visited us two years ago. '*Bari Amma*, I don't feel like going back,' he had said. 'But I can't help it.' Nobody wanted him to go. We pleaded with him to stay back. But he was adamant. He stayed for two months.

'Now what will happen to that ill-fated widow and their children?' *Amma*'s words are still ringing in my ears.

Perhaps *Amma* is remorseful. Maybe I am wrong. Perhaps there is no repentance in her heart to commiserate with the bereaved family. Maybe *Amma* was jealous of Kamal's prosperity and, at the same time, saddened by his death. Such mixed feelings. . . . But why not?

On the last occasion when Kamal *bhai* was leaving for Pakistan I went to the railway station. *Bhabhi* and the children were in the waiting room. We went to the office of the Assistant Station Master to get Kamal's passport stamped. He was a Sindhi refugee. He gave Kamal *bhai* a startled look. 'Are you living in Karachi?' he asked.

'Yes.'

'I've also come from Karachi. Lalvani is my name. You know Rafiq? His tea stall? It's just there as you come out of the station. Give him my *salams*. Tell him I remember him a lot. Both of us belong to Hyderabad. Pay him my regards. And there is Abdul Sattar, T.C., at the Karachi railway station. Tell him you had met me and that I remember him a lot.'

Lalvani kept asking all sorts of questions about Karachi. 'There was a popular restaurant at Bunder road. Is it still there? Mr Latif was then a head clerk at the D.S. Office. Is he still in service or retired? He was a very good man, very helpful.' Kamal kept replying with 'yes' or 'no'. He made his escape at the first opportunity.

'Let's have tea at some tea stall outside the station,' Kamal *bhai* suggested to me.

We drank tea from an earthen cup. 'How one pines to drink tea from an earthen cup in Karachi! One can't get such delicately flavoured tea there. I like the tea at two places in Gaya—the station tea stall and at Basudev's *dhaba* near the police station. This time I found Basudev's *dhaba* closed. It seems he has left the city.'

'May I tell you, Khwaja, migrating to Pakistan was a grave error. If only I had paid heed to *Abba*'s advice! I am neither here nor there. Sometimes I think that a united India would have been to everybody's advantage.'

I heard him in silence. He talked like an old man who had turned senile. There was not much point in thinking of the past.

THE LAST WISH

The country's partition was an accomplished fact. Kamal *bhai*'s migration to Pakistan was also a reality.

When the train steamed out of the station I saw Lalvani running towards Kamal *bhai*'s compartment.

He kept running and shouting, 'You must convey my *salams* to Rafiq and to Abdul Sattar. Don't forget Latif. Tell them that I still remember them. Make sure my name does not slip your memory. You'll remember, won't you? Lalvani. . . . That is. . . .'

For sometime I saw Kamal waving at us until the train was reduced to a dot. The platform was deserted but Lalvani stood there panting heavily. Life can be so strange and play such tricks. Lalvani, whose veins were saturated with thoughts of Karachi, was in Gaya. And Kamal, who pined for the breeze of Gaya, was destined to stay in Karachi for the rest of his life.

Kamal *bhai*'s talk at the railway station left me perplexed. His support for the Muslim League was well known. I had heard him raise slogans like: 'We shall have Pakistan!' 'Quaid-e-Azam Zindabad!' A huge procession was taken out on the occasion of Mohammad Ali Jinnah's visit to Gaya. Kamal *bhai* was at the head of it.

Those days the Muslim League was gaining ground and the Hindus and Muslims were polarized politically. But was there any difference in the daily lives of the two communities? None. They were plodding along in much the same way. . . . Just as *Amma* and *Chhoti Ammu*. Their squabbles went on, but there wasn't a point of estrangement.

A person related to us was branded as a Nationalist Muslim. He was not active in politics, though he was deeply interested in political affairs. He was a bitter antagonist of the Muslim League and disapproved of the Pakistan movement. He was older than me and Kamal *bhai*. He subscribed to the Congress ideology and followed Mahatma Gandhi and Maulana Abul Kalam Azad. He had heated discussions with Kamal *bhai*. His name was Ahmad Imam but was nicknamed Gandhiji by many people. We also started calling him Gandhi *bhai*.

Once at a Muslim League meeting held in our *mohalla*, Kamal *bhai* recited Iqbal's famous poem carrying the lines:

Cheen-o-Arab hamara, Hindustan Hamara,
Muslim hein hum watan hain, sara jahan hamara.

He sang well. He had a musical voice. His song was received

with thunderous applause. At the end of the meeting Gandhi *bhai* dropped in at Kamal's house, more to pull his leg than to praise him. He said to him, 'Couldn't you think of any other poem to recite? Iqbal is more of a philosopher than a poet. Sometimes he is unable to understand the anguish of a human heart.'

'As if you understand Iqbal's poetry! Most of it goes over your head.'

Kamal *bhai* said this angrily. But everything was soon forgotten. At that time I was too young to appreciate Iqbal's poetry. But later, when I was able to capture the essence of his poetry and read it in the context of our political and social problems, I was inclined to agree with Gandhi *bhai*'s viewpoint. When I heard Kamal *bhai*'s feelings at the Gaya railway station, I felt Gandhi *bhai*'s judgement on Iqbal's poetry made sense. Kamal *bhai* considered himself a Muslim cast in Iqbal's mould. Perhaps that's why he had not felt a wrench on abandoning his home in India. But could he completely tear himself apart from his birthplace? It was clear from the expression on his face that his emotional attachment with Gaya could not be snapped.

Once when Gandhi *bhai* had remarked that Iqbal's philosophy was inconsistent with humanism, it did not seem like that. His *Mard-i-Momin* was a replica of Nietzsche's superman. It was Nietzsche who had given birth to Hitler. Gandhi *bhai* maintained that one day Iqbal's *Mard-i-Momin* would also plunge the world into disaster.

Gandhi *bhai* and Kamal *bhai* held endless discussions, sometimes ending in bitterness. Others would also join in. Mostly, Gandhi *bhai* had to go it alone. The Muslim League ideology had percolated so deep in the minds of the people and had spread so extensively that few people could escape its deleterious impact. Whereas Kamal *bhai* would have a dozen people to buttress his viewpoint, Gandhi *bhai* had to face their onslaught single-handedly.

This was about a year and a half before the country's partition. The Nationalist Muslims held a meeting at the Town Hall. Many leaders came to participate. The Muslim League planted its agents in the audience to disrupt the meeting. Kamal *bhai* was one of the agents provocateur.

I had started taking interest in politics. I was present at this meeting. No sooner did the proceedings start the League volunteers started their game. Gandhi *bhai* and others tried to pin

THE LAST WISH 143

down the mischief-mongers. This led to an exchange of hot words and ultimately to blows. While this was going on someone turned off the main electric switch and the meeting changed into rioting. Gandhi *bhai* was severely beaten up by the League volunteers. He had to stay in bed for many weeks. Kamal *bhai* summed up the whole thing saying, 'Such is a traitor's lot. This is how he always ends up. If he betrays his people, will they put garlands round his neck?' It was Gandhi *bhai*'s good luck that he escaped. On their part, the League volunteers took it for granted that they had killed him.

Gandhi *bhai*'s and Kamal *bhai*'s conversation generally revolved round one point. Kamal *bhai* maintained that the Muslim way of life was radically different from that of the Hindus. Their culture, language, mode of dress, food habits, religion, customs and traditions were very dissimilar. The Muslims were a separate nation. Their culture could not remain safe in undivided India.

Gandhi *bhai* countered his arguments by contending that except for their religions, there was no difference between the Hindus and Muslims. The difference, if any, was superficial. There were far greater differences between the numerous Hindu sects. The same was true of Muslims. 'Have you ever considered that the life of an average Muslim, right from his birth to his death, runs through the same gamut of customs and rites, which are akin to those of an average Hindu,' Gandhi *bhai* would ask. Celebration of birthdays, bridal songs, even death rites had strong similarities in both the communities. The two-nation theory was nothing but a web of illusions in which innocent Muslims were being trapped. It would result in wholesale disaster.'

Gandhi *bhai*'s arguments were no doubt weighty. If I was able to stay clear of communalism and the poison spread by the Muslim League, it was because of Gandhi *bhai*'s thinking. It was a matter of great surprise that Kamal *bhai* and lakhs and lakhs of Muslims of his ilk failed to notice the validity of his arguments.

It was a still greater surprise, nay an irony, that Gandhi *bhai*, a bitter enemy of communalism who had narrowly escaped death at the hands of communalists but had kept the flame of communal harmony burning by shielding it with his feeble hand, was ultimately killed by a Hindu soon after the country's partition.

These memories crowd my mind at the news of Kamal *bhai*'s death. Then they suddenly converge at a point. At the Gaya station the special train for Pakistan is bursting at the seams with passengers. Those who have come to see off their near and dear ones far outnumber the passengers. Kamal *bhai* is one of them. He is going of his own sweet will, bidding good-bye to this land forever. Two weeks ago he could not have imagined that he would be going. He is not leaving under duress. The decision is his own. He believes he is right. He has no regrets. And yet he seems lost. His mind says that he is right; yet his heart quails. He is haunted by an unknown fear.

Gandhi *bhai* is also on the platform. The train starts moving and thousands of eyes watch the receding train till it is lost to sight. A sense of vacuity fills the hearts of those on the platform. Gloom descends over them. Gandhi *bhai* bursts into tears. The words he uttered between sobs still echo in my ears. 'He will have no country to call his own,' Gandhi *bhai* had said. 'Like the wandering Jew he will roam from place to place. He will belong nowhere. He will pine for the soil of his own country and long for its lulling breeze.'

Then I recall what Kamal *bhai* had once said, 'The days pass in earning a livelihood. It's the nights that are so oppressive. In the stillness of the night a mysterious sense of desolation creeps over me. You have to go back from where you have come, a voice keeps saying. It is more a feeling than a voice. But when and how? There is no answer.'

Qul was performed on the fourth day after Kamal *bhai*'s death. In the same room where Abba's *Qul* took place years ago. Joss-sticks were burnt. The Holy Quran was read. *Milad* was held to seek peace for the departed soul. The poor were fed. By afternoon, the rites were over. The flurry of activity and its accompanying noise subsided.

I sat alone in the sitting room mulling over the viccissitudes of life. The same rites were performed years ago when *Chhote Abba* died and much before him when *Abba* passed away. But there was something else over and above these rites which we could not observe in the case of Kamal *bhai*.

On the evening of *Qul* we carried joss-sticks and a flower *chadar* to *Abba*'s and *Chhote Abba*'s graves. We recited the *Fateha* and returned home. But alas, we could not visit Kamal *bhai*'s grave thousands of miles away. And the distance could not be calculated in terms of miles. Swept by waves of emotion, I wondered what

THE LAST WISH

Kamal *bhai* thought of during his dying days? His house? His childhood? The lanes and alleys of Gaya? Did he think of *Abba*, his brothers and sisters and his mother? Who could tell how many candles of memory lit up in his mind! Or maybe, no thought crossed his mind. Maybe the fearsome shadows of death swallowed up all the memories.

The same day we received *Bhabhi*'s letter in the evening mail. She had written: 'Perhaps he had a foreboding of death. He knew he was not going to live. From the day of his illness he kept repeating, "Take me to *Amma*. I don't want to die in the desert of Karachi. Bury me across the river Falgu. In the graveyard where *Abba* and *Bare Abba* lie buried."'

I felt as if time had come to standstill.

Hazrat Yusuf (Muslim name for Jacob), the Maulvi *Saheb* was saying, 'spent the major part of his life in Egypt. He died at the age of hundred and ten. On his deathbed he wanted his family to assure him that they would not bury him in Egypt. Instead they would wait for the day when the Banu Israel, as prophesied, would return to power over the land of his ancestors. Then they would carry Yusuf's bones and consign them to the soil of his ancestral land. True to their word, members of *Hazrat* Yusuf's family mummified his body and preserved it in a coffin. During the reign of Moses when the Banu Israel (the clan of Israel) migrated from Egypt, they carried the coffin with them and buried *Hazrat* Yusuf's body in the land of his ancestors.'

'Maulvi *Saheb*, what came to Yusuf's mind? Why did he make such a request?' Kamal *bhai* asked the Maulvi *Saheb*.

'You must know that *Hazrat* Yusuf was also a king, a ruler of Egypt. He had prestige, power, fame, and wealth. He lacked nothing. Had all of it in abundant measure. But there is something else above all this, the pull of one's own country. The soil of one's own country beckons a man. But you will not understand,' the Maulvi *Saheb* said.

Who could tell that Kamal *bhai* would have to repeat what Yusuf had said to his clan of Israel? But then, God had promised Yusuf that he would be restored to the land of his ancestors. God made no such promise to Kamal *bhai*. I had realized long ago that Kamal *bhai* lived by leaning against the crutch of a great lie. Soon, he recognized this lie. He had thrown off this mantle of falsehood, and realized the validity of what Gandhi *bhai* said long ago. Kamal *bhai*'s face would then not fossilize into just one face, but rapidly transform into myriads of them. They were not the faces of Hindus or Muslims. They were human faces which, torn from their roots, looked so pathetic—faces which the evil-minded and selfish man's diabolical conspiracies had cast into hell.

Translated from Hindi by Jai Ratan

The New Regime
KRISHNA SOBTI

Krishna Sobti, born in 1925 in Gujrat (West Punjab), had her early education in Simla and Delhi. Partition forced her family to move to India. Well-known for her short stories, among them 'Badalon ke Ghere', 'Yaron ke yar' she achieved much acclaim with her novel *Zindaginama: zinda rukh* (1979), a memory of the ethos and ambience of pre-partition rural Punjab. It received the Sahitya Akademi Award (1980). Her other novels, *Dar se bicchudi*, *Surajmukhi Andhere ke* and *Mitro Marjani*, explore the woman's world, often in an urban setting.

'Sikka Badal Gaya' is one of her earlier stories on the transformation that partition wrought.

Dawn was breaking when Shahni reached the banks of the river. A *chadar* of *khadi* thrown over her shoulders, she held a rosary between her fingers. A roseate glow was spreading over the expanse of the sky. She took off her clothes and carefully put them aside chanting, 'Shri Ram! Shri Ram!' Entering the water she scooped the water in her cupped hands and made her obeisance to Surya. Next, she sprinkled water on her drowsy eyes and immersed herself in the flowing water.

The water of the river Chenab was cold as ever. Wave upon wave rose. Far away on the hills of Kashmir the snow had started melting. With the swirling waters fell hunks of mud from the banks into the river. But for some unknown reason the vast expanse of sandy waste stretching from the river far into the distance lay mute and still. Shahni put on her clothes and looked around. Not a shadow lurked anywhere. But in the sands down below, she saw footprints. Apprehensively she looked around.

'Sikka Badal Gaya' from *Kitne Toba Tek Singh*, ed. Bhisham Sahni, (Delhi: People's Publishing House, 1987), pp. 92-7.

An eerie feeling gripped her in the sweet stillness of dawn. For the past fifty years she had been bathing at this very spot. What a long period! Shahni recalled how on this very bank she had one day come as a bride. And today . . . today Shahji was dead. Her highly-educated son was also gone. She was lonely and disconsolate in Shahji's big and magnificent *haveli*. But no . . . why should such thoughts trouble her early in the morning? She was still very worldly-wise, still in love with life.

Shahni took a deep breath and walked towards her home through the millet fields chanting *Ram, Ram*! In the distance, she saw smoke spiralling up from some neat, mud plastered houses. *Tun, tun*! the bells round the bullocks' necks jingled. . . . Even so, she felt the atmosphere was stifling. Even the Jammiawala well was not working today. All of this belonged to Shahji. Shahni raised her head. The vast stretch of land belonged to her. Everything around was hers—a living testimony to Shahji's prosperity. The fields, studded with numerous wells, starting from the outskirts of the village stretched far into the distance. The fertile soil yielded gold year after year. She went to the well and called out, 'Shera, Shera! Husaina, Husaina!'

Shera knew who it was. Who else would, if not Shera? He had grown up under Shahni's care after the death of his mother Chaina. He quickly pushed the wood chopper under the heap of rubble. Holding his *hookah* in his hand, he called out to Husaina, 'Aye . . . Sena! Sena! Sena!'

Shahni's voice had shaken him up. Just then, he had thought of an opportune moment to enter the dark attic in the upper storey of the *haveli* for stealing the chests of silver and gold and other pieces of jewellery. Shahni's intrusion upset his plans. Should he take his anger out on her? Or, on Husaina?

'*Eh*, are you dead?'

'May God bring you death.'

Setting aside the *ata* container, Husaina emerged. 'Here I am,' she fumed.

'You have already started fretting. The day has not even begun.'

By then, Shahni heard Shera fuming at Husaina. 'Husaina, is this the time to quarrel?' she said gently. 'If he loses his head you should keep your cool.'

'Keep cool?'

'A man is a man. But have you ever asked him why he starts hurling abuses from early morning?'

Shahni gently caressed her back. 'Mad girl,' she laughed. 'You know it, his wife is dearer to me than . . . Shere!'
'Yes, Shahni?'
'It appears those Kulluwal people came here last night.'
'No, Shahni,' Shera said haltingly. He seemed agitated.
Shahni ignored Shera's reply. She was visibly concerned. 'I don't see any good in what's happening. Shahji would have certainly handled the situation. But. . . .' Shahni knew what was happening around her. She was deeply touched. Tears came to her eyes. Shahji died years ago. But something new, something different was beginning to agitate her. Perhaps old time memories.

Suppressing her tears she looked at Husaina and gave her a faint smile. Shera wondered why Shahni was talking in such a vein. He knew no power on earth—not even Shahji—could avert the impending calamity. It was destined to happen. But why not? Shahji had filled up his coffers by extracting interest from one and all. It was said that he weighed bags filled with gold. The very idea angered Shera. Suddenly he thought of the wood chopper. He looked furtively at Shahni.

No, no, no. In the recent past Shera had committed thirty to forty murders. But he was not such a mean person as to . . . No, he mustn't do any harm to Shahni standing before him. He thought of those cold nights when Shahji reproached him. He would then lie down in a corner of the *haveli* and sulk all night. And then, under the light of the hurricane lantern, Shahni would appear with a bowl of hot milk. 'Shera, Shera, get up. Here's some milk for you. Drink it.'

Those hands trembled with motherly affection. He found her smiling at him as he looked at her face that morning, a face furrowed with years.

Shera was stirred to his depths. What harm had Shahni done to him? He should have settled scores with Shahji. Why her? He must instead protect her. But the last night's plan? Why did he agree to the overtures of Feroz?

'Everything will proceed according to plan. We'll distribute the loot.'

'Shahni, come, I'll escort you to your house.'

Shahni got up. She walked ahead of Shera lost in her thoughts. He walked behind with determined steps, glancing furtively to his right and left, his companion's words still ringing in his ears. But killing Shahni? What good would that do him?

'Shahni!'
'Yes, Shere!'
He wanted to tell her about the impending danger. But how?
'Shahni!'
Shahni raised her head. The sky was filled with smoke.
'Shere!'
Shera knew it was arson. They wanted to set Jaglapur on fire and they had done so. Shahni was tight-lipped. Many of her relatives lived in that village. . . .

They reached the *haveli*. Shahni stepped into the vestibule with an empty heart, not even noticing when Shera was gone. She was old, frail and alone. There was nobody to look after her. She just lay there listlessly. The afternoon came and went. The *haveli* was desolate and quiet. Shahni just couldn't get up. She felt as if she was losing control over the place. Shahji was the rightful owner of the house. . . . But no, her possessive instincts had not slackened. Nor her attachment to what belonged to her husband. Evening came and yet she did not get up. Suddenly, Rasuli's voice startled her. . . .

'Shahni! Shahni! The truck will soon come to take you away.'

'The truck!' Shahni could not say anything more. Her hands groped in search of support. News spread throughout the village. 'Shahni's *haveli*. . .' a woman said in a choked voice. 'Such outrageous treatment! How horrendous!'

Shahni stood there like a statue. 'Shahni, we couldn't imagine that this could ever happen,' said Nawab *bibi* in an emotion-choked voice.

Shahni was shattered, but was unable to express her feelings. She heard Begu *Patwari* and the *beldar* talking down below. Realizing that the critical moment had arrived, she came down quickly but could not walk across to the vestibule.

'Who's there?'

Who was not there that day. The whole village—which once used to dance attendance at her slightest bidding—had gathered. She considered her tenants as her kith and kin. But today nobody was prepared to stand by her. A big crowd, including the farmers of Kulluwal, had turned up. She had an inkling of this early in the morning.

Begu *Patwari* and Ismail, the priest of the mosque, had other ideas. They came and stood near her. Begu found it difficult to face

Shahni. Clearing his throat he said in a low voice, 'Shahni, this is how Allah had willed.'

Shahni's feet faltered. Her head swam and she leaned against the wall for support. Is this way Shahji had left her behind? Begu stood there looking at the feeble, lifeless Shahni. After all nothing could be done now. With the change of government a different coin was in vogue. . . .

It was not a small matter to throw out Shahni from her own house. The entire village was there, right from the main door of the *haveli* upto the outer meeting room. Shahji had built that room to commemorate his son's marriage. Important decisions concerning the village were taken there. The idea of plundering the *haveli* was also mooted in that room. Shahni knew but feigned ignorance. She had no rancour in her heart. She never thought ill of anybody. What she did not realize was that now a new coin was in circulation. . . .

It was getting late. Police-Inspector Daud Khan came up swaggering. He stopped abruptly on seeing a shadowy figure in the vestibule. It was the same Shahni whose husband had put up tents for him on the bank of the river during his official visits to the village. It was the same Shahni who had gifted a gold ornament to his fiance at their first meeting. When he had called on her the other day to discuss the Muslim League affairs, he had said: 'Shahni, they are going to build a mosque at Bhogowal. You will be required to contribute three hundred rupees.' Shahni obliged.

'Shahni!' Daud Khan called out.

Shahni stood there.

'Shahni!' The police officer approached the vestibule. 'We are getting late, Shahni.' He then lowered his voice.

'Keep something for the way if you like. Have you got a bundle to carry with you? Gold, silver?'

'Gold, silver!' Shahni said shakily. 'Child, all this is for you. My gold lies in every part of my land.'

'Shahni, you are alone. Keep something with you. Some cash at least. These are bad times. You never know. . . .'

'Bad times?' Shahni smiled through her tears. 'Daud Khan, will I ever live to see better times?' she asked sarcastically.

Daud Khan had no answer. He repeated: 'Shahni, you must carry some cash.'

'No, child, I don't love money more than this house. The money belongs to this place and will stay here.'

Shera came up and stood by her side. Seeing Daud Khan talking to Shahni he suspected he might touch her for some money. . . . 'Khan *Saheb*, it's getting late,' he said.

Shahni was startled. Getting late? In her own house? She had been the queen of this big house dating back to her ancestors. How could they be so audacious as to pounce upon her own victuals? No, she wouldn't let such a thing happen. Getting late indeed! The words kept ringing in her ears. So be it, Shahni said to herself. She would not depart from her ancestral house crying. She would go with fanfare, in style. She would step out of the vestibule with her head held high—the place where she once entered as a queen. Controlling her faltering steps, she wiped her tears with the end of her *dupatta* and came out of the vestibule. Women, old and young, started to cry. Their benefactor, who had stood by them through thick and thin, was going away from her own house forever. None could measure upto her standard. God had bestowed his blessings upon her. She lacked nothing. But it does not take long for fortunes to change.

With her head covered, she cast a final look at her *haveli* through her tear-dimmed eyes. The heritage she had preserved after Shahji's death was now slipping out of her hands. Oh, what a betrayal! She joined her hands. This was her last *darshan*, her last salutation. She would not set her eyes on this *haveli* again. She was overwhelmed. She should have wanted to see every nook and corner of the house, but was feeling so dwarfed. But she refused to look small before those in whose eyes she had remained so exalted. The inevitable had happened, and she had bowed before it. As she receded from the vestibule, tears welled up in her eyes and fell to the ground. The lady of the house was going away. She kept walking till the high mansion was left far behind. Daud Khan, Shera, the *Patwari*, women and children trailed behind.

The truck was full. Shahni approached the truck dragging her feet. People looked on, crest-fallen. Even Shera, who had so often dipped his hands in blood, was heart-broken. Daud Khan stepped forward to open the door of the truck.

'Shahni, say something before you go. Blessings from you always comes true.' Ismail wiped his tears with the end of his turban.

'May God keep you safe and secure. May He bring you happiness.'

That small gathering started crying. There was no hatred in Shahni's heart. And they . . . they had not been able to keep

Shahni with them. Shera touched Shahni's feet. 'Shahni, nobody can do anything for you. Even our government has changed and has been replaced by a new one.' Shahni put her trembling hand on Shera's head and blessed him. Daud Khan made a gesture with his hand. Some old women hurriedly embraced Shahni. The truck moved on.

Her ties with the place snapped. Its soil was going to deny her sustenance. The *haveli*, the new sitting room, the upper storey, all flitted past Shahni's eyes. She was aware of nothing else. Was it the truck that was moving or she who was moving? Daud Khan cast an uneasy glance at the old Shahni. Where would she go? What would be her destination?

'Shahni, don't think ill of us. We are helpless. If only we could do something for you. Times have changed. Rulers have changed. New coins are now in vogue. . . .'

When Shahni reached the refugee camp at night she mused over the changed situation. 'So the Raj has been overthrown! But will the currency also change? But how? That I've left behind.'

And Shahni's eyes brimmed over with tears.

The night was raining blood on the village surrounded by green pastures.

Perhaps the Raj was being overthrown. Perhaps, a new currency was replacing the old one.

Translated from Hindi by Jai Ratan

How Many Pakistans?
KAMLESHWAR

Kamleshwar (b. 1932), one of the famed trio of the 'Nai Kahani,' shot into prominence with the publication of *Raja Nirbansiya*, a story which explores the protagonist's agonizing experiences in a *mofussil* milieu. He has ten novels, ten collections of short stories, besides a large number of film scripts to his credit. In the 1970s he edited a monthly journal *Sarika* and before that *Nai Kahaniyan*.

Kitne Pakistan? (How many Pakistans?) is typical of Kamleshwar's simple yet incisive prose, and his insight into the hidden layers of reality, which are then reconstructed in a disturbing manner.

What a long journey! I don't understand why I keep thinking of Pakistan over and over again. It almost imposes itself upon me.

Salima, have I ever been unfair to you? Then why this self-infliction? You laugh. But I know it is barbed laughter tinged with poison. Not touched with the fragrance of the henna bushes whose buds blossom in the gentle breeze in the moonlight. I am amused at the very thought. Salima, do you remember the day when you had said, 'Like the breeze I am also fancy free and sometimes even touched in the head.'

I'm sure you remember that. Women never forget. Do they? They only make a pretence of forgetting. Otherwise, life would be unbearable. I feel odd when I call you Salima or take you for some other woman. I would instead like to call you Bano, the girl who brought me henna flowers with their fragrance mingled with her breath. You would hold the flowers near my nose and blow over them. 'They give out fragrance when you blow over them,' you would say. Bano, I felt intoxicated. A little touched in the head. Now I hesitate to call you by that name. I wonder if you would ever like to be reminded of that name,

'Kitne Pakistan?' from *Kohra* (Delhi: Rajpal and Sons, 1994), pp. 89-106.

or the sound of it. But why be so punctilious? What's there in a name, after all?

That night I wanted to go up the stairs to your room and ferret out something from you, remind you of something you seem to have forgotten. But how could you forget? You don't, you remembered everything.

Oh, God, who can tell how many more Pakistans were created with the creation of that one Pakistan? It's such a mix up. Things have become more complicated.

That night was no different from other nights. I don't know whether it was the sound of the *pipal* tree in the courtyard behind our house or the voice of Badru *Mian*. 'Qadir *Mian*,' the voice had said, 'this blasted Pakistan has at last come into being. This sister's lover, Pakistan!'

That moonlit night was horrendous! You lay naked in the courtyard down below, bathed in moonlight while the *pipal* leaves kept rustling in the breeze. And then came the voice of Badru *Mian*, 'Qadir *Mian*, this blasted Pakistan has come into being.'

Friend, my life's long journey has three stages. The first was when I was intoxicated by the fragrance of Bano's henna flowers. The second when I saw Bano lying stark naked in the moonlight. The third when Bano had asked, 'Is there someone else with you?'

'Yes, there was someone else.'

Bano, what made that wavering, blind moment end in a laugh? What did I do to you? Why this streak of vengeance? On me? On Munir? Or was it on Pakistan? Who were you trying to humiliate, me, yourself, Munir or. . . ?

Why should Pakistan come between us again and again? Pakistan conveys nothing to me or to you. It is a mere appellation given to a dreadful reality. What a reality! A reality that sets us apart and then draws a wedge of silence between us. A reality that makes people insensitive to the families, communities and religion of others. They have no feelings for the suffering of others, their joys and sorrows. Perhaps this void, this lack of feeling has assumed the name of Pakistan. It is like a henna flower without hue. Devoid of fragrance.

Listen, had it not been so, I would not have left Chinar and wandered around. Why would I lead the life of a dervish? The same Chinar with its henna flowers. From the Mission School where the henna flowers blossomed, we would walk down to the *pipal* tree on the bank of the Ganga and eat tamarind fruit. We would sit on the broken ramparts of the Raja Bhartrihari Fort.

How can I forget the evening when Zamin Ali, the hospital compounder, came to my grandfather and said, 'I know it's not true, but convincing the people will be difficult. Send Mangal away for a few days. If not, people will continue to gossip about his affair with Bano. Their marriage is out of the question. Yet the affair may lead to a Hindu-Muslim riot.'

I felt miserable. How could I leave Chinar? But then, I was compelled to. Oh, those beautiful Chinar nights, the flowing Ganga, the boats loaded with Kashi-bound pilgrims, the ruins of the Bhartrihari Fort, the thatch-roofed octroi post where I waited for Bano. I wondered whether she would be able to come along the lanes fissured by the receding flood water. Whether she would make it to the bank of the Ganga. Sometimes she would come. Sometimes she would not. But I waited and waited!

Little did we realize that they now considered us adults and looked askance at our meetings.

It never occurred to us that our coming together could cause communal tension. But that was how things stood. We did not know. How could we? We never talked about such things.

The three stages of my life's journey passed without my knowing. At no stage did we pause to talk to one another. Not even when the fragrance of henna buds permeated the air in the moonlight and went to our heads. Or, when I saw her naked in the moonlight. Nor when she asked me, 'Is there someone else with you?'

Henna flowers, Chinar, my house, your house. The brick-paved lane which went past my house and through the *bazar* ran along the river bank upto the portals of the old Bhartrihari Fort. The octroi post stood at the turning of the road that led to the Fort. Here the passengers got off the boats at the Ganga *ghat* and paid their toll. Mumbling Ram's name under his breath all the time, the octroi clerk accepted the duty in kind—fish, crabs, mangoes and the like. Ten times a day he would offer holy water to Lord Shiva's idol under the *pipal* tree, and then returned to the shed where he would coach four children under the thatched roof.

Near the octroi post the road bifurcated, one led to the Fort and the other to an unpaved path, virtually a web of channels whose water was absorbed by the river sands. I called them Bano's lanes.

At the end of Bano's lanes, a cobbled path led to the Mission

School. Housed in an old bungalow dating back to early British days, the path to the bungalow was lined up with a long henna hedge. Wild belladonna bushes grew all around in a *maidan* beyond.

These belladonna bushes caused me a great deal of anxiety. When feelings ran high on account of our affair, Bano made it to the octroi post. She said, 'Mangal, if Maulvi *Saheb's* flunkies take the law in their hands and try to clip my wings, I'll swallow belladonna and go to sleep. Don't be a coward and desert me. If you do, don't forget that the Ganga flows nearby.'

She was gone before I could explain how matters stood—about the turmoil in my house. Unknown persons threatened grandfather in the *bazar*. He feared that some day Muslims might kill me or attack our house at night.

Bano, Pakistan had already been created. But your father, the drillmaster, was still writing *Bhartrihari Nama*.

'He's crazy, this drillmaster of ours,' people would say. 'Imagine a Muslim writing in praise of a Hindu raja. This man could not be a Turk. He must be a low caste convert to Islam.' That was the moment when we realized that there are Muslims and Muslims. Everybody claimed that their ancestors had migrated from Iran and Turkey and had settled here. The local Muslims had ostracized the drillmaster but felt responsible for Bano's welfare. As if they were her real mentors.

Bano did not know the law of the land. I did. Bano's father was feckless. He believed in toeing the line, following the *Maulvi's* dictates. He did not assert himself. Nor would he stand by his convictions. He did not think independently. One day he came to my grandfather and burst into tears. But he continued to write *Bhartrihari Nama*. I got to know about this closely-guarded secret just when I decided to leave town. While passing the octroi post for the last time, the clerk slipped a piece of paper into my perspiring hand.

It was a frightfully dark night. Fear seized everybody. The shadow of death lurked. Shouts of '*Ya Ali!*' triggered off trouble, bringing bloodshed in its wake. Even the Ganga was in spate that night while the *pipal* tree on its bank swayed violently. A fierce wind whistled through the ruins of the fort. My grandfather had escorted me to the railway station with the help of half a dozen Hindu youths—yes, I have to say, Hindu youths—so that I could board the train without a mishap and save my body and soul.

At first they decided to send me to my maternal uncle's house in Jaunpur. But ultimately they packed me off to Bombay. I was to take up a job in the railway workshop where my uncle was also employed.

Bano, it was a dreadful night. I was turning my back on my own house in disgrace. My mind was torn by a fierce conflict. At times I thought I go back, pick up a hatchet and kill all those Muslims of yours, paint the road red with their blood and win you over. And if I failed, I would kill you and drown myself in the Ganga.

The town lay in a swoon. My grandfather was warned that I should not be seen the next morning. They went into a huddle till late into the night. By the time they finished there was just the goods train to Mughalsarai.

I was ashamed and scared. I knew that the drillmaster did not object to our affair, though he had kept mum. He hadn't abandoned his work on *Bhartrihari Nama*. Perhaps, if he had discontinued there wouldn't have been much of a hullabaloo.

I was escorted to the railway station by half a dozen Hindu youths. We avoided the main *bazar* and followed the deserted Fort road to the station. The octroi clerk, lantern in hand, slipped a piece of paper into my hand. A parcel train, the last of the night, was scheduled to pass through at two-thirty. I could go on to Mughalsarai. My grandfather was nervous. My comrades were scared, humiliated and vengeful. They were ready to wipe out the Muslims if they had their way. It was feared that the Hindus would start rioting in the morning as soon as these youths returned from the station, and tear the sleeping Muslims to pieces. Bano, how painful it was for a Hindu to be a Hindu. The parting that night was extremely painful. There was a chill in the air. The floor of the railway platform was very cold. The Vindhya Hills and the pine trees across the railway station seemed to be brooding in silence.

How can I tell you all this? I lost my peace of mind after being thrown out of my own town. I thought of those lanes along which Bano came to meet me. I would wait in vain for her at the octroi post. I would traverse the same lanes impatiently. On seeing the henna flowers, I would console myself. Maybe Bano came thus far before retracing her steps. Maybe somebody did not let her come. Frankly, it was only then that Pakistan had come into existence as far as I was concerned. It had pierced through my heart like a dagger. The breeze over the town seemed to have been lulled into immobility, leaving Bano marooned within the precincts of the town.

I reached the point of no return. Even if Bano was restored to me, she would have perhaps meant nothing to me at that time. I was so befuddled and cheerless. The inevitable happened.

I read that piece of paper on the train. I realized *that* she had no words of comfort for me. Just like the drillmaster. I learnt from the same piece of paper that the drillmaster continued to write *Bhartrihari Nama*

> Why have you become a mendicant
> Renouncing your friends, soldiers and courtiers?
> Why have you taken to a life of poverty,
> leaving behind narcissus and poppy?
> Why have you donned saffron robes
> In place of expensive shawls of silk?
> Why do you go from door to door,
> Singing God's name?
> You have wandered afar to Kamrup, Dhaka and Bengal
> What kind of madness is this to renounce your sceptre and crown?

Call it madness. Brocade, shawl, silks, narcissus, poppy flowers—were real. So were the *pipal*, acacia, henna and belladonna flowers. Pakistan was also a reality. But what meaning did *this* Pakistan have for us?

The train was hurtling along, making me a dervish in my own town. Never again did I have the urge to return home.

I sensed that the drillmaster must be feeling stifled in Chinar. Bano? I wasn't so sure. I was sure of one thing—that she couldn't have drowned herself in the Ganga. She must still be there, happy or unhappy, warming someone's bed like a devoted wife. Colouring her hands with henna, praying for her husband's health, looking after her children and their petty needs. Happy or remorseful, she must have relegated everything into some corner of her mind, never to be recalled again. And what she could not forget must have transformed into Pakistan, bringing time itself to a standstill.

Well, Bano, what was to happen has already come to pass. From Mughalsarai I came to Allahabad and then to Bombay. My uncle found work for me at the Kurla Railway Workshop.

From there I went to Poona. I worked in a hospital workshop manufacturing artificial limbs. I had a strong feeling that I would not feel at home at Chinar, nor would my people live there in peace. And nor Bano for that matter. But I never imagined that my grandfather would go away to some distant place with the other families.

As a matter of fact everybody seemed to have lost interest in Chinar. The Chinar we had known no longer existed. When something known as Pakistan comes into existence the crops wither, the sky is sundered into pieces, the clouds no longer bring rain and the wind does not blow.

After a few years, my grandfather wrote to me. He had migrated to Bhiwandi along with some families of farmhands and carpenters in search of new pastures. He hoped to live close to the green fields, a blue sky and rain-laden clouds. I learnt a little later that Bano's family also went along. But what kind of opening could a drillmaster have in a place like Bhiwandi? Grandfather's decision made some sense to me. He was a cotton merchant. Bhiwandi offered good prospects to carpenters also. But for Bano's father?

I learnt about Bano from grandfather. This was in Poona. He told me in passing that the drillmaster accompanied him to Bhiwandi to secure a job at a local school. He told me that Bano was married to a young man who was an excellent handloom weaver. He was specially good at weaving silk cloth.

I could see that he was trying to sound casual. He completely blacked out the information that Bano's family also lived in his house in Baje *Mohalla*. Did the drillmaster do so to wipe out his sense of guilt? I wanted to meet Bano to find out for myself. But I was in no mood to do so. I felt miserable when I learnt that she lived in Bhiwandi and was married. Grandfather had subtly hinted that it was not advisable for me to visit the place.

And what if I went and gave vent to my pent-up feelings? In that case another Pakistan would have exploded in my heart and I would have barged into Bano's room in a fit of fury.

Or, if I tried preventing Bano from sleeping with her husband? Or, if I drove him out of Bhiwandi just as I was driven out of Chinar?

Of course, grandfather and the drillmaster had reassured each other that they were above reproach. But I was not so easily convinced. They had lost nothing. I was the one who had suffered.

I hid my face behind a mask, my hands were gloved and there was a dagger concealed under my waist. And I kept wandering from place to place.

Soon, Bhiwandi was also riot-stricken. Of course, Bano and I were not responsible. Distrust was rampant there too. I had not visited Bhiwandi for the simple reason that Bano's sight may have triggered off another riot from my side.

Yes, I did see Bano at long last. But in bizarre circumstances!

MOONLIT NIGHT AND BANO

I reached Bhiwandi a fortnight after the riots. As I entered the city, I noticed heaps of debris and charred houses clustered together, tense with fear. The air still smelt of ashes. An acrid smell mixed with that of burnt earth pricked my nostrils. Bano, you must have smelt it, too. Is there anyone in this country who is not familiar with the smell of ashes?

It was late in the evening when I got off at the bus stand. All was quiet. No sign of panic anywhere. Three policemen stood chatting under a big cinema hoarding. Most buses were empty and silent. No passengers were heading towards Sange Maneer, Ali Bagh, Bhorwarda. There were no passengers even for Shirdi. No taxis bound for Thane. The roads were deserted. Under the tinshed of the bus stop, a few policemen bunched together like a small family of gypsies. One would not have known that they were cops but for their guns which were stacked next to them, like sugarcane stalks. There was some activity in the nearby *dak* bungalow where the Collector was camping.

What is it like walking through a riot-torn city? You may have some experience. I don't. Desolate streets. Eerie silence. You see; yet there is nothing to see. Or, you see things intensely but without any sense of human kinship. Why do all human bonds snap? Why does one lose faith in humanity?

It was a small town and yet it was difficult to reach Baje *Mohalla*. Anyhow I found my way and located the house. But silence prevailed everywhere. Life in such sinister silence?

The upper storey of the house was plunged in darkness. Had it not been a moonlit night, I would have been scared out of my wits.

The door was ajar and I stepped into the courtyard. There were two water pitchers lying in a corner. Near them were two shadows, apparently of two women. One was naked from her waist upward. The other sat by her side massaging her breasts, her hands moving up and down her bosom. I could not understand what was this woman up to, but I distinctly made out the contours of a naked female form. Bewildered, I retreated.

Coming out into the street I met the drillmaster. He recognized me straightaway. But he stood there like a dumb creature, not knowing how to greet me. What kind of overture should he make? Allude to the years gone by? Tell me how he had come to know me? Before he could open his mouth, I asked about my grandfather.

'He left for Chinar the day before.'

'The day before?' I repeated in disbelief.

'Yes, he didn't want to stay back. Many other families have also gone away.'

I suddenly realized that in spite of all that had happened, my grandfather could still opt for Chinar but not the drillmaster. He left Chinar for very different reasons. He was exiled because of adverse circumstances; he had found that it was not easy to swim against the tide. As for me, I was forced to abandon my home just because a handful of people turned hostile.

I was perplexed. How to conduct oneself without my people? How and where to seek refuge in an unfamiliar, riot-torn city? With Bano around, the drillmaster would not put me up for the night.

'Has grandfather taken his things with him?'

'No, most are still here.'

'Has he locked up his rooms?'

'Yes, but I've got a duplicate key,' he said hesitatingly.

'In that case I would like to stay here for the night. I've got to return by tomorrow evening.' I knew I was forcing myself on him. But I had no choice. A stranger in the city.

The drillmaster returned with a key and a candle. He led me upstairs by a side staircase, opened the lock to let me in. 'Have you eaten?' he asked.

'Yes,' I said and went into the room.

'Let me know if you need anything.' Without waiting for my answer he came down the stairs. The author of *Bhartrihari Nama* was shrewd enough to know how to make his moves. He had used the expression 'let me know' instead of 'come and ask me'.

Bano, what a strange night! You didn't even know that I was there. The drillmaster would not have told you. If the police had not come to our house early next morning, you would have never known whose shadow was hovering over the terrace all night. Everything was very quiet.

It was a moonlit night, airless and still. I decided to move to the terrace to escape the oppressive heat of the room and sleep in the open. I waited for the footsteps but gave up after a while.

The tree behind the house was bathed in moonlight. From my cot I looked into the courtyard below. What I saw took my breath away.

There were two beds in the courtyard, one occupied by Bano and the other by her mother. My heart missed a beat on seeing her. Bano was lying in the moonlight, her sari pulled down. Her exposed breasts were like full blown balloons. She lay writhing like a half-dead fish.

'*Hai Allah*!' Bano groaned.

'Try to sleep,' I heard her mother plead.

'They are going to burst,' Bano wailed and squeezed her breasts as if she wanted to crush them.

Her mother came over to her. She pressed her breasts. Milk squirted from them, drenching her naked body, pearly drops trickling down her waist.

What a sight! I was stunned. Fearful, life seemed to be ebbing out of my body.

I kept pacing up and down. I was remorseful. Then I fell asleep and dreamt of youthful breasts hanging all over the sky.

I had just slid into sleep when I heard noises in the neighbourhood. Someone's wails rose above the pervading noise. This was followed by the cry, 'Qadir *Mian*, Pakistan has come into being. The accursed one is born!'

If the sacred *pipal* tree had not stood there, I would have thought it was a ghost's voice from the nether regions. I would have tried to escape. But having experienced such weird scenes already I could not trust my eyes. What a nightmare! I saw the sky raining blood, dead bodies running in the dark, and blood sprouting from headless torsos. I saw people dancing naked in the *bazar*.

I woke up in the morning with a heavy head. My eyes were red, the hands and feet numb. I got up because the police had come. The drillmaster trembled with fear.

'Some policemen are looking for you,' he said.

'Why?' I asked.

'They have orders to interrogate every visitor to the city.'

I was enraged. Did anyone ask about me when I was driven out of my own town at an unearthly hour? Why was I going? Where was I going?

Bano, what is Pakistan? Its abode is in the mind, which manifests itself when one fails to understand man in his fullness, and conceives of him as a lopsided entity under the stress of time.

The police took me to the police-station. I was grilled.

They wanted to know why I was there. What could I tell them? Why does one visit places? The police would have kept harassing me had the drillmaster not answered all the questions. His being a Muslim lent credibility to his account.

We went out and sat on a log of wood by the roadside. I had turned pale. The drillmaster wanted to give me time to collect myself. Neither of us spoke. Then the drillmaster broke the ice. 'Badru has gone crazy,' he said. 'He has been sitting under the *pipal* tree after the riots broke out. His looms were burnt. It was he who was calling out to Qadir *Mian* last night. Didn't you hear?'

Three people sat next to us near the *Teenbatti* crossing. Perhaps they had been to the police station to stand bail. They had such hangdog looks. The *maulvi* was fearful. 'The Prophet had said that the trumpet shall sound thrice,' he said to the people next to him. 'When the trumpet sounds for the first time the people will quail with fear,' he said. 'At the second call everyone will perish. And when the trumpet sounds the third time, everyone will stand before God to be judged. This is how it is going to happen. The first trumpet has sounded. . . .'

'Are you still writing your *Bhartrihari Nama*,' I asked Master *Saheb*.

'Yes,' he said, 'and listen . . .

I am a wanderer,'
Here only for a night.
Talk, so that the night passes quickly
And the day dawns.'

He looked around after reciting these lines. Yellow flowers grew in the cracks on the roof. Birds hopped in the thick grass like small fish. They carried blades of grass in their beaks and picked them up as they fell. Master *Saheb* watched them indulgently.

I broke the silence and asked, 'Last night . . .'

'Yes, that was Badru,' Master *Saheb* said. 'He has gone mad. All his looms were burnt. And now he keeps cursing all the time sitting under the *pipal* tree.'

'And in the house....' I ventured to ask. 'Is everything all right with your family?'

It was then that the drillmaster unfolded Bano's story. 'She is not too well,' he said. 'She gave birth to a baby at Dr. Sarang's Nursing Home, three days before the riots started. The rioters set fire to the Nursing Home. Mothers with newborn babies jumped from the first floor to save their lives. There were nine mothers. Two died along with five babies. Bano lost her baby while trying to jump. Somehow she was rescued and brought home. She is better now but the milk in her breasts is a terrible problem.'

We sat in silence for some time. 'I think it's time I returned to Poona,' I said at last.

'Better go to Chinar instead. Your grandfather may be looking forward to meeting you.'

'Why, is he unwell?'

'Yes, he lost one of his arms. It was the rioters' doing. They had come to attack us. A pitched battle took place right in front of this house. Your grandfather saved us all. He rushed into the street and in the mêlée the rioters chopped off his arm. But he continued to use this arm as a weapon, fighting until he was unconscious. He was treated in hospital.'

'What about his arm?' I asked shaken to my core.

'His arm is missing, but he is alright. He said he would continue his treatment at Chinar. God is merciful. You must go and look him up.' The drillmaster covered his face with his hands.

What a bewildering turn of events! I feared I would go out of my mind. What kind of world did I live in? Who were these people? Were they really men or ghosts? Now, only a cripple looked normal, wearing a terrifying look.

I came back to my room and lay down. The drillmaster went to his room. Then I heard some voices from the courtyard below. Bano, her mother, father and Munir were arguing.

'Why are you hell-bent upon living here? I just don't understand.' It was Munir speaking.

'You'll never understand,' Bano retorted. 'I lost my child on this soil and I must get it back from here. Then, I'll go with you wherever you want me to.'

I peeped through the railing. A lean and thin Munir trembled with rage. 'Do what you like for all I care,' he fumed. 'Go and have a child from anyone you please.'

I was dumbfounded. Was Munir alluding to me? Maybe I got him wrong. Bano spoke again, furious. 'As if you are capable of giving me a child. You are only good at selling your blood and buying hooch.'

Smack! Perhaps Munir had slapped Bano. Hot words were exchanged. 'Don't I know,' Bano shouted back, 'why you make these frequent trips to Bombay? It is to sell your blood and buy liquor. Then you lie in bed shivering the whole night.'

What did I hear? A Pakistan seemed to be shedding tears within her. We were all harbouring a Pakistan in our hearts. We were all crippled, half-alive. Pakistan was here to nag each one of us, to torment us, to tear us apart, bit by bit, reducing us to cripples.

Oh, what a dreadful moonlit night! Overcast with gloom, I left Bhiwandi unceremoniously in the same way I had fled Chinar. I got into a taxi going to Thane. From Thane I took a bus to Bombay and then on to Poona by train. I was down with fever in Poona and stayed in bed for several days.

Bano, I wanted to forget everything. I wanted to withdraw into my shell to divine what I really was and how meaningless life's journey could be. Though bloodied and crippled, man still lives on.

In this desolate loneliness if a voice rings through the darkness, 'Is there anyone else there?' how would you respond? No one knows for certain, not even you, Bano.

IS THERE SOMEONE ELSE?

About five months later, my grandfather informed me that he had returned to Bhiwandi. His business was not doing well because of the Sindhis and the Marwaris who had entered the market in a big way. The market was generally dull and a large number of handlooms were lying idle. My grandfather's walk had become stilted because he had lost an arm. He humorously remarked that people had nicknamed him *tonta*. He didn't have much to say except that Munir had gone to Bombay with Bano. He didn't know whether he was still there or migrated to Pakistan. The drillmaster was slightly demented. He did drill exercises at home and wrote the story of *Bhartrihari* at school.

If I had not gone to Bombay that day, I would have not have run into Bano. What a painful meeting! I was so ashamed of myself. She must have formed a very poor impression of me, thinking that I regularly visited prostitutes. To tell the truth, Bano, I did visit them and often attributed my waywardness to you.

Passing through Bombay *en route* to Bhiwandi, I broke journey at Bombay for a day or two. I ran into Kedar, an old Bombay friend, at the station. We decided to spend the evening together. Bano, you were far removed from my mind. We had a few drinks at Colaba, took a leisurely stroll and stopped in front of the Handloom House. From here we entered a side lane, somewhat like a Bohra locality, very open and clean.

The building where we stopped had a lift. But we preferred the stairs. I was out of breath by the time we reached the fifth floor. I could smell food being cooked in some apartments. Pausing to take a breath, we resumed our climb to the sixth floor. Kedar stopped in front of a door and rang the bell. The flat did not appear tidy.

The door opened. Still panting like hippies we stood before a Sindhi. The room he led us into was sparsely furnished. Cheap sofas rested against the walls. The Sindhi kept wheezing.

I was restless and went to the window for a breath of fresh air. I saw dirty rooftops stretching far into the distance. The Sindhi placed a bottle of Coca-Cola before me and then took Kedar to a corner of the room where I had a fleeting glimpse of a woman in black veil. But I couldn't listen to their conversation.

The two disappeared. After a minute or two, I heard Kedar's laughter from the adjoining room.

The Sindhi reappeared after a while, still wheezing. 'Beey. . . ? Care to . . . ?' The rest of the words were carried away on his breath.

'I wouldn't mind,' I said.

The Sindhi asked a boy to fetch a bottle of beer. He did not join me.

'You . . . Bombay?' he asked checking himself.

'I've come from Poona.'

'For pleasure?' he asked.

'No, I had some work here.'

'Business?'

'No, personal. I'm on my way to Bhiwandi.'

The Sindhi sat there breathing heavily. All of a sudden Kedar showed up. The Sindhi rose to his feet, swayed heavily as if he was caught unawares. I felt uneasy; so I gulped down the remaining beer. Kedar was paying for my beer when the door of the adjoining room opened and a woman's hand held out a bunch of keys before Kedar. Seeing me beside the Sindhi whose chest was working like bellows, a voice asked, 'Anyone else?'

Yes, there was. Someone else was very much there.

After a blind, tremulous moment you recognized me. Your lips suddenly curled up in a venomous smile, dripping contempt and poison. Or was it just a figment of my imagination?

I wish I knew on whom you were wreaking vengeance? Against me, Munir or Pakistan? Or against yourself?

I went downstairs, Kedar close on my heels. I wanted to climb the stairs again and ask, 'Bano, was our relationship destined to end this way?'

Where do I go now? Which place, which town, which city? Where do I hide? Moving from place to place, could I ultimately land somewhere away from Pakistan? A place where I could live in the fullness of life, with my longings and desires. . . .

But that is not to be, Bano. I discover a Pakistan at every step. Bano, it plunges a knife in your body and mine. We bleed and feel so betrayed and humiliated. But it continues to be.

Translated from Hindi by Jai Ratan

Asylum
AGNEYA

S.H. Vatsyayan 'Agneya' (1911-87), an outstanding Hindi poet, also made a seminal contribution as a fictionwriter, essayist, critic, editor, journalist and translator. Pioneer of the Experimental and New Poetry Movements, he brought a modernist sensibility to contemporary Hindi literature. Though often castigated for being too self-possessed and even formalist, he has a notion of literature's social function. In a preface to *Sharanarthi* (short story collection) he wrote, 'These stories will justify themselves if they can leave even a bit of benevolent influence on today's polluted social psyche.' Recipient of the Sahitya Akademi and Bharatiya Jnanpeeth Awards, *Kitne Navon Men Kitne Bar*, *Hari Ghas Par Kshan Bhar* (poetry), *Apne Apne Ajnabi*, *Nadi ke Dweep* and *Shekhar: Ek Jeevani* (novels) are among his notable works.

The story 'Asylum' is typical of Agneya's play with situations and language, leading not to a catharsis but to an identification with the ironical ambivalence of the situation.

'No, Davinderlal*ji*, such a thing can never happen.' The lawyer Rafiquddin was emphatic, but his worried expression betrayed his true feelings. 'No, Davinderlalji, such a thing can't happen,' he repeated. Davinderlal expressed his helplessness. 'Each one of them has left,' he said. 'I have no apprehensions about you. But you know very well that when fear grips people and they start fleeing, the atmosphere changes all around. Each person starts suspecting the other and regards him as an enemy. You are, no doubt, held in high esteem in this *mohalla* but I can't vouch for the outsiders? You can see for yourself the incidents that take place everyday. . . .'

Rafiquddin cut him short. 'No *Saheb*, we'll lose credibility. Tell me, does it make sense to abandon your own home and be a refugee in your own city? It is our moral duty to protect the minority. If

'Sharandata' from *Ye Tere Pratirup* (Delhi: Rajpal and Sons, 1961), pp. 47-60.

we can't protect our neighbours, how the hell can we defend our country? I am convinced that even in parts of Punjab where the Hindus are in a majority, not to mention in other parts of the country, people must be reacting in this way. Please don't go. You mustn't. I take the responsibility of protecting you. Well, what more can I say? I give you my word.'

One by one the Hindus in Davinderlal's neighbourhood moved away. Invariably he would bump into someone on the street in the afternoons or in the evenings and ask, 'So, *Lalaji* (or *Babuji* or *Panditji*), what's your decision?' Pat came the reply, 'What's there to decide? We are staying put here. Time will tell. . . . ' Next morning or evening Davinderlal would discover that they had packed some of their essential belongings and left quietly. Some left Lahore for good, while the others moved to Hindu localities in the city. Four houses to the right of his own house were deserted. The new owner of the open space next to them was a Muslim *gujjar* (he kept milch cattle and sold milk). On one side were tied his buffaloes, while on the other lived simple Muslim craftsmen. The houses between Davinderlal's and Rafiquddin's on the left were unoccupied. Beyond Rafiquddin's house was Mozang's den. Next to it, sprawled a locality inhabited by Muslim fanatics.

Davinderlal and Rafiquddin were old friends. They would discuss each departing neighbour. Finally, one day, Davinderlal hinted that he was also thinking of going. Rafiquddin was jolted. 'You too!' he cried in a pained voice.

Rafiquddin prevailed upon Davinderlal to stay on. He agreed to warn him if there was any foreboding of trouble and make arrangements for his safety. Davinderlal's wife had left a few days ago for her mother's house in Jalandhar. He had written to her not to return. Only Davinderlal and his servant Santu, a lad from the hills, were left behind to fend for themselves.

But this state of affairs did not continue for long. On the fourth morning, Davinderlal found that Santu had deserted him. He made some tea for himself. Just then Rafiquddin gave him the disquieting news that the entire city was gripped by violence. Before long the goons of Mozang would be on a rampage, fanning out in groups. There was no time to move elsewhere. Rafiquddin suggested that Davinderlal collect his valuables and shift to his house.

Davinderlal had no 'valuables' to take care of. His wife had taken the jewelry with her to Jalandhar. Some cash was stashed away in the bank. His liquid assets were not much. Of course a householder regards everything in the house as valuable. It took Davinderlal some time to decide. Within an hour he moved into Rafiquddin's house with his trunk and bedroll.

The mob reached Mozang at about three in the afternoon. In the evening, Davinderlal saw people entering his house. They broke open the lock and ransacked it. It was a wholesale loot. At night they saw flames rising in several places. The smoke made the humid summer night more suffocating.

Rafiquddin too, like Davinderlal, watched in silence, defeat writ large in his eyes. Only once he remarked, 'What a day. And that too in the name of freedom! *Ya Allah!*'

But when a person is thrown out of his own house by God, he does not even find shelter in his own lane.

Davinderlal was forced to stay indoors. Only Rafiquddin ventured out into the city. There was no question of attending to his practice. He would just go around, do the daily shopping, and return home to relate the day's news to Davinderlal. Both would go into a long huddle and discuss the country's future. Soon Davinderlal discerned a note of anxiety in Rafiquddin's voice; a sort of pain which he was unable to define with certainty: was it exhaustion, gloom, detachment, or a sense of defeat? God alone knows!

The city wore a deserted look. Dead bodies lay rotting everywhere. Lots of houses were looted and set on flame. Some prominent citizens went to a leading doctor who commanded respect and requested him to visit various *mohallas*. They thought his words would restore sanity and also attend to the patients. The doctor agreed. He visited two or three *mohallas*, and then went to a Muslim *basti*. He had barely bent over to examine a patient with his stethoscope, when the patient's relative stabbed him in the back. . . .

A railway employee in a Hindu *mohalla* gave shelter to numerous refugees. He dutifully sought the police help to protect their belongings. The police in turn arrested those people along with the railway employee. They took away the women. The railway employee's house was looted and burnt down. They were released after three days. Two armed policemen were deputed to escort them home. Hardly fifty steps from the police station the armed guards opened fire on them. Three women were killed. The railway employee's mother was wounded. His wife collapsed and lay on the road unattended.

The atmosphere was vicious. Hate and anger was whipped up and communal frenzy spread everywhere. Religious fanatics had a field day. The guardians of law and the bureaucrats made things worse. Davinderlal often wondered whether he and Rafiquddin were the only sane people. Davinderlal realized that the oblique hints by Rafiquddin in his conversation were becoming explicit—hints, coarse, yet filled with shame.

Several hundred Muslim refugees sought shelter in a Sikh village situated along the tentative border between Hindustan and Pakistan. The people of neighbouring villages and of Amritsar made life difficult for them. But then the residents of three Sikh villages decided to escort the refugees to the Amritsar railway station, from where they could move to a safe Muslim locality. About two hundred and fifty Sikhs, brandishing *kirpans*, formed a cordon around them and escorted them to the railway station. Not a single refugee was injured.

Rafiquddin narrated this incident. 'Each one of us finds himself at a dead end. Sometimes one suffers alone. But in this case an entire village proved true to their word in the end. Kudos to them. The refugees were escorted without a mishap.'

Davinderlal nodded in agreement. But the first sentence that came to his mind was, 'True, there is something called helplessness. A man ploughing a lonely furrow has often to bend.' He gave Rafiquddin a sharp look, but Rafiquddin did not take his cue.

Six or seven people met Rafiquddin one evening. He took them to his sitting room and talked on and on. They whispered mostly. Sometimes their voices rose to a high pitch. The words 'cussedness', 'treason', 'Islam', reached Davinder's ears. Davinder did not ask what the discussion was all about. But when Rafiquddin tried to walk past with a long face, he could not resist. 'What's the matter? Is everything right?'

Rafiquddin gave him a tense look. He did not utter a word. Instead he lowered his eyes.

'I know you have to suffer this humiliation because of me. You have taken a risk. Let me go. Don't risk your life. I'm grateful for what you have done. I'm indebted. . . .'

Rafiquddin placed his hands on his friend's shoulders.

'Davinderlal*ji*. . . .' He started breathing heavily. Then suddenly he went inside the house.

At dinner Davinderlal insisted: 'If you don't allow me to go, I will have to leave without letting you know. Please let me know what is going on. I want to know the truth.'

'They threatened me, what else?'

'What kind of threat?'

'Are there different kinds of threats? They want a quarry. By making threatening noises if they can. Otherwise by brute force and arson.'

'So it has come to that? That is why I must go away. I'm alone. I can fend for myself. I'll just slip out. You have a family to look after. They are bent upon destroying everything.'

'They are just *goondas*.'

'I'll leave today—'

'How is that possible? After all I prevented you from going. I have a responsibility towards you.'

'You did so with the best of intentions. Now, you have no further obligations.'

'But where will you go?'

'I'll see. . . .'

'No, that's not possible.'

The discussion went on for long. Ultimately Davinderlal agreed to move to the safety of a house belonging to Rafiq's Muslim friend.

Davinderlal was lodged in a garage hidden behind a row of trees. This was in Sheikh Ataullah's compound. Not exactly in the garage, but in a small and narrow room adjacent to it. The room had a small courtyard in front and was enclosed by a brick wall. Maybe it was once used by a car driver. A small door opened into the courtyard. There was no other opening, not even a window. The room had a string cot on one side and a mud pot in an alcove. The floor was smeared with earth. A small pit was dug on one side near the corrugated iron gate of the garage. Near the gate was a heap of lime mixed with clay. From it and the mud pot the purpose of the pit was evident.

The trunk and bedroll were placed in a corner of the room. The courtyard gate was shut and locked. For a moment he stood listlessly. Here was a taste of India's freedom! Before independence, a foreign government gaoled people for their passion for freedom. Now, solitary confinement was the fate of those who wanted to stop internal feuds in order to safeguard freedom. At that moment Davinderlal's instinct of self-preservation took over. He looked around to see what was in the garage-cum-room.

The garage was not bad; it was just a bit smelly. He could shut the door and keep the smell out. Mercifully, there was enough water to wash his hands and face. The room was not bad except that it was not well lit. He could not read. In any case he had no books to read. The light filtering in from the verandah was good enough for him to perform his daily chores. At the end of the courtyard lived the Sheikh.

Davinderlal started thinking. One was free to sing or shout in British jails. But here one had to keep mum.

Then he remembered having read that prisoners kept pigeons, squirrels or cats as pets to overcome their loneliness. Or they studied the ways of ants and spiders to keep their minds occupied. To make friends with mosquitoes? The idea did not appeal to him.

Moving to the courtyard, Davinderlal looked at the sky— the sky of an independent country. He could see the smoke from burning houses going up like a prayer. And there was the sandal paste mark too. But it was red, the colour of blood.

Suddenly he saw a shadow on the courtyard wall. It was a tom cat. 'Come, come!' he called out. But the cat kept staring at him with unblinking eyes. Pleased, and no longer lonely, Davinderlal spread out his bedding on the cot and went off to sleep.

They sent him food once a day, after nightfall. It was sufficient for two meals. The pots in the garage and in the room were also filled up at that time. A young man brought the food. He was Sheikh *Saheb*'s son. He did not say a word. When Davinderlal asked about the city the first day, he merely gave him a quizzical look. When asked if the city was peaceful, the young man shook his head. When asked how things were at home, he nodded implying that all was well.

Though he could make do for two meals with the food brought in, Davinderlal decided to eat just once a day. He would eat and leave the rest for the cat. The cat was friendly and would take a bone or two into the courtyard and chew it there. It would come and sit by Davinderlal's side and start purring.

This is how he spent time until darkness descended on the house. In the morning he would exercise. He spent the rest of the day playing with pebbles, watch the sparrows on the courtyard wall, or listen to the cooing of pigeons in the distance. At times he heard voices from the Sheikh's house. He soon started relating the different voices to the inmates of the house. The woman with the raucous voice was most probably the Sheikh's wife. The woman with a shrill voice, having a rough edge, was an elderly woman. Probably a poor relation. The lilting feminine voice which responded to the name 'Zaibu' was obviously Sheikh *Saheb*'s daughter. There were two male voices also—one of them being Abid *Mian*'s, Sheikh *Saheb*'s son, who brought him food. The other voice was heavy, viscous and leathery, like fat on raw meat. That was Sheikh *Saheb* himself. Davinderlal could hear his voice but could not make out what he said. Only a shrill voice can be understood from a distance.

Zaibu's voice was so soothing and unpretentious. Davinderlal would conjure up visions of her youthful appearance. What awful thoughts for an old man like him to entertain! He wondered if somebody with such an appealing voice would spread the poison of hatred among the people?

Perhaps Sheikh *Saheb* was head clerk in the Police department. Maybe, Rafiquddin thought, that a policeman's abode would be the safest place for him. This reasoning was quite plausible but had given rise to many problems. It wouldn't be at all surprising if all the people in such a household were spreading poison. . . . While eating, Davinderlal wondered who had cooked what, who had packed the food for him? Perhaps the woman with the shrill voice. He liked to imagine that Zaibu had a hand in packing the food. He would tend to eat more and more.

One day Davinderlal noticed a qualitative change. Instead of the large Muslim *rotis*, there were small, featherweight, round Hindu *phulkas*. In addition to the usual course of meat, there was also a big helping of *rabri* , a sweet. This was special, because he had earlier only been served *phirni* or *shahi-tukra*. When Abid left, Davinderlal picked up a *phulka* and then put it back. For a second, the picture of his own house flashed before his eyes. He picked up the *phulkas* again from the *thali* and put them back. He was startled.

A crumpled piece of paper lay hidden within the fold of the *phulka*. Davinderlal unfolded and smoothed out the piece of paper. It contained nothing.

He was going to roll up the paper into a ball and throw it away. Just then he held back. He moved to the courtyard and the faint light to scrutinize the paper more carefully. A sentence was scribbled on it: 'Feed the dog before eating.'

Davinderlal tore the paper into pieces, crumpled them, and buried them in the pit outside the garage. Then he returned to the courtyard and started pacing up and down.

He didn't know what to do. He was numb. He just thought of Zaibu.

'Zaibu' . . . 'Zaibu' . . . 'Zaibu!'

He went back and stood by the *thali* of food.

He was supposed to eat that food—Davinderlal's food. It may not have come from his house but it was from a friend's. From the house of his host, his saviour's.

From Zaibu's house.

From Zaibu's father's house.

Is there a dog here?

Davinderlal started pacing the room.

A shadow moved across the wall of the courtyard. It was a cat.

Davinderlal took the cat into his room. 'Look, son, you're my guest as I'm Sheikh *Saheb*'s. Am I right, son? What he wants to do to me I want to do to you. It doesn't behove me, but I'm going to do it. I don't know whether he wants to do it to me. Maybe he does, maybe not. I just don't know. Oh, it's such a rigmarole. Well, you eat the leftovers every day. Today I'll eat what you leave for me. Yes, that's right. Here, have this food.'

The cat had a go at the meat. Then the *rabri*.

Animals instinctively know what food is wholesome for them and what is not. Otherwise, how would they survive? This instinct is more pronounced in cats than in other animals. That's why they are not tamed as easily as dogs.

Suddenly the cat snarled furiously and leapt out of Davinderlal's lap. Howling, it leapt over the wall and landed on the roof of the garage where it started writhing in acute pain. It was a pathetic sight. The cat groaned and groaned until life ebbed out of it.

Davinderlal stared at the food. He kept looking without seeing. He stood stock-still, his eyes riveted on the *thali*.

Freedom! Brotherhood! Country! Nation!

One had forced him to stay back and insisted he would be given protection. But eventually he was turned out by his benefactor. The other had offered him shelter—and poison.

He was also warned that he was being poisoned.

What audacity!

Davinderlal's heart was filled with self-pity. The shocking incident could not be forgotten by leaning against the crumbling wall of politics but only by thinking of one's ordeal philosophically.

It dawned upon Davinderlal that the real danger in this world was not the power of the evil-minded but the feeblemindedness of the virtuous. The ingrained timorousness of the virtuous wrought the greatest evil. Dark clouds did not usher in the night. Night came when the sun faded.

He picked up the *thali* and placed it in the courtyard. Then he drank some water and started pacing up and down. He was thinking.

Next, he entered his room and opened his trunk. Rummaging through the trunk he took out some documents, a few photographs, a bank passbook and a large envelope. He shoved them into the pocket of his *sherwani* and buttoned it up. He moved to the courtyard again and put his ear against the wall, listening.

Then he jumped over the wall and landed on the road— He did not know how he did it.

What happened thereafter is not just a story or a combination of events spinning themselves into a story. Events remain inconclusive. Only stories are rounded off with conclusions. Human logic, commonsense, virtuosity, aesthetic sense, all go into the making of a story. People call it fiction and derive pleasure from wholeness. But incidents in real life are the result of some uncanny power, not strictly based on human reason. Call it fate, nature, coincidence, the supernatural or God. That is why man fails to comprehend these mystifying things easily. By that token, perhaps it is not necessary to spell out how Davinderlal fared after jumping over that wall.

One has to add that a month and a half later when Davinderlal relayed a message to his family over the Delhi radio giving his address, he received a letter from Lahore: 'A thousand thanks to God who helped you to escape. I ardently wish that the persons whose names you had broadcast over the radio are united with you. I seek forgiveness for what *Abba* did or tried doing. I must tell you that I foiled his evil design. This was no favour. You are not under any obligation. My only request is that if you find someone from the minority community in a similar situation you must help him out. My example is before you. Not because the person happens to be a Muslim but because of human considerations. After all you are, like everybody else, also a human being. *Khuda-Hafiz.*'

The greasy, raucous voice of Sheikh Ataullah: 'Zaibu, Zaibu,' echoed in Davinderlal's mind. So also the cry of the cat, groaning and writhing on the roof of the garage, turning into a prolonged sigh and trailing into silence.

Davinderlal crumpled the letter into a ball and flicked it away.

Translated from Hindi by Jai Ratan

Lajwanti

RAJINDER SINGH BEDI

Rajinder Singh Bedi (1910-84) was an outstanding short story writer in Urdu, who had the unusual knack of creating a well-knit, effective and lifelike tale out of seemingly trivial occurrences. One of his widely-acclaimed short stories is called *Garm Coat* (Warm Coat—that is, an overcoat). Described as an artist par excellence, he was able to impart new nuances to the word and phrase he selected to express particular situations and moods. Ismat Chughtai (1915-91), another brilliant fiction writer, said of Bedi in a *Mahfil* interview: 'He's got style, and characters too.... His *Ek Chadar Maili Si* is a beautiful and integrated picture of a human being. His language, some say, is very defective, but I find it very attractive. The story has the forcefulness of a thunderbolt.' *Ek Chadar Maili Si* (literally, 'a rather dirty sheet') won the Sahitya Akademi Award in 1966. (trans. by Khushwant Singh, *I Take This Woman*, Hind Pocket Books, Delhi, 1967).

On his association with the Progressive Writers' Movement, Bedi commented: 'I was taken into it at first. I didn't know until I was told that I was a "Progressive" writer and that the others were also "Progressive" writers. But it's partly true that I was, for I did write about the life of the common people and was truthful about the life I had lived and knew.... Later, when the movement was struck with a sort of formalism, I realized that Progressive writing was also part of a larger doctrine or ideology which was being propagated through us.'

'This is the plant of touch-me-not; it shrivels up at a mere touch....', so goes a Punjabi folk song.

The country was partitioned. A myriad wounded human beings staggered out of the shambles and wiped away the blood that still stained their bodies. Then they turned their dazed eyes towards

From *Contemporary Indian Short Stories* (Series II) ed. Bhabani Bhattacharya (New Delhi: Sahitya Akademi, 1st edn. 1967), pp. 172-183 those whose bodies were yet whole and unscathed but whose hearts were torn, bleeding.

In every *mohalla* of the city of Ludhiana rehabilitation committees were set up. The work of giving relief to the displaced and the dispossessed, of settling them in jobs, on lands and in homes was carried on with an intense fervour. But there was one phase of this problem which was yet neglected and the programme that sought to tackle this aspect carried the slogan: 'Rehabilitate them in your hearts!' This programme was, however, staunchly opposed by the inmates of the temple of Narain Baba and the orthodox, conventional people who lived in that vicinity.

To give impetus to this programme, a committee was formed in the *mohalla* of Mulla Shukoor which lay near Narain Baba's temple. Babu Sunder Lal was elected secretary of this committee, by a majority of eleven votes. It was the considered opinion of *Vakil Saheb*, the Chairman of the old *moharrir* of Chauki Kalan, and other worthies that there was no one who could perform the duties of secretary with greater zeal and earnestness than Sunder Lal. Their confidence rested perhaps on the fact that Sunder Lal's own wife had been abducted—his wife whose name was Lajo or Lajwanti, the plant of touch-me-not.

At early dawn, when Sunder Lal led *prabhat-pheris* through the half-awakened streets, and his friends, Rasalu, Neki Ram and others sang in fervid chorus: 'These are the tender touch-me-not, my friend; they will shrivel and curl up even if you so much as touch them . . .' it was only Sunder Lal whose voice would suddenly choke; and in utter silence, as he mechanically kept pace with his friends and followers, he would think of his Lajwanti whom wanton hands had not only touched but torn away from him—where would she be now? What condition would she be in? What would she be thinking of her people? Would she ever return? . . . And as his thoughts wandered the alleys of a sharp and searing pain, his legs would tremble on the hard, cold flagstones of the streets.

But presently the stage came when he ceased to think about his Lajwanti. His own pain and suffering had been transcended and it had become one with universal suffering, the pain of all mankind. To escape the sharp sting of his own agony, he had plunged into social service, seeking to alleviate the agonies of others. Yet, whenever the inspired voices of his friends rang out, shaking the misty silence of the mornings, his own voice failed and he thought:

How delicate is the human heart, indeed! A mere touch and it cracks like the most fragile glass, withers like a leaf of *Lajwanti*! But in the past he himself had maltreated *his* Lajwanti often enough and he had not infrequently thrashed her, even without the slightest pretext or provocation.

Sunder Lal's Lajwanti was a gay and slim girl of the village—a daughter of the soil. Her skin had been tanned to a deep musk by too much exposure to the sun. But within her was some strange source of verve and vitality, a resistless joy and effervescence. Her restlessness was that of a dew drop which rolls about on the large *arvi* leaf. The slimness of her body was not because of ill-health; on the contrary, it was a sign of good health. Sunder Lal, who had a tendency to obesity, had felt diffident at first; as he discovered that Lajo could bear any burden, submit to any form of pain and suffering and even to occasional bouts of thrashing, he had gradually increased his maltreatment of her. Presently, he became so confident of her capacity for tolerance that he even lost sight of those frontiers at which the tolerance and patience of any human being can crack up. Lajo was indeed helpful in making Sunder Lal forget those frontiers, in making them dimmer, ever nonexistent. Since she was naturally unable to remain sad and pensive for long, she could not resist her brightly and naive laughter at the slightest smile on Sunder Lal's face, even though they might have quarrelled most bitterly just a little while before. And her only truce term would be: 'If you beat me again, I shall never speak to you.'

On each such occasion it would be evident that she had forgotten all about even her most immediate torture. Like other girls of the village, she believed that all husbands treated their wives in that manner. If any woman showed the slightest independence or rebelliousness, the other women would themselves condemn their subversive sister. A finger to their noses, they would proclaim: '*Le*, is he a man that he cannot control a chit of a woman?' And this maltreatment by husbands, abuses and thrashing, had become an accepted convention among the womenfolk, even a theme for their songs. Lajo herself used to sing: 'I shall not marry a youth from the city for he wears boots and my waist is slim and slender!' But at the very first chance Lajo gave her heart away to a youth from the city whose name was Sunder Lal. He had come to Lajo's village with a marriage procession and had whispered into the groom's ears: 'Your sister in law is spicy, my friend; your wife must also be pepper!'

Having heard these words of Sunder Lal, Lajo forgot that he wore heavy, ugly boots and that her waist was so very slim.

These were the memories that came winging through the years as Sunder Lal went about leading *prabhat-pheris* along the streets. And as these pods of nostalgia cracked and opened, Sunder Lal thought: For once, if only for once, I get my Lajo back, I shall enshrine her always in my heart. I shall tell others that these poor women were blameless, that it was no fault of theirs to have been abducted, a prey to the brutal passions of rioters. The society which does not accept these innocent women is rotten and deserves to be destroyed. . . . With all the eloquence at his command he pleaded and preached that such women should be given the status that is accorded to the wives, the sisters, the mothers and the daughters in a home, and that not even by hint or suggestion should they ever be reminded of the heinous torments to which they had been subjected. Their hearts were torn and bleeding, for they were delicate, tender like the plants of touch-me-not.

So, to give a practical shape to the programme whose slogan was 'rehabilitate them in your hearts,' the committee of *mohalla Mulla* Shukoor organized many *prabhat-pheris*. The ideal time for them was four or five in the morning—there was then no din and bustle in the streets, nor any problems of traffic. Even the pariah dogs who kept watch all night were now quiet. Drowsy citizens in their cozy beds would mumble: 'Those people again!' And sometimes with patience and sometimes with irritation they would listen to the inspired orations of Babu Sunder Lal. Women, safe and out of harm's way, lying complacent like cauliflowers, with husbands by their side like stems, would mutter in protest at the disturbance. Somewhere a child would open his eyes for a moment, and thinking that the sad chorus of the propagandists was just another song, he would fall asleep again.

A word, however, settles in a niche of the mind, and even when one wakes up it does not pass. All day long it moves through the mind like a blundering stranger. Sometimes, men do not even understand it but keep on repeating it to themselves, mechanically. And it was because such words had by now settled in the minds of the people that, when Miss Mridula Sarabhai brought over some abducted women by virtue of an exchange pact between India and Pakistan, several men of the *mohalla* of *Mulla* Shukoor volunteered to rehabilitate the women in their homes. The kinfolk of these women went to the outskirts of the town near Chauki Kalan to meet them. For a long moment the abducted women and their relatives stared at each other like strangers. Then, heads bent low, they walked back together to tackle the task of bringing new life to ruined homes, and Rasalu and Neki Ram and Sunder Lal shouted fervently: 'Mahendra Singh *Zindabad*! . . . ' 'Sohan Lal *Zindabad*!'. . . . They kept on shouting till their throats became hoarse and dry.

But there were some amongst these abducted women whom their husbands, fathers, mothers, brothers and sisters refused to recognize. On the contrary, they would curse them: Why did they not die? Why did they not take poison to save their chastity? Why didn't they jump into the well to save their honour? They were cowards who basely and desperately clung to life. Why, thousands of women had killed themselves before they could be forced to yield their honour and chastity?

Little did these people know that those who had lived through the horror and shame had shown a terrible kind of bravery. One of the women, whose husband would not take her back, vacantly mumbled her own name to herself: *Suhagvanti*, the married one. . . . Another, seeing her young brother in the crowd, cried out: 'You do not seem to recognize me Behari, but I have taken you in my lap and fondled you as a child.' And Behari, too, wanted to cry out to her but he looked at his parents and the parents looked at Narain Baba, and Narain Baba looked up at the sky which, in fact, is no reality but an illusion, the frontier of our sight beyond which we cannot see.

But Lajo was not amongst the abducted women whom Miss Sarabhai had brought in a military truck in exchange for the abducted women of the other country. With gradually dwindling hope, Sunder Lal saw the last women descend from the vehicle and in silence he turned back and with added zeal redoubled the activities of his committee. They did not go out for *prabhat-pheris* in the mornings, only, but started to bring out processions in the evenings as well. And sometimes they would convene a small meeting in which the chairman, the old pleader Kalka Prasad, would make a speech like the orations of the Sufi saints. He would cough ceaselessly and strange noises would come from the loudspeakers and Neki Ram, the *moharrir* of the *Chauki*, would get up to say something; but whatever he said, quoting copiously from the holy scriptures, went against the cause that he sought to plead. And seeing the battle being lost because of this unintended confusion, Sunder Lal would stand up but he would be able to speak no more than a sentence or two. His voice would choke, tears would ooze out of his eyes, the lump in his throat would stifle all the fervent words he had wanted to utter, and he would sit down again. On all such occasions, a strange hush would fall on the meeting and the few words which had broken forth from the depths of Sunder Lal's heart would prove more effective than all the sermons and advice of Vakil Kalka Prasad. But the people—they shed tears only at the meeting, and emotionally sated by this catharsis, they returned vacantly to their houses.

One day the members of the committee came out to carry on their propaganda in the evening and gradually arrived at the stronghold of the conservatives. Devoted and god-fearing men and women were crowded on the cement platform round the *pipal* tree outside the temple and Baba Narain Das was reciting to them that particular passage from the *Ramayana* where a washerman had turned out his wife from his house, saying 'I am not like Raja Ramchandra who has accepted Sita even after she has lived for years with Ravana.' And, hearing that, Ram turned out the true and faithful Sita even though she was then pregnant. 'Could there be better proof of justice and morality?' Narain Baba asserted: 'Such is the true *Ramrajya* in which even a washerman's words are respected.'

The procession which the committee had sponsored stopped near the temple. Sunder Lal heard Narain Baba's last words and said: 'We do not want such a *rajya*, Baba!'

'Shut up ! Who the devil are you?' Shouts of angry protest came from the crowd of devotees. But Sunder Lal stepped forward undaunted.

'Not one of you can stop me from speaking what I want to say.'

Again a chorus of shouts came. 'Quiet ! We will not let you speak!' And a voice could be heard: 'We'll kill you, if . . .'

The soft and mellow words of Narain Baba came then: 'You do not understand the greatness of our scriptures, Sunder Lal!'

'Maybe,' said Sunder Lal, 'but one thing I do understand, Baba. A washerman's voice was heard in *Ramrajya* but those who desire *Ramrajya* are not prepared to hear the voice of Sunder Lal.'

The hostile ones now shifted their position. 'Let's give him a hearing.'

Sunder Lal started: 'Undoubtedly, Sri Ram was a great man, a divine being; but why was it, Baba, that he believed the words of a washerman and not of his wife and queen?'

'Sunder Lal, you would not understand the greatness of such a gesture.'

'You are right,' Sunder Lal answered. 'There are many things in this world which I do not understand. Yet, in my humble opinion, the true *Ramrajya* is that in which a man cannot be cruel even to his own self. To be unjust to yourself is as big a crime as to be unjust to others. Today, Ram has again rejected and expelled Sita from his house because she has passed some time with Ravana. But what was Sita's fault? Was she not the victim of treachery and betrayal, like so many of our mothers and sisters? Is this the case of the truth and untruth of Sita, or of the baseness and brutality of Ravana, the demon King, who had ten human heads and one more, the largest, that of a donkey?'

'Today our sisters have been turned out of their homes through no fault of theirs . . . Sita . . . Lajwanti. . . .' Babu Sunder Lal could not speak any further. Tears gushed from his eyes. Rasalu and Neki Ram picked up all those red banners on which that very day the boys of the school had neatly cut out the slogans and pasted them; and with cries of 'Long live Sunder Lal Babu! 'Babu Sunder Lal *Zindabad*!' they left the place and moved ahead. Somebody in the procession shouted, 'Long live Mahasati Sita' and another voice shouted, 'Sri Ramchandra . . .'

A babel of voices surged up in protest, 'Quiet, quiet!' In a few moments, months of the assiduous work of Narain Baba in the cause of religion went to waste: a good section of his audience joined the procession which was headed by Vakil Kalka Prasad and Hukam Singh, the *moharrir* of Chauki Kalan, who tapped the ground with their old sticks, raising a clear, reverberating sound, the sound of challenge and condemnation. And somewhere amongst them was Sunder Lal, tears still running from his eyes. Today his heart was wounded afresh and his companions were singing with a zest greater than ever before: 'These are the tender leaves of touch-me-not, my friend, they shrivel and curl up even if you so much as touch them. . . .'

The strains of this lusty chorus were still ringing in the ears of the people, it was not yet dawn and the widow living in House No. 414 of *mohalla Mulla* Shukoor still lay on her empty bed turning and twisting her body, when Lal Chand, who belonged to Sunder Lal's village in Pakistan, came running to Sunder Lal's house and cried excitedly:

'Congratulations Sunder Lal!'

'What for?' Sunder Lal put some sweet tobacco into the *chillum*.

'I have seen Lajo *bhabhi*!'

The *chillum* fell from Sunder Lal's hands and the sweet tobacco was strewn all over the floor.

'Where . . . where did you see her?' Sunder Lal caught Lal Chand's shoulders and shook him vigorously.

'On the frontier of Wagah.'

Sunder Lal's hands dropped lifeless from Lal Chand's shoulders and after a pause he only said: 'It must have been somebody else.'

'No, brother,' Lal Chand reassured him. 'It really was Lajo *bhabhi*. . . .'

'How could you recognize her?' Sunder Lal was gathering the tobacco lying on the floor and rubbing it between his palms. 'What are the identifying marks?'

'A tattoo-mark on the chin and another on the cheek.'

'And a third on her forehead,' added Sunder Lal. He could see all the tattoo-marks on Lajwanti's body, marks that she had fancifully got pricked into her body while yet a child—they were like the tiny green grain on the body of the plant of touch-me-not. Like that plant, Lajwanti used to curl up with shyness whenever he touched those tattoo-marks with his finger; at such moments she would get lost and recede into herself as if all her secrets had become exposed, as if some hidden, unknown treasure of hers had been pillaged.

Sunder Lal shivered with a strange fear and felt warmed by the holy fire of his love. He clasped Lal Chand's arm and asked eagerly, 'How did Lajo reach Wagah?'

'Don't you know that abducted women from India and Pakistan are being exchanged?'

'What happened then?' Sunder Lal hunched up and repeated: 'What happened then?'

Rasalu, too, got up from his cot and coughing in the typical manner of smokers, he said, 'Has Lajo *bhabhi* really come?'

'Pakistan delivered sixteen women at Wagah in exchange for sixteen from India,' Lal Chand continued. 'But one problem arose. Our volunteers objected that the women delivered by the Pakistanis were mostly old or middle-aged. Then the volunteers of the other side brought forth Lajo *bhabhi* and pointing at her they cried out: "Do you call this woman old? Can even one of the girls you have given us compare with her?" And there, as she stood assaulted by a myriad eyes, Lajo *bhabhi* was trying to hide her tattoo-marks. . . . Then the quarrel increased. Both parties decided to cancel their offer. I shouted "Lajo . . . Lajo *bhabhi* . . ." Then our own army men drove us back.'

Lal Chand showed Sunder Lal his elbow where he had been hit by a stick. But Sunder Lal seemed to be looking at something very far away. May be he was thinking: Lajo came and yet she did not come! . . . He felt as if the violence that had marked the partition was still alive and active: only its garb had changed. The only difference was that people did not even have any sensitivities left. If you asked a man: Do you know that in the village of Sambharwal there was one Lahna Singh and his sister-in-law, Banto . . . immediately the reply would come—'Dead !' And the man would walk away, as if nothing had happened.

A step ahead were the cold-blooded traders in human merchandise who bartered human flesh and human emotions. And in much the same manner as people who buy cattle at a fair assess the age of a cow or a buffalo by pushing aside its snout and testing the teeth, they put up women as saleable commodities in the public squares and marketplaces, making exhibition of their beauty and their youth, of their most precious and most intimate secrets, of their dimples and tattoo-marks, to the gaze of the buyers. Violence had by now become normal and natural to these merchants. There was a time when, at the fairs, transactions were settled under the cover of a handkerchief—behind the veil the fingers of the buyer and the seller met, concluding the change of ownership. But now the handkerchief, too, had been taken away and deals were struck upon sight—the sellers and the buyers had bid adieu even to the courtesy and conventions of trade. This buying and selling, this trade looked more like a tale of old in which are described the sales of women in the slave markets of free and prosperous cities. On both sides of the market stand naked women of various climes, contours and complexions, and the Uzbek passes through this array, stopping before one and then another, disrobing them even in their nakedness, his eyes prying into the betrayed secrets of their nudity. Then he approaches one of them, touching a body with a probing finger, and where the finger touches the flesh, a rosy dimple is made and around it a pale circle and then the rose and the pale rush and run into each other, fusing and changing places. The Uzbek moves ahead and the rejected woman, heavy with the acceptance of defeat, in utter shame and lassitude, clutches her loosened undergarment with one hand and with another tries to hide her face from public gaze. . . .

Sunder Lal was getting ready to go to Amritsar, the border town, when he received news of Lajo's arrival. The suddenness of the news unnerved him. Impulsively he stepped towards the door, then withdrew. He would have liked to spread out all the placards and banners of the committee and sit on them and cry. But this was neither the time nor the occasion to crack up under an unrestrained expression of his emotions. Like a man he stood up to the conflict that ravaged his heart, quelling what sought to break through. Slowly he made his way to Chauki Kalan, for it was there that the abducted women were being delivered.

Lajo stood facing Sunder Lal, trembling with fear. She and none but she knew Sunder Lal, knew that Sunder Lal had always maltreated her. Now that she was back after having lived with another man, she dared not imagine what he would do to her.

Sunder Lal looked at Lajo. A black *dupatta* was draped on her head and round her body, worn in a typical Muslim fashion, one end of it thrown across her left shoulder—it was a matter of habit, mere habit. She had made friends with Muslim women, thus finding an easy chance to run away from her captor. And as she came she was thinking about Sunder Lal desperately and had no time to think of the dress she was wearing, nor of the manner in which she wore it; she was in no condition to distinguish between the 'basic difference' between Hindu and Muslim cultures and bother whether she had put the end of the *dupatta* on her left or right shoulder. And now she stood before Sunder Lal, trembling with hope and despair, with joy and terror.

Sunder Lal felt the impact of a shock. He saw that Lajo's complexion had become fresher and brighter, that she now looked healthier—she had almost become plump. Whatever Sunder Lal had thought about her had turned out to be wrong. He had imagined that her suffering and torture must have reduced Lajo to a mere skeleton and that she would not even have the strength to utter a few words. But, now, the thought that she had been happy during her stay in Pakistan, which was evident from the brightness of her skin and the plumpness of her body, struck a blow at his heart. He kept quiet, however, for he had sworn to himself that he would keep quiet at any cost, though he could not understand why she had chosen to come back to him if she had been so happy with that other man. May be, he thought, the Government of India had forced her to come here against her wishes. But why was it that Lajwanti's musk face was now pale and bloodless? He had no answer. He did not know that it was suffering which made her look plump: her flesh had loosened from her bones and sagged. This was a kind of plumpness which is but an illusion and which makes a person pant if required to walk but a few steps. . . .

Such were the thoughts that flashed through Sunder Lal's mind as he took the first look at the abducted woman. But he faced these thoughts bravely, sealing them off at their very source. Several other people were present and one of them cried out: 'We shall not accept the women who have been spoilt by the Muslims.'

But this voice was soon lost in the zestful slogans raised by Rasalu, Neki Ram and the old *moharrir* of Chauki Kalan. And above these slogans and very different from it was the cracked and powerful voice of old Kalka Prasad who coughed violently and spoke vehemently at the same time. He was fully convinced of this new truth, this new reality and this new purification: he had learnt a new *Shastra* and wanted others to share with him this new knowledge and enlightenment.

Surrounded by all those people, their slogans and their speeches, Sunder Lal and Lajo were returning to their house and it looked as if once again, after thousands of years, Ramchandra and Sita were returning from their long period of exile and entering the city of Ayodhya.

Even after Lajwanti's return Sunder Lal continued the programme of the committee with unabated enthusiasm. Both by word and deed he had fulfilled and justified his own faith in that programme. People who had looked upon Sunder Lal's work only as an expression of sentimental idealism now began to be convinced of his earnestness and sincerity. His action had made some of them happy while the conservatives still felt sad about it. Most of the women of *mohalla Mulla* Shukoor, except the widow living in House No. 414, dreaded coming to Babu Sunder Lal's house.

But Sunder Lal cared neither for the applause nor the condemnation of the people. His queen, the darling of his heart, had come back to him and the yawning chasm of his loneliness had filled up. Sunder Lal had enshrined the golden image of Lajwanti in the citadel of his heart and himself stood at the doorway, keeping street watch lest the image was again lost. And Lajo, who had once crouched in terror at Sunder Lal's maltreatment, had now begun to open up because of his unexpected kindness and fineness of behaviour.

Sunder Lal did not call her Lajo any more but always addressed her as '*devi*'—goddess! Lajo became inebriated with an unknown joy. Intensely she desired that she should pour out all that had happened to her and while narrating her tale of torture she would let her 'sins' be washed away in tears. But Sunder Lal always shrank from hearing her story, so that despite her new freedom Lajo still crouched behind some strange apprehension. And when Sunder Lal went to sleep, she would gaze at his face for long spells. And whenever he caught her in the act and asked her the reason, she would only mumble. 'No!' 'Just like that!' '*Unhun!*' Sunder Lal, tired after a long day of leading the processions and preaching, would go to sleep again. Once, in the beginning, Sunder Lal had asked Lajo just one question relating to her 'dark days'. 'Who was he?'

Lajo had cast down her eyes and answered: 'Jumma!'—And then, fixing her eyes on Sunder Lal's face she had wanted to say something more, but Sunder Lal was looking at her with strange eyes and softly caressing her hair. Lajwanti's eyes had dropped again and Sunder Lal whispered the question:

'Did he treat you well?'

'Yes!'

'He never beat you?'

Lajo dropped her head to Sunder Lal's chest and said: 'No. . . .' And then she spoke again: 'He never beat me and yet I was terribly afraid of him. You beat me often but I was never afraid of you. You will never beat me again—will you?'

Tears gushed to Sunder Lal's eyes. Moved with shame and repentance, he cried, 'No, *devi*, I shall never again beat you, never.'

'*Devi!*' thought Lajwanti and tears started flowing fast from her eyes too.

Then she wanted to reveal all that had happened to her but Sunder Lal said: 'Let the past be the past. Since you are not to blame for what has happened.'

'So, all that was in Lajwanti's heart remained gagged, stifled. She curled up sobbing in her helplessness and gazing at her body which had become the body of a *devi* and not her own—not Lajwanti's. She was happy, very happy, indeed, but it was a happiness that was stung by doubt and uncertainty. And as she lay in bed, she would often sit up, startled, as if in moments of sheer ecstasy one was suddenly jerked back to consciousness at the footfall of an intruder. . . .

Ultimately, when quite some time had passed, doubt no more remained an intruder but took the place of joy, not because Sunder Lal had again started maltreating her but because he treated her much more kindly than before. It was a kindness that Lajo had not expected from him—she wanted, desperately, to become the same Lajo who would quarrel on a trifle and, all at once, be friends again. Now the question of a quarrel between them did not arise for she was a *devi* and he her worshipper. And Lajo would look at herself in the large mirror and think that she could not be the same Lajo ever again. She had got back everything and yet she had lost everything—she was rehabilitated and she was ruined. Early each morning Sunder Lal would slip away from Lajo's side and go down to join the *prabhat-pheri*. And quietly would Lajo creep to the window and listen tearfully to his voice in the chorus:

> These are the sensitive plants, my friend
> They curl up and shrivel at the merest touch. . . .

*Translated from Urdu by Rajinder Singh Bedi**

---

* I have italicized the Hindi and Urdu words. Otherwise, Bedi's own translation is reproduced without any editorial change.

Pimps
RAMANAND SAGAR

Ramanand Sagar is a filmmaker now known primarily for his TV serials *Ramayana* and *Krishna*. His novel, *Aur Insaan Mar Gaya*, depicts the trauma of partition in graphic details. "Pimps" deals with retrieval/restoration of women in society after they have been allegedly 'defiled' by the 'enemies'. Sagar shows how women are always at the receiving end—first they suffer at the hands of the aggressors and then in at hands of the members of their own community where they do not find acceptance or succour.

The Muslims raided our village at dawn. I was collecting dry twigs on the bank of the river as grain stalks were scarce that year for lack of a good harvest. Our village was situated on the other bank of the river on a slightly higher plane. The river bank on that side was very beautiful with a row of *sumbul* trees spreading far. In my childhood I used to climb to the highest branch and happily watch the glistening waves of the river rolling further and further. I used to swim in the river a lot. At thirteen or fourteen, I could swim from one bank to the other in a single breath.

She was weaving such apparently unrelated things together as though she was muttering to herself amidst a sweet dream.

Anand could see all these things dancing in her eyes—the glistening, shimmering waves of the river, the long row of *sumbul* trees and a small girl swinging like a creeper amidst red, conical flowers. He watched, spellbound, this drama being staged. So much so that the girl became self-conscious and her dream broke abruptly. The string snapped, as it were, and she came out of the romantic trance to the world of bitter reality.

'Bhaag in Burdafarushaon Se', from *Fasadaat ke Afsane*, ed. Zubair Rizvi (Delhi: Zehn-i-Jadid, 1995), pp. 88-94.

"The Muslims came on boats to raid our village from the other bank of the river. Gathering wood, I had reached quite close to the bank. My husband was collecting wood at some distance. I did not see the boats coming, but only heard some voices—"

'*Subhanallah*, what a lusty maid!'

'Well, the beginning is quite auspicious!'

"I turned to see three, four hefty Muslims wielding small axes advancing towards me. Many were still disembarking. Behind them several other boats were approaching the shore. A cry escaped my throat. Throwing away the wood I began to run. I called out to my husband only to find that he had started running before me and quite far off. Perhaps he saw them disembarking before I did and escaped with his own life instead of attempting to save me.

"I also ran with all my might, but . . ." She paused for a few moments.

When she resumed, her voice had become thinner. "Like me, several other women of the village fell to their captivity. We saw the corpses of old men and youths of the village lying around. Among them there was no one from my family. I realized that it was very wise for my husband to run away. He saved himself and took our little darling, Prem, along with him. Several women had the corpses of their husbands in the houses where they were working as slaves to other men. I was happy that my husband was alive, so was my son, and . . ." She was overwhelmed with emotion and could not go on.

"They took hold of our village. For a whole month we remained captives in the hands of strangers in our own houses. . . . Then one day we learnt from their conversation that this side of the river had gone to India. On the following day they got the news of some approaching army, collected all the women, put them in boats and took them to their own village on the other side of the river.

"Ten to fifteen men sat around each woman. They had already sent to their village the meagre belongings that we had in our houses. We were the last item that they brought along with them.

"For me, the happiness at the deliverance of our village from their hands surpassed my agony at being brought to their side. This was probably because I secretly hoped that he would return home now as the village got back its freedom. His own home, his own village—which were just on the other side of the river and which I could see all the time. In fact, I would keep on gazing at that side ever since I had been brought here.

"During those days the river Ravi was in full spate, spreading on both sides. But it seemed as though the other bank was approaching closer to me. My spirits rose with every passing day and inspite of the distance the objects on the other bank got clearer and clearer. And . . ." She wanted to pause for a second but it was beyond her at this stage of the narrative to do so even for a moment.

"And then one day I actually saw Prem playing on the bank, alone. He could not walk yet; he would take two steps and go down. Perhaps his father was gathering wood nearby. I was terribly angry with him. The waves were dancing, with every sign of an imminent flood and he had left the boy alone to play on the bank! Shouldn't he have looked after him properly until my return? I was restless. I just wanted to go to him once to say that he should not leave Prem alone on the bank of the river. But it was not possible to go even for a moment. Those brutes kept us on a tight leash all the time."

She got up to drink water but when she started her narrative once again, it seemed as though her throat had gone dry. Sitting like a statue Anand kept listening and she continued in her monotone as though there were no listeners.

"Suddenly it occurred to me he might be looking for me. He was wandering about that big *sumbul* tree where I was gathering wood on that fateful day. Today water had reached that spot. Did my husband tell him that I was lifted from there? I felt sad at this thought.

"He had not yet learnt how to talk coherently. But on my return when he would utter in his childish stammer the one-word sentence, 'Muslims?', what reply would I give him? What would he be thinking now, looking for his mother around the shady *sumbul* tree. How piteously he would be calling out for me—ma, ma . . .

"'Your ma's heart bleeds for you, my son', escaped from my lips involuntarily and I became restless.

"In the meantime, while trying to walk he tottered and fell down. The waves were almost touching him. I could not bear it anymore and jumped out of the window of the two-storey building from where I was watching him and landed on the roof of the adjacent house. I had no idea how the grass-roof caved in and how I reached the ground in a tattered state. The only thing I remember is that the spot where I touched the ground was a garbage dump. But where was the time to pause and ponder? Without so much as a thought I made straight for the river.

"I swam while my eyes were fixed on that spot. I saw my husband come running and lift Prem from the ground to his lap. I could breathe freely again but felt exhausted. At that moment I heard great commotion on the side of the river from which I came. Turning back I saw that all the Muslims of that village had gathered. Then I realized what I had done and the consequences that would follow if I was caught.

"All eyes were fixed on me. I gave up swimming and surrendered myself to the mercy of the waves. Then I took a long plunge so that they would think I was drowned.

"As I heaved up my head once or twice to take a breath I saw that Prem was returning home sitting in his father's lap. I yearned to call out to them to stop and take me along. We would go home together from the place where you had lost me one day. But at that moment I thought of the Muslims on the trail and pretended to spread my limbs like a drowning person, allowing myself to be buffeted by the waves.

"Having repeated this twice or thrice, I began to swim properly once again and realized for the first time that I had not eaten well for the last couple of days and that I did not possess the earlier strength. I had reached the middle of the river but felt I could not swim anymore. I might have been hurt as I jumped from that house and the injury started tingling after contact with cold water. Then I thought of Prem and my husband and tried to imagine how Prem would cling to my bosom as soon as he saw me and suck my breast to slurp milk as he usually did. After that it seemed as though I was swimming on the strength not of my hands but my breasts.

"By the time I reached the other bank it was almost evening. My village was further up. Yet as soon as I put my foot on the shore, my exhaustion and weariness seemed to have vanished. At last I was free and back on the Indian soil. My soul began to dance in happiness. I cannot put into words my heart's feelings at that moment. I just felt that someone was sitting there and dancing. And I, despite the heavy wet clothes, was speeding towards my village. The wet clothes got on the way, my steps staggered as they fell on uneven ground but I did not stumble or slip even once and kept running.

"Several lamps were burning in my village as though people had arranged for illumination on my homecoming. Above the lamps I could see the light in our two-storey house. In the whole village only we had a two-storey house. My in-laws were traders for generations. That is why everyone in the neighbouring villages knew them. I was approaching my house and thinking that on that following day people from several neighbouring villages would come to congratulate them on their release from the hands of the oppressors. People would talk about my daring and courage. Women would come to see me having traversed that river of blood all alone and stayed alive. And Prem? He would ask his single-word question, 'Muslims?' which encompassed in itself a multiple of questions. What then . . .? I had already decided that I would have a tiff with my husband that very night on why he had told the child all these things. Why didn't he tell him that I had gone to my mother's? But he would reply . . . 'how could I because your mother herself had been here looking for you? Taking Prem in her arms she had kept on sobbing for a long time'. And I thought how happy my mother would be. She would come running as soon as she got the news. This time also she would cry, but out of happiness. Whenever I returned from my parent's house to that of my in-laws, she would cry inconsolably. But she would not allow me to stay at her place for long. She would always say—'After marriage, the daughter should not stay with her mother. It is her good fortune if she dies at the feet of her husband in his own house'.

"I was deep in thought and did not know when I had reached the door of my own house. My husband was putting the latch to the outer door. He did not know that it was the time to open the door to his heart while he was closing the door to our house. I thought of a mischief—I would knock the door repeatedly and as he would open it asking 'who's there?' I would hide myself. I would keep on doing so as long as he did not emerge out of the house looking for the thief behind the haystack where I was hiding. And then . . . But it so happened that when I knocked, he stayed inside and asked, 'who's there?'. As I remained silent, he repeated his query but did not open the door.

"I realized that he was still living under the shadow of the past. He would not open the door just like that. My heart went out to him. I could not remain silent after hearing his voice and said, 'It's me, Nirmala'. My voice was feeble—almost like a whisper. But he heard it all right because he hurriedly exclaimed, 'you!'. After this there was silence—complete silence as though the pulse of the world had stopped. That one moment of freezing silence seemed like an age. Another such moment passed, but the door did not open. Perhaps he could not believe his ears.

"I had heard that people sometimes lose consciousness when they receive a sudden good news; some even die . . . . I got scared and started banging the door—'open the door, oh please, open the door. It's me, Nirmala . . . Nirmala . . .'

"Eventually the door opened, but it was not my husband." Once again she fell silent as though she was scared. She looked at Anand in such a way as though she saw him for the first time. The story had taken such a turn at this point that Anand was compelled to sit up.

"Who was it, then?" he asked, agitated.

"No, he was not my husband", she repeated in her dull, uninflected voice. "He was not the person who took my hands in the full view of the assembly, the one who had made several promises along with the chanting of *mantras* at the time of our marriage. Well, as far as the physical features went, he was the same, but . . . . I don't know what had got hold of him. First, he seemed not to recognize me, then asked in a deadpan voice, 'why have you come here, now?'

"It was as though someone had thrust an ice-cold knife into my heart. The blood in my veins turned into snowflakes, my tongue went dry like a piece of wood. What could I tell him—why I had gone there . .

"Meanwhile I heard the sound of father-in-law's *kharaun* as he came into the courtyard. As usual, he was wearing the *patka* bearing Lord Rama's name all over. I advanced and touched his feet but he did not give me his blessings. He threw a questioning glance at his son and then at me. Then he muttered, 'Ram, Ram' as though he was invoking the Lord in order to avoid my polluting touch.

"After this there was deathlike silence. We three were afraid of looking at each other in the eye. With every passing moment I was being overwhelmed by a sense of sin. So much so that in the deadly silence I gradually felt that someone was branding me with a hot seal in every part of my body as a proof of my sin and I could see each mark under my wet cloth. It seemed to me that my clothes gradually dropped off my body and I stood naked before my father-in-law. Then an irresistible force got hold of me and I snatched the *patka* bearing Lord Rama's name from my father-in-law's body and wrapped it around mine . . . . Still I was naked.

'She's gone mad, poor thing', my father-in-law said in sympathy.

'Indeed, she's mad', my husband confirmed, 'otherwise she would not have come here just like that.'

'No, I'm not mad yet, but now I'll certainly go mad', I screamed.

'Hush! softly . . .' said my father-in-law in a subdued tone. 'People will wake up. They know that you're dead.'

'That's a lie. They know that the women of our village were carried away by them', I said spiritedly.

'Maybe. But everyone says that his daughter has jumped into the river to save her honour.'

'So, no one will take his daughter back?'

'Who keeps the ghost of the dead in his house?'

'*Hai* Ram, what great injustice!' I started crying.

'It's not injustice, it's the way of the world. No one can live here without honour', my father-in-law reasoned with me, 'you used to read the *Ramayana* everyday. Didn't Lord Rama abandon Sita for the sake of family honour? Moreover, mother Sita was a chaste woman.'

"'Mother Sita was chaste' was thrown at me sarcastically like a live ember which made all my earlier marks burn once again. My heart cursed the sages who wrote the *Ramayana*. Did they write it for this? Is it for this reason that the Hindu wives are instructed to read the *Ramayana* everyday? Did the sages make god of every husband so that he can perpetrate his injustice under the guise of honour?—And my husband, 'the best embodiment of honour in Man' was standing there mute and listening.

"I was not at all angry with him. He ran away like a coward while his wife was being made a captive right before his eyes. What else could he do now when I was being abandoned for the sake of family honour?

"As I was leaving the house, my father-in-law was all praise for me. 'It was very wise of you to come here in the darkness of the night. Otherwise the honour of an old family would have been ruined'. He also consoled me—'There's no reason to feel sad. We have taken our full revenge. We have carried away many more of their women than they had ours.'

'And you have settled them at your homes?' I flared up.

'Yes. It's a matter of pride to keep them in our houses', the chest of my father-in-law swelled in pride and he said, indicating to the inner part of the house, 'we've got two of them here.'

"I could not listen to him anymore. It seemed to me that I had so long been trapped among pimps and procurers.

"I fled from there and began to run. But where could I go after all? From my experience I had learnt that the same fate awaited a decent woman everywhere—be it India or Pakistan. Both the countries belonged to men who had ripped apart the thin veneer of decency and began to dance around the naked body of women. There was no safe haven for a woman. Like the land they had also divided our bodies among themselves. But none among them was probably ready to accept a woman who was a mother.

"I was still running. There was no shelter for me. The whole stretch of Indian land was stained at places with the blood of women who were raped by both India and Pakistan in tandem. They were partners in this brutality and I wanted to go far beyond their clutches.

"Before me was Ravi and she also seemed trapped. She was held by India on one side and Pakistan on the other and her sacred waves were moving further and further in the effort to save their honour. I had found my companions. I thought they would take me along and save me from dishonour. I was totally worn out and unable to run alone. So I threw myself into her lap, but . . . . She left me behind. Probably because I was not chaste like her. I had been robbed of my chastity!!!"

Translation from Urdu by M. Asaduddin

The Dunghills
MUMTAZ MUFTI

Mumtaz Mufti wrote his first story in 1936 and has since published a number of collections, including *Anarkali, Chop* and *Gahma Gahmi*. Before settling in Pakistan, Mumtaz Mufti lived in Bombay. He was moved by the killings and appalled by India's hostile and belligerent attitude towards Pakistan. In his preface to *Ismaraiyaan* in July 1992, he recalled the 'Nip in the bud policy' of the Indian government.

These stories, along with seventeen others in *Ismaraiyaan*, were written between 1950-52. In his stories, commented Muhammad Sadiq, historian of Urdu literature, 'the human interest is usually subservient to psychoanalysis, and instead of getting his material from life he gets it from clinics'.

Seeing her, the young cyclist stopped at the road's turning. He placed his feet on the ground and dismounted. He gave his cycle a quizzical look, as if it had suddenly broken down. She smiled at the young man provocatively. And then, as was her habit, she turned to Gehna and began to giggle and chat with her. It was not the first time this had happened. Cycles, ridden by young men, invariably developed some snag and came to a sudden halt! The pedestrians either suddenly froze in their tracks or slackened their pace considerably. Once there, some would begin to twirl their moustaches, some would just blink and some nudged their companions out of nervousness. At other times, someone would sing a romantic song at the top of his voice. Feigning total indifference, Sarwari would giggle and go on chatting with Gehna.

On such occasions, Sarwari experienced strange emotions: she felt as if she were sitting on a rainbow and swinging in the air....

'Gobar ke Dher' from *Ismaraiyaan* (Lahore: Feroze Sons, 1993), pp. 268-79.

as if she were going down, cascading like a mountain stream and the trees growing on the slopes were bending down and looking at her. . . . The flowers were smiling . . . the branches were winking at each other . . . the bushes joined their heads and were talking about her while the universe stood and waited for her gentle nod.

The rush of these delicate emotions intoxicated her, the curve of her lips seemed so evocative.

'Sarwari! . . . Sarwari!'

Amma's voice startled her.

'Dress up my child!' a voice came from the courtyard below. 'Do you hear me?'

Sarwari's smile froze. . . .

She felt as if a gust of cowdung stench had swept over her. The road receded into a haze.

The colourful swing snapped and stood suspended in midair.

She clutched at her heart.

'Why don't you answer?' The softness had gone out of *Amma's* voice.

'She has!' Gehna replied seeing Sarwari looking glum.

'Where has she gone?' Amma growled.

'Upstairs,' replied Gehna. . . . 'At least answer her!' she chided Sarwari in a gentle tone.

'I have heard her all right, haven't I?' she shouted in exasperation, and then cursing her fate she sat by Gehna's side.

Gehna knitted her brow and said, 'What comes over you? Why do you behave as if you're going to die?'

'It is a daily torture!' Sarwari grimaced.

Gehna said, 'You have only to go somewhere in the locality itself.'

Sarwari pulled a long face and pursed her lips.

'You prude!' Gehna teased.

Heaven knows what came over Sarwari when she heard *Amma* use the words 'dress up'. Suddenly her wit and vivacity disappeared, and some unnamed fear seized her. Instead of 'dressing up', she wanted to hide in a corner and cry. At such times she felt averse to *Amma*. *Amma*! She hated her; in her eyes *Amma* was a witch. She intensely desired to run away; far away where no *tongawalla* could come and knock at the door and where *Amma*'s leechlike soft voice telling her to 'dress up', didn't reach.

In such a mood she turned to the courtyard of the opposite

house where the bearded gentleman lived, one who passed the street everyday, late at night, head bent. . . . On reaching the threshold of his house, he would call out in a deep voice: 'Sarwar!'. . . . Whenever Sarwari heard his voice, her heart sank.

But soon clinging to the rising tide of hope she would begin to float and feel as if she had reached the safety of the shore. *Amma's* house appeared like a violent whirlpool, while her neighbour's courtyard seemed to be a welcoming shore. . . . And that shore would start creeping towards her. Sarwari wanted to cling on to it and be spared the constant refrain of 'dressing up.' Seeing her respectable neighbour, she was reminded of past memories.

That small village on the lush green slopes of a hillock near Madhopur and their spacious house, plastered with clay, oxen tied on one side and her goat on the other, with chickens scratching the dust for something to peck at. On the other side were two huts in which they lived—father, mother, brother and she. Green fields spread far and wide; a stream flowed through from one end to the other. On the hilltop was an enamelled road stretching like a white ribbon, twisting and turning. Cyclists plied, but their cycles never broke down at this turning. Nor did they tarry to smile at her. The passersby simply kept going and she kept watching them recede farther and farther into the distance. Then bored, she would go back to the courtyard and keep the chickens away from the goat.

'Sarwaran!' She would sometime hear the deep and full-throated voice of her father. For a moment she would stand still and then, head bent, she'd go and listen to him. But soon thereafter she would return to the same place to watch the passersby.

'Sarwaran!' Her mother's voice. Again she looked unconcerned, as if no one had called her. 'Sarwaran! Are you putting the cowdung cakes onto the hearth or not?' Her mother screamed from a distance. Infuriated, her mother came rushing in and grabbing her arm, said: 'Will you do some work or keep standing here all day long?'

'I want to wear new clothes,' she would pester her mother.

'What! Wear new clothes! . . . Just look at your face! . . . Be off!' Sarwari's mother kicked her back, and the girl left sighing and sobbing.

'Why is she crying?' her father asked.

'She says she wants to wear a new shirt,' the mother shouted.

Her father came out stroking his beard and said: 'Come on, leave her alone!' And then Sarwari ran and clinging to her father's strong arms, felt protected.

Those were the days when she longed for new clothes, everyday. But her mother always responded by thrashing her soundly. She didn't then know what 'dressing up' meant. But now it was no secret to her. How good her mother was! Once she used to curse her. And now this *Amma*! . . . This witch! . . . 'Dress up my child!' A pounding sensation gripped her temples. . . . But then something happened and her mood changed. From the far end of the street, the bearded gentleman, holding his pointed black beard on his broad chest, would come walking slowly. How slowly and gracefully he walked! Sarwari wanted to run to him and to his strong arms, and save herself from this demeaning routine of 'dressing up'. . . .

Her mother had begun to say: 'Our Sarwari has grown up.'

'Just listen! Aren't you concerned?'

'Look! Here is this young daughter in the house and you seem to have little idea what to do about it!'

'I say it's time you started worrying about her dowry!'

To begin with, the father just coughed and kept quiet; then he just said '*ahum*!' and, holding his beard in his hand, started thinking. At last he would talk to mother in hushed tones. Sarwari did not understand what had happened. As far as she was concerned, nothing had changed. Even now she put the cowdung cakes on the hearth, fed the chickens and watched passersby from the parapet. In what way had she grown up? Mother had gone out of her way to create confusion. Yet when she heard her mother talk, she was swayed by a strange emotion. When she walked before her father, she stood on her heels to look taller and, when she came up to her mother, her chest would swell.

She had no idea what happened when you grow up. But she longed to grow. She knew that after that girls wore such lovely clothes, smeared their palms with henna. The village boys smiled when they looked at them and, feeling shy, the girls looked for a place to hide.

Sarwari too wanted someone to look at her and smile, so that she too felt shy and ran to hide herself. Only, no one did that.

Occasionally she felt shy and ran to hide herself. But what use when no one was looking? Her mother had needlessly raised such a hue and cry that 'she is growing up.' Was she? Now, Kaneezan was really grown up. Everyone passed through her street while going to the fields, and stopped in their tracks the moment they caught sight of her. It was exactly like everyone stopping at the turn of the road in front of their house now.

At that time how she wished that all those people walking the road would just look at her and stop! Even now such happenings gave her immense pleasure. The only difference was that far from feeling shy, she would smile back and tease them by chatting and giggling with Gehna.

How she wished to stand by the window with people going their way and ogling at her as they fumbled and stumbled. She wished that their mouths would open wide with wonder, their lips quiver, their cycles stop. Moreover, here, it was the city-folks who tripped—college boys wearing suits and ties, *babus* in white pants, agile young men in their stylish *achkans*. God knows whether these people were capable of doing anything except fumbling and stumbling. Each time she 'dressed up' and went out in a *tonga*, she felt she was going to meet one of these fumblers, and her heart would begin to beat with a strange longing and desire.

But that was a thing of the past when she had just come to *Amma*'s house. Now she knew full well who would meet her on reaching her destination—the same lips dangling like leeches, bloodshot eyes and a vast heap of dung with its inevitable stench . . . . Oh! As soon as she thought of that, she was reminded of the day when the peace of the village was shattered by sudden shouts and cries: 'They have come! . . . They have come! . . .' And then all hell broke loose.

She ran blindly and barefoot, in the fields. . . . Away from that enamelled road, far away. . . . And then she hid near a pit full of dung with a roof erected with grass and straw.

For a few hours she heard the sound of screams and bombs. And then suddenly frightened by the approaching sound of a heavy tread, she thrust herself into a heap. The sound of the footsteps came close to her, and then gradually faded. But she remained hidden in the dunghill. All around her was a sky of dung and a universe full of stench. A deathlike silence presided.

Although once in a while the sound of crackers was heard, followed by a scream, yet the same silence returned. A sky of dung, walls of dung, a river of dung and a sweet and soft smell. And then out of the dunghill. . . . A leg emerged from the other side. Her heart missed a beat. But she didn't have the strength to run. She clung to the wall of dung in front of her. . . . She was still watching apprehensively when the dung assumed a clear shape.

'Kala!' she cried out.

Without even looking at her, Kala fell flat on the ground and groaned. Blood was oozing from his leg.

'Water! . . . Water!' He cried.

Sarwari looked at the village sweeper Kala. And then started searching for water. There was surprise and impatience in her eyes. Kala's anguished groans subsided into a soft murmur. Silence . . . Death . . . Darkness. . . .

She woke up. Someone was screaming close by. Then she heard iron striking iron. Overawed, she closed her eyes. 'They have come! They have come!' Hearing Kala's dreadful cries, she opened her eyes. Kala had come close to her, then closer, and at last he clung to her. At first she tried to move away. But finally she became like a stone. The voices faded and stopped.

She woke up with a start. Two dark hands clung to her like little snakes. It seemed as if a leech was sucking her blood. . . .

Sarwari shuddered. Apart from that, she didn't have the strength to move. Kala moved closer and closer. God knows whether he wanted to forget those dreadful voices or find relief from the intense pain in his wounded leg. Then something like a dark marquee stretched over her and an ebony hatchet struck. . . . Sarwari's heart almost stopped beating with fear.

The old soldier who had taken her under his wing used to collect rations for her from the camp. Late at night the same old man begged for sympathy. A scornful smile spread over her lips. Another Kala virtually begged her to give him relief from the pain of a hidden wound. For a moment the memory was freshened. . . . The pitch dark marquee stretched over her and the ebony. . . . She closed her eyes. Her body was ice-cold.

It happened again a couple of times. . . . The same marquee with the same leech . . . the same little snakes and the stench of dung. But now she couldn't care less. Now she was in her own

Pakistan, where she never heard the sound of crackers or the hue and cry of life or death. Everyone was sympathetic. Everyone wanted to help her. And then in the misty atmosphere of the night, under the shadow of stars, near some dunghill, he begged for sympathy; trying to forget some sorrow, the mouth of some leech searched for her. At such times she felt like a log of wood.

In the atmosphere of self-gratification that prevailed at the camp, an old woman showered her with love and brought her delicacies from the city. That old woman had never tried to seek her sympathy and Sarwari had begun to think of her as her own mother. That was why she began to call her *Amma*, and one day when *Amma* really pressed her hard, she agreed to live with her like her daughter. When she'd just shifted to *Amma*'s place, she was simply surprised by her love and affection. Gehna smiled at her naivete, and said: 'How strange! She pretends as if she doesn't know what it is!' Sarwari had no idea what Gehna was talking about!

Then one day Amma dressed her in lovely clothes, sprayed her with perfume, arranged her hair stylishly, dolled her up with powder and rouge and then took her out in a *tonga*. It turned out to be the same old dunghill . . . soft and sweet smell. . . . That was the day when she realized that actually *Amma* too was a leech, and an old and seasoned one at that.

That day when she came back looking a little frightened, Gehna said to her: 'Come off it! Now drop this pretence and stop behaving as if you didn't know what was in the offing.'

That incident shattered her dream and she began to think: 'Was there no one around who could rescue her from the dung's stench?' No, there was no one. Wherever she turned, she saw a dunghill from which one or the other leech was trying to stick onto her.

She rose. The moon was traversing the sky. On the horizon the clouds assumed menacing shapes. She felt as if she had to live all her life right here . . . in this very house in *Amma*'s company . . . under this dunghill. She went and stood by the parapet. From there she looked down on the street. 'Is there no one who can rescue me from this dunghill?'

Someone was coming from the opposite side. . . . A strong, broad body, trimmed beard and bent head; as if he were coming from a mosque. Her hopes were raised. Sarwar! The respectable neighbour knocked at his door.

Her heart began to pound, as if it had recognized the voice. But, in a few days, she realized that it was well nigh impossible to reach her neighbour.

His house stood apart in the corner of the locality. The nearest was about four or five houses westwards. To come out of her courtyard and reach the house was simply not possible, because the old woman either kept it locked or slept on her string cot there.

Then, gradually she was lulled by silk garments, garlands of flowers, perfumes, and powder and rouge. Her attention was drawn by the passersby fumbling as they saw her nudging a companion or pretending that their cycles had broken down. New desires awakened in her heart. Her smiles became more alluring. She learnt to communicate through the corner of her eye and became adept at casting provocative glances. Still, whenever she rode in a *tonga* at *Amma*'s command, all those nice smells, that leechlike marquee, and those dreadful, pouncing little snakes were reduced to a dunghill. And then wave after wave of pain and revulsion would begin to rise from every pore of her body.

That day, while dressing, her eyes reflected a grim determination. Her heart beat fast.

'Will you hurry up or not? Can't you see the night is already far gone?' *Amma* shouted.

'That is exactly what I am doing!' She ground her teeth.

'You have been doing that for ages!' Then turning to Gehna, she said: 'Have you given her the flower bracelets or haven't you? That *bubu* loves flowers. See to it that she wears them. And look! While going out I will lock the door. We don't have to go far. I will be back in no time. Do you understand?'

When *Amma* closed the door and busied herself locking it, it suddenly occurred to Sarwari that this was her chance. 'I pray to God that, that man turns out to be a decent fellow. May God grant me my wish.' But the street was completely deserted. God knows where the man was. Her heart pounded. The door to his courtyard was right in front, and was open.

'My, my! What has happened to this lock?' *Amma* was grumbling.

She started walking silently, and entered the courtyard with one swift stride. A string cot stood on one side and she hid herself behind it. 'Thank you, my Allah!' She said folding both her hands and looking at the ceiling.

'Oh! Where are you?' The old woman shouted. 'Sarwari! . . . Sarwari.' Where has she gone? The voice of the old woman came nearer and nearer.

Sarwari held her breath. 'Oh my Allah! Oh my Allah!' she watched the ceiling. The voice of the old woman started fading. 'Oh my Allah! Save me from this old woman . . . just once!' she prayed.

She felt as if months had passed standing there. Tick! Tick! Tick! . . . She heard the clock ticking inside. Her heart started beating violently once again.

'My, my! This is the limit!' The voice of the old woman was heard again. Sarwari again folded her hands. The sound of the old woman's footsteps came nearer and nearer. Suddenly, the door banged open and she entered. '*Babuji*! . . . Oh Babuji!' Sarwari's body had already turned still and motionless like a stone.

'What is it?' The respectable neighbour with a beard came out.

'Has the girl come here? Has she?'

'No, she hasn't!' he replied.

'That is strange! Just now she got ready to come with me. God knows where she took the wrong turn by mistake and went astray.'

'She didn't come here,' he said.

'I thought perhaps . . . but don't worry,' the old woman put her hand on his heart and smiled meaningfully. 'I will find her in a moment. Where can she go? Such a sweet kid. Where can she go?'

'She is sweet,' he laughed.

'I will go and fetch her. Keep your door open.'

'All right.'

All of a sudden Sarwari felt that her stiff body had begun to melt like wax and flow like a stream of water.

A strong gust of the dung's stench swept over her. She saw a big pile of cowdung cakes behind the cot and an ebony coloured leech making its way out of the dung. She stood still for a moment.

Then she jumped forward as someone embraced the heap of dung.

A scream arose, followed by laughter . . . 'Hi! Hi! Hi! . . .'

'So! There you are!' The old woman ran towards her. 'What kind of joke is this?'

'Joke! Hi! Hi! Hi!' she laughed like a mad person.

And then she fell heavily on her neighbour's strong and broad body.

And instead of the smell of cowdung, the atmosphere was filled with the jasmine scent.

Translated from Urdu by A. S. Judge

An Impenetrable Darkness
MUMTAZ MUFTI

Amar Singh opened his eyes. Darkness was beginning to descend everywhere. He found it difficult to breathe. Nor could he jump out of bed. He seemed to have lost control, over his own body. Terror-stricken he closed his eyes again.

Heavy and dark clouds were hovering over him. He opened his eyes out of fear and panic.

Suddenly he felt a sharp thrust on his right side. He groaned with pain and then sat up.

He was surprised. In spite of the heavy, ominous feeling overwhelming him, his body could still bounce up, as if it was fitted with springs. He examined his body. In the vast expanse of darkness he felt like a fragment of cloud , . . . a fast floating fragment.

Amar Singh looked around nervously. Darkness was dissolving into mist. In that misty atmosphere stretching far into the distance was a dark floor with dark pillars. On top of these pillars hung round, yellow objects emitted smoke. Behind the pillars were hazy-looking curtains, and beyond the curtains was the outline of houses.

He felt the familiar surroundings, but couldn't quite place where he was or fathom why he was lying there. All of a sudden he wondered, 'Who am I?' But he was unable to recollect who he was. How strange he didn't have any idea about his own identity.

Beep! Beep! He heard the a horn somewhere in the distance.

Beep! The sound was familiar. Suddenly he remembered: Radio! Yes! He yelled with pleasure. He was repairing the radio and had come home early that day. His food was in his tiffin-

'Ghor Andhera' from *Ismaraiyaan*, pp. 226-45.

carrier. Where was his tiffin-carrier? He sat up and looked around, but saw no trace of his tiffin-carrier.

Beep! Beep! Something was approaching from somewhere far away, a dark, dreadful thing. Oh! It was an army truck! He felt scared and impulsively got behind a tree.

Seeing soldiers with cocked guns in the truck he recalled that these were days of disorder and disturbances and that he should be cautious. Even as he realized this, dark shadows began to encroach upon him from every direction. He probed his left side. Sword? Where was his sword? His tiffin-carrier and his sword. He began looking for his sword.

All of a sudden he came to a stop. In front was a cannon. 'It is a gas station!' he murmured, gazing at it intently. He didn't remember anything; everything seemed new and unconnected.

It is the same gas station I pass everyday with my tiffin-carrier and sword. But what happened? Yes, they were all closing their shops and running, and the worker from the printing press stood there staring at me. I felt like greeting him and asking him how he was. But his face was tense. All of a sudden everyone was staring at me. And then a dark dreadful apparition pounced on me and an object flashed like lightning at my side. At that very instant I felt the excruciating pain at my side.

'What happened after that?' He tried hard to think. 'It was hazy and dark. And all of them fled as if I had turned into a ghost. I wanted them to stay with me. I felt scared by myself. And that oppressive darkness started gathering around me.'

Why did the worker from the printing press run away like that? Actually, when a bomb exploded in the printing press the other day, I had sympathy for the workers. I longed to go there and find out how they were.

But, why was I frightened? Perhaps he was also scared of me or maybe, of my sword. But he was like a fellow-worker. Then, why the fear? Why? . . . The sword I held was for my self-defence. But Kartar Singh's comment had struck home. I asked him: 'Kartar! Why don't you carry a sword?' He replied, 'I am embarrassed to do a thing like that. It is such a shame to carry a sword among completely innocent, unarmed people! If I did that I would be haunted by some terrible fear.' But then I carried my sword with me as a matter of habit.

No, no! The printing press worker certainly wasn't scared of my sword. But then why did he strike me? That shooting pain. And then every limb of my body hurt.

Amar Singh felt the terrible pain and because of its intensity he fell down in a heap near a dark pillar. Layer upon layer of oppressive darkness began to press down on him until he felt he had lost control over his body.

Who knows how long he kept lying there. He was woken by the sound of *ghungroos*. A *tonga* was heading towards him. A *tonga*? At this time? And then, for no logical reason, he leapt on to it and settled on its back seat.

'No! No!' Seeing a shadow leap into the *tonga* the *kochwaan* was startled and started shouting. 'No! No! I'm not a Muslim. I am only a *kochwaan*. A *tonga* driver!'

'A *kochwaan*?' Amar Singh looked at him with surprise. 'So?' The *kochwaan* said. 'So what? I am trying to tell you that I'm nothing! Nothing at all!'

'Nothing? Oh!' Amar Singh seemed mystified. 'And I . . . I. . . .'

'You! . . . You!' Just then the *kochwaan*'s eyes fell on Amar Singh's long hair and he began to shout: 'No! No! I won't go to Krishan Nagar! I didn't want to go there that day, either.' The *kochwaan* spoke through suppressed sobs. 'I never wanted to. Even though each one of them was ready to give me ten rupees. But sir, what is the value of money? Here today and gone tomorrow. . . . I wouldn't have gone there for anything. . . . But then seeing tears in the old woman's eyes I was reminded of my own mother.' Who knows from where drops of water fell on Amar Singh's hand. 'In Amritsar they had told her that. . . .'

'What?' said Amar Singh looking at his wet hand.

'What?' The *kochwaan* was startled. 'Nothing, nothing at all. All these shops, these mansions . . . nothing at all!'

'But what about the old woman?' Amar Singh mumbled.

'The old woman? Oh! That old woman. The old woman with tears. . . . I told her, come, mother, I will take you there. She blessed me just like my own mother used to.'

'Then?'

'Then? There were too many of them, far too many. They surrounded me. The old woman started cursing them, then started imploring them not to harm me. When nothing worked she began to cry. But they remained unmoved. Why did her tears not effect them? Wasn't she like a mother to them? On the other

hand why was I so moved by her tears? Why? Speak up! After all, you, too, belong to Krishan Nagar. You tell me!'
'Who? Me?' Amar Singh winced inwardly.
'They dragged the old woman off the *tonga* and surrounded me.' The *kochwaan* heaved a deep sigh. The horse stopped, glanced at him and then let out a prolonged whinny. 'Had they killed me no harm would have been done,' the *kochwaan* murmured, 'but they raised their hand against the mute Moti.' He looked at Moti with moist eyes. 'Moti was no Muslim!'
Moti let out another whinny. A prolonged, painful sound, stirred uneasily and then it started on its way again.
'All of them,' said the *kochwaan*, 'were the same people who covered their ears at the very mention of causing injury to a living being. I know that because I've spent my whole life at the stand in Krishan Nagar. And all of them attacked Moti with spears and swords.'
Suddenly he was silent.
All around the air was filled with the sound of sobs and moans. Moti trotted on slowly groaning with pain. Amar Singh sighed deeply from time to time and the *kochwaan* was lost in contemplation of the horizon. All of a sudden the *kochwaan* started mumbling. 'Then, darkness, impenetrable darkness. . . .'
'Stop!' A policeman standing on the road shouted, 'Stop!'
Startled, the *kochwaan* began hunting for the horse's reins. But before the *tonga* could come to a halt the policeman clambered on to it.
'Where are you going?' he demanded in an authoritative manner.
'Me?' replied the *kochwaan*. 'Where am I going? Well, *Babuji*. . . .' He gave Amar Singh a questioning look. Amar Singh didn't know what to say. 'Me? You mean us,' and he fell silent.
'I can't understand a thing,' the policeman mumbled to himself. 'But I must get there or all of them will die of hunger.' He got up. 'I must go, I have to save them. But where do I go? Where?'
'Perhaps to the police station,' said the *kochwaan*.
'No, no! I've just come from there.'
'Yes, yes!' said Amar Singh, for the sake of saying something.
'Where have I to go to?' The policeman asked Amar Singh. 'Speak up!' he said, 'otherwise, each one of them will die of hunger.'

'What difference does it make?' The *kochwaan* sighed. 'After all, what difference does it make?'

'No, no!' the policeman shouted, 'You shut up! They don't have a single grain with them and will die of hunger. I was going to report this to the police station when they told me not to go that way. I would get killed. Fools! I had to give the report. Otherwise all of them will die.'

'Then?' questioned Amar Singh.

'Then, stones started raining down from the roofs. And then. Darkness. An impenetrable darkness. They were laughing. Fools! They didn't realize that I had to go there immediately and do my duty. I will haul them up for that! If I don't handcuff all of them my name is not. . . . My name? But I don't know my name. Speak up! Tell me my name. And where do I have to go? What? You refuse to tell me? All right, I will book you for that.' Saying this, he alighted from the *tonga* and began to shout: 'Stop! Stop!'

Moti gave a loud whinny and quickened its pace.

'No, no!' The *kochwaan* shouted. 'We are not going to Krishan Nagar, son! We are heading towards Shahalmi.'

'Don't go to Shahalmi. Don't.' Someone stepped forward and held the horse's reins.

'Shahalmi!' Overcome by a strange feeling the youngman who emerged from somewhere and caught the horse's reins started shouting. 'Fire! Fire!'

'*Bhagwan*!' Amar Singh shouted.

'*Bhagwan*!' the young man said angrily.

'No, no! *Bhagwan* has already deserted us. Now only *shaitans* live here. Flames don't leap out of dry bricks! where *Bhagwan* is present'.

'Yes!' Amar Singh muttered. 'This world belongs to the *shaitan*. Run, run away from here!'

The young man laughed and laughed till tears came to his eyes. 'Ramlal tried to run away, to escape from the window. What a shower of bullets there was! Nothing but the sound of booming guns and our Madho! God of clay, who would hear nothing. Poor Ramlal didn't know what was going on. He thought it was a display of fireworks. And then he himself exploded like a firecracker.'

'Then?' enquired the *kochwaan*.

'Then?' he winced. 'Then the walls began to collide, the sky caved in and the earth was steeped in darkness. Darkness. An impenetrable darkness.'

'Stop! Stop!' he shouted. 'I have to save Dina. Dina! Dina!' He left shouting. His voice could be heard from far away.

'Dina! Dina!' Holding the reins in his hands the *kochwaan* sat in complete silence. Amar Singh mumbled something. Raising his head, Moti stared at the horizon. Everything was still.

'Dinu!' someone called. 'Dinu.' An old woman appeared from nowhere. 'Where is my Dinu?' She came close to the *tonga* and stopped. Then, turning to Amar Singh, she burst out: 'You have killed Dinu! You are his murderer. Kill! Kill me, too!'

She planted herself in front of him stretching her body to its limit.

'No, no!' Amar Singh began trembling.

'Catch him!' She rushed forward towards the *kochwaan*. 'Catch him. He is a murderer!'

The *kochwaan* sat where he was, watching her face.

'No one listens to me! No one!' She began shouting. 'They, too, didn't listen. They had long beards, *khaki* uniforms. Disguised as policemen, they surrounded us. And all of them—Allahditta, Ghafura, Rahim—went to them to lodge a complaint. Oh! Allah! But all were shot dead. Their bodies were seared like roasted corn. And then they came and surrounded us. And then they killed Dina . . . Kill me as well!' 'I cannot live without my Dina. Kill me as well!' she shouted again. All of a sudden she buried her head in her hands. 'Oh, my head! My head!' And she sat down crying.

Moti turned its head and looked at the *kochwaan*. Tears flowed down its cheeks. The *kochwaan* looked at the sky and drew a deep breath. Amar Singh began to let out subdued groans. The sound of his groaning echoed everywhere.

'Dina! Dina!' A voice came from somewhere far away.

'Coming!' the old woman cried out. 'I am coming. I am coming.' She disappeared into the darkness.

All of a sudden Moti let out a scream and began to gallop.

The lights at the top of the pillars flickered. Groans rose from the oppressive dense darkness. Down below, the dark road was convulsed with sobs.

'You keep her,' an old man begged. 'For *Bhagwan's* sake, keep her. But let me go, spare my life. I am old. What will you gain by killing me?' His beautiful daughter listened to her father in astonishment.

'No, no! This child is not mine!' An old woman shouted. 'Believe me, sister. He is not mine! How long can I keep carrying him with me? Looking after him at such a time is really killing me. I am completely exhausted.' The child looked at her utterly perplexed. His lips were open, as if to say 'Ma!'

'What are you doing, *Sardarji*? No! No! My name is Kaushalya. See, the tattoo on my wrist in Hindi!'

'Ha! Ha! Ha!' The man laughed. 'What difference does it make?' The Sardarji's face was swollen with lust. His leechlike lips advanced towards Kaushalya.

'How can you do this? No! No!' Kaushalya tried to extricate herself from his grip.

'I am not a Sikh!' he laughed. 'This long hair is not real!'

'I will tell them that I was ruined by my own people.' Her voice became almost inaudible, as if someone had gagged her. And then a dark, ugly, naked man trapped her in his arms.

The *tonga* came to a halt.

In the grey darkness Amar Singh saw a huge cage with shadows moving within. Nearby sat some coolies. A luggage cart appeared from nowhere and rolled towards the coolies. Amar Singh clutched at his heart. All of them will be mowed down. But the cart passed by and the coolies continued sitting there as before. Amar Singh was flabbergasted. He could not understand these strange events. Dogs jumped through opaque walls effortlessly; crows flew through Moti, as if there was a window in its body. Intrigued by these mysterious occurrences, he came and stood by the coolies.

An old coolie shouted: 'Your luggage is your headache! We won't carry it for you!'

'She, too, begged me . . . begged, and I took pity on her. And that box! How heavy it was! It slipped from my shoulder. Then, God knows how it happened. Thunder, lightning. The coolie's face was distorted with horror. Fragments of an object flew like missiles. And then there was nothing but darkness.'

Coo! Coocoo! the train's whistle was heard.

'I have to go. I must!' Amar Singh burst out. 'I won't stay here!'

'Amritsar! Amritsar!' he shouted with joy.

'Amritsar!' came a horrifying reply. 'Amritsar!'

Confused, Amar Singh looked around. A severed head was flashing its teeth near the footrest of the train.

A woman popped her head out of the train. Her breasts had been chopped off. A child was still hanging on to them. The woman pointed towards her breasts and said: 'Amritsar!'

Amar Singh was confused. He looked at her and said: 'Amritsar!' And then, frightened, he rushed into a compartment.

The walls were covered with splashes of red. Down below, bundles of flesh were lying in puddles of blood. Fearful, Amar Singh withdrew to a corner.

The severed head on the seat opened its eyes. Seeing Amar Singh, its eyes popped right out. 'No! No! I am not a Muslim. I swear by the Prophet.'

Slipping from the seat the severed head fell on the floor, rolled through the door and came to rest on the platform.

'*Alhamd-illalah,*' came an elderly voice.

'*Alhamd-illalah...*'

All of a sudden there was an outcry. The bundles of flesh began to move. The limbs stirred.

'Oh! My leg. My leg!'

'For God's sake, kill me. Kill me!'

'Pakistan!'

'Pakistan!' a voice echoed on the platform.

Terrified, Amar Singh fled from the compartment.

Human limbs were creeping on the platform.

Severed heads were rolling like balls.

'Pakistan!' A severed head stood on its neck and shouted 'Ha! Ha! Ha!' The horrible laughter echoed from every direction. Pearls started dropping from the eyes of the severed head.

The old man whose arm had been slashed, smiled. 'Pakistan!' There was much longing in his smile.

'*Alhamd-illalah!*' Someone nearby whispered. 'Allah be praised, we have reached.'

'Reached?' A young woman laughed. 'Reached!' There was irony in her laughter.

'Thank God,' said the old woman creeping forward on her elbows. And then, tired and exhausted, she fell down flat.

Amar Singh turned his face away. He was surprised to see the *kochwaan* by his side. '*Kochwaan!*' he exclaimed. But the *kochwaan*'s gaze was fixed on the old woman.

The *kochwaan* advanced towards the old woman and supporting her, said: 'Get up. Come on, get up!'

'Lift her first.' She pointed to the young woman lying at her side. The lower portion of her body hung loosely from the rest of her. The *kochwaan* felt he could not lift her on his own. 'Where are your companions?' he asked the young woman.

'Companions!' There was contempt in her voice. 'Companions! They were all there!'

'There?'

'They were all standing right in front of me,' she said with intense hatred. 'They saw me with their bulging eyes. Oh! Why didn't their eyes split open! Faith! Valour! These are lies. To save their own lives they lied and sacrificed their honour.' She burst into laughter and then fell down.

'Water! Water!' she cried, dragging herself.

Amar Singh looked around. Seeing a water sign outside a compartment he ran. He found the compartment deserted.

'No, no!' A child hiding in a corner cried. I am not thirsty. I haven't asked for water!' He started weeping. 'Don't kill me. Don't, I won't ask for water. I am not thirsty!'

'I won't ask for water!' Amar Singh looked at him with surprise.

'No! No!' Dry crusts appeared on his lips. His dehydrated tongue hung out. '*Papa . . . Papa. . . .*' His eyes were petrified. '*Papa . . . Papa. . . .*' Amar heard voices from under the seats. He bent down to have a look under the seats. '*Papa . . . Papa. . . .*' Scores of dry lips were moving, their tongues hanging out. '*Papa. . . ,*'

'No, no! I am not a Muslim.' Someone screamed on the platform.

'Companions! Ha! Ha! Ha!' The woman laughed.

'*Alhamd-illalah*! We have reached.'

'*Alhamd-illalah.*'

Amar Singh began to float. He wanted to escape to somewhere far away where there was no Shahalmi, no Amritsar, nothing at all. To somewhere far away where those voices couldn't reach. Then the voices started fading into complete silence.

The sky was overcast with dark clouds. The air was humid and it started to drizzle. The lightning flashed somewhere near the horizon, followed by complete darkness. The earth seemed desolate. Intermittent feeble voices were heard, at times getting louder, and then a scream, followed by silence. Groans and sobs, screams and whispers punctuated the silence that prevailed.

'Dina! Dina!'
'Fire! Fire!'
'I am a Muslim. I swear by my *dharma* that I'm a Muslim.'
'Pakistan! Ha! Ha! Ha!'
'Rawalpindi! Amritsar! Shahalmi!'
'I am not thirsty. No! No!' Scores of dry lips with wooden tongues hanging out. '*Papa! Papa!*'

Having been on the run all the time, he was exhausted. But the voices lingered on, as if chasing him with a vengeance. Crushed and defeated Amar Singh closed his eyes and collapsed.

After sometime he opened his eyes. Scores of animals lay dead, their bellies swollen, as if they had gorged themselves until they dropped dead. The outline of a village was visible through the mist. Somewhere dogs howled. Broken and battered trucks stood by the road. Kites and vultures hovered overhead . . . so many vultures! He had never seen so many at one place.

Amar Singh started walking towards the road and halted near the vultures. The vultures seemed frozen, as if they had lost the power to move. Once in a while, one of them stirred and fluttered its wings but the body remained stationary. Pink bundles were lying at their feet, and there was a strange odour in the air. He felt nauseous and moved away towards the shed. The lamp was still flickering inside, casting a dim light on the room. There was desolation all around—the desolation that comes after a great upheaval and gives birth to a dreadful silence, a silence which reeks of screams and sobs.

Perturbed, Amar Singh was about to leave when a little girl emerged from behind the door. 'She is sleeping,' the child stuttered. 'Sleeping . . . goes on sleeping . . . she doesn't wake up.'

'She is sleeping!' Amar Singh repeated the child's words with surprise.

'Yes!' The little girl said, pointing to the middle of the floor.

She lay sprawled on the floor with her outstretched arms and legs. 'But her clothes?' Amar Singh rubbed his eyes. White body and golden hair, splattered with red, as if she had gone to sleep after the Holi revelries. Her bluish, swollen breasts were limp.

'She is sleeping,' the child cried. Then she ran towards the woman and called out, '*Ammi! Ammi!* See! She is sleeping. *Ammi* is ill.'

'Ill!' Amar Singh repeated.

'Yes!' she said. The dacoits came here, but they protected *Ammi* and saved her. They were very nice people. They said *Ammi* will be all right soon. And then they massaged her.

'Massage?' For the first time he looked closely at the woman. 'All of them kept massaging *Ammi*'s body,' she said. '*Ammi* went to sleep feeling better.'

Amar Singh saw a smile across the woman's lips, a sardonic smile. 'They've gone to fetch a doctor,' said the girl.

'Oh!' Amar Singh felt dizzy. He preferred the darkness outside to the lighted shed, and the story told by the silence of the vultures more tolerable than the childish prattle of the innocent girl. Bewildered, Amar Singh stumbled out.

'*Ammi! Ammi!*' the voice of the girl came from inside. But Amar Singh was running away, far, far away from there.

He stopped suddenly, surprised to see Moti trotting on the road in front of him. Sitting in the *tonga* was the *kochwaan* with his head between his hands.

'Moti! Moti!' He shouted, and then ran after the *tonga*. He leapt on to it and sat on the back seat. The *kochwaan* remained lost in his own world, unaware of Amar Singh's intrusion. But Moti whinnied with pleasure and then, suddenly, strayed from the road towards the fields.

The fields were deserted. Here and there cattle picked out the ripe ears of corn, but seemed tired of grazing. Seeing Moti in the open field, a dog tried barking at him but no sound emerged and even its body seemed inert. Chickens treaded over the scattered intestines carelessly. A dreadful silence descended over the entire settlement. Moti stopped with a sudden jerk which shook Amar Singh from his seat.

The *kochwaan* raised his head. 'No, no! My child, we won't go to Krishan Nagar. No, we won't!' Moti didn't stir. After a while the *kochwaan* sat down with his head in his hands.

Amar Singh walked on to the village. A tall man, standing at the main gate of the *haveli*, smoothed back his moustache and beard and then popped his head out and said to Amar Singh: 'Suspect something? If you do, then come in and have a look.' He pointed towards the *haveli*. 'There aren't any Muslims in my house. I never gave refuge to them. Do you hear me? Buzz off, you scoundrel!' He rushed back into the *haveli* and slammed the door shut.

'Ah! Ah!' a voice came from inside. 'Oh! My head! My head! Hold me! No! No! There are no Muslims in my house.'

'No Muslims here,' came a childish voice. 'It is only Chaida's *Abba*, and not a Muslim. He is very nice. Chaida is my friend. It is her father.' Suddenly, the child gave a prolonged scream, and then the whole house went quiet.

All of a sudden something rankled Amar Singh's mind and he ran towards the *tonga*.

He shook the *kochwaan*. 'Run! Run away from here! You are in Krishan Nagar!'

Moti whinnied, and turning and tossing restlessly, broke free from his harness and bolted.

'Moti! Moti!' the *kochwaan* shouted, but Moti had already fled. The *kochwaan* wiped his eyes with the hem of his shirt.

'Why do you keep staring at me?' shouted Amar Singh. 'Go away. Run. Run away from here!'

'To where?' the *kochwaan* asked, looking at his battered *tonga*.

'Pakistan!'

'Pakistan! Ha! Ha! Ha!' Laughter echoed in the atmosphere.

The *kochwaan* looked at his *tonga* again and murmured in a low voice, 'My companion.'

'Companions!' A voice came from the darkness and the woman with the swollen flesh crept out in front of him.

'Companions!' She laughed. 'What a lie! They all stood watching the scene, as if it was a special show!' She fell down, her neck twisted and arms became stiff.

'Chaida! Chaida!' The innocent child came out of the *haveli*. 'Your father is here. Inside. . . ' All of a sudden the child's glance fell on Amar Singh.

'No! no! He is not a Muslim. He is only Chaida's *Abbaji*.'

'Be quiet!' she said. 'Quiet! *Ammi* is sleeping . . . sleeping. . . . They were very nice. They massaged *Ammi*. *Ammi* got well and went to sleep.'

'*Kochwaan*! *Kochwaan*!' Amar Singh dragged him off the *tonga*. 'Come, let's run away.' And both started running.

'But where to? Where?' The *kochwaan* stopped and looked at the fleeing Amar Singh.

'Where?' Amar Singh repeated and suddenly stopped.
She was standing in front of him, blocking his path.
'Kill me!' she shouted. 'Finish me off! I am a Muslim. Kill me!'
They drew back in surprise at the sight of her extraordinary youth and beauty.
'Why don't you go to Pakistan?' Amar Singh shouted.
'No! No! I won't. Kill me if you want to but I won't go to Pakistan. I beg you in the name of your *guru*. Kill me! Finish me off! My life is useless!'
'Where are they—the two of them?' She began to rave. 'I had left them right here in this field, fighting with their swords. A brother was fighting with his own brother for me . . . for me . . . .' She fell silent and started looking around triumphantly.
'Who were they?' asked Amar Singh.
'They were two brothers who came to rob our house!' The young woman looked at him, reproachfully, as if blaming him for his ignorance.
'They martyred all my five brothers and then advanced towards my mother. I don't know what happened to me. I flung off my *dupatta* and stood in front of my mother. "Kill me. I am a Muslim. I spit in the face of *kafirs*." And I spat at them. They stopped. One of them said to his brother: "All this loot is yours." And holding me by my wrist, he said, "This is my share." Saying this, he left the house dragging me along and brought me to this field. Then he looked back and found his brother still following him. "Stay where you are!" said the elder brother holding my hand.'
'Give her to me.'
'Idiot!' shouted the elder one.
'She is mine,' said the younger brother.
'What about all that loot?' said the elder one.
'I spit on it.' The elder brother hit him. The younger brother drew his sword. Both began to fight. I kept sitting and watching, and they kept fighting over me.'
'Then?' said Amar Singh.
'Then, a car stopped on the side. I ran. They continued fighting. They killed my brothers and sisters, ruined our house. But they did not deceive me. And that imposter from Pakistan! He said to me: "Come, let me help you to reach the camp." And . . . and I was ruined after reaching Pakistan. "No! No! I won't go to Pakistan. Even if you kill me."'

Two severed heads rolled in the field.

'She is mine,' the smaller head clashed with the bigger one.

'Mine!' shouted the bigger one and the two heads collided violently with each other.

'Run! Run!' Amar Singh shouted.

'Where?' the *kochwaan* looked around him in sorrow.

'No! I won't go!' cried the beautiful woman. 'It is better to die here than to go and lose your dignity in Pakistan.'

'No! No! It's not true. Don't stay here. Don't stop here.' A young woman emerged from nowhere. 'My name tattooed on my wrist in Hindi—is Kaushalya. He took no notice at all. He knew me. He was our neighbour. But he said he was a Muslim. A Muslim with long hair. *Ha*! *Ha*! *Ha*! Muslim *Ha*! *Ha*! *Ha*!'

She laughed—a poisonous laugh. 'It's a lie. There is no Muslim, no Hindu, no Sikh. Only beasts live here. Beasts!'

'Don't be crazy!' shouted Amar Singh. 'Run away from here. Run away!'

'To where?' The *kochwaan* raised his head.

'Where human beings live.'

'Human beings!' the other woman laughed. 'Where do you look for human beings? Where? There aren't any!'

'I won't run away!' the young woman cried. 'No! I have to give birth. Give birth to a human being.' She pointed to her stomach.

'Give birth?' the other woman looked at her in surprise.

'Yes! I, you, we. . . .'

'May God grant you your wish,' said the *kochwaan*.

'God!' the other woman laughed heartily.

'How I wish He had the power to do that.'

'I will do it!' the young woman cried out.

'A human being! A human being!'

'Who called me? Who is it? In this dense darkness?' An old man—wearing a *langoti* and holding a stick—emerged.

'Who is it?'

'A human being!' The man with the *langoti* sighed deeply.

'Who are you?' asked the young woman.

'I am nobody. No one at all.'

'Nobody?' The *kochwaan* looked at him in surprise.

'Peace. Peace!' The old man said in a gentle voice '*Bhagwan*!'

'*Bhagwan*!' The woman looked at him. 'No. No! Not

Bhagwan, but a human being!' she cried out. I am going to give birth to . . .'

'You! Blessed are you mother!' said the old man and raising both his hands he bowed his head before her.

'I will help you,' said the other woman, and both of them made their way into the field.

'A human being! A human being!' Voices came from far away.

'A human being! A human being!' The vultures, scared, started to scream.

'A human being!' It seemed as if thousands of bees buzzed over the flowers. And the sound became louder and louder.

'A human being! A human being! A human being!'

Translated from Urdu by A.S. Judge

The Alien
BADIUZZAMAN

'Is Khaje *Babu* in?' I heard a familiar voice.

I knew Janva wanted me to read her the letter from Chakko.

I had just returned from college and my body was drenched in perspiration. The sun had set but it was still very hot. I had cycled for four miles under the scorching sun. I felt exhausted and longed to keep lying in the cool, pleasant dark room for sometime. Janva's voice really riled me. For that matter, I was put off by the thought of reading Chakko's letter. He was an illiterate who made others write for him. It was quite a job deciphering the handwriting. On top of that there were spelling mistakes and grammatical errors galore. Reading his letters was no less arduous than reading legal documents. To begin with, it was quite a strain to read those letters but now I have mastered his handwriting. Even if I was unable to read a couple of words, I could still capture the spirit of a particular sentence. That my guess work was generally correct was borne out by Janva's nods.

This business of reading letters has gone on for the past eight or ten years. Ever since Chakko had picked up a quarrel with his father and left this place. First, he wrote from Hazaribagh, then from Jhumri Tallaiya and before that from Kodarma. Then he went away to Calcutta. He was still there. He would come home once in six months or so and make it a point to meet me.

Janva, whose real name is Jainab or Zainab, is Chakko's widowed sister. After her husband's death, Chakko looked after her family: it was quite a strain on his resources. He did not send any money to his father but made it a point to send her thirty or thirty-five rupees each month. His daughter also lives with Janva along with her father, other brother and sister.

'Pardesi' from *Chautha Brahmin* (New Delhi: Praveen Prakashan, 1982), pp. 31-46.

'Is Khaje *Babu* in?'

'Oh, I can't escape Janva,' I muttered and got up. The door opened onto the street. Janva stood there holding an envelope in her hand. She handed me the letter without comment and sat on the threshold.

The handwriting was the same. So also the style of writing. It was indeed a letter from Chakko. But the envelope bore Pakistan's postmark? What was all this? I was curious. For a moment I forgot that Janva was right here, waiting for the letter to be read out. Then I saw Janva's anxious look. I read out the letter.

'Many *salams* to *Baba* from Abdur Shakoor and *salam* to Jainab *bua* and blessings to my brothers. May I tell you that with God's blessings we are all safe and sound here. I pray to God for your safety and welfare. You must wonder why I went away to Pakistan from Calcutta without informing you. Well, Ilahi Master in whose shop we were working said that he was going to open a tailoring shop in Pakistan, and that he wanted the workers to go with him. I was in a fix. He didn't even give time to seek your advice. Within four days we landed in Dhaka. Ilahi Master's brother-in-law lives there. He was the one, so we learnt in Dhaka, who had enticed Ilahi Master to come to Pakistan. We came here leaving behind a well-established business. We live in a hovel-like room in Ilahi Master's brother-in-law's house.

'Ilahi Master has not yet got a shop. He is frantically in search of one. We wish he gets one soon with the grace of God.

'We are getting so jittery, sitting idle.

'Let Baba and Janva know that I am well. There is nothing to worry. The money will be sent as usual. Write regularly. Dhaka is a nice city. It is full of Bengalis. They hate us. "Where have we come from?" They keep asking. I had worked with Ilahi Master for so long that I could not say "no" to him. It is raining heavily. Gaya must be very hot. Write in detail about everybody in the *mohalla*. Convey my *salams* and good wishes to everyone. One thing more, Moharram is just round the corner. When the Moharram procession is taken out offer them five rupees on my behalf as usual, every year. My *salam* to Baba. *Salam* to Zubaida and blessings from her Baba. And love to Mustaqeem and Yasin.'

When I finished reading the letter I found tears in Janva's eyes. . . . All along she had kept wiping her tears with her *anchal*.

'Khaje *Babu*, so you see for yourself how stupid Chakko is.

Father, brother, sister, they were all here, yet he took it into his head to go to Pakistan. *Babu*, our bad luck. What else can one say?'

I kept silent. What could I say? Janva took the letter from me and went away, wiping her tears.

Chakko's letter made such strange reading. He had been living away from home for a long time—at Hazaribagh, Jhumri Tallaiya, Kodarama, and then at Calcutta. All these places were located in Hindustan and people of our *mohalla* often went there in search of livelihood. But Dhaka was an altogether different country. It is not as if people from our *mohalla* had not migrated to Pakistan. But they had gone soon after partition. Most of those who went were educated, prosperous or held jobs. Life in the *mohalla* turned dull after they were gone. With the establishment of Pakistan their number dwindled further. Only the weavers, tailors, carpenters, masons, builders and the like stayed put. In fact their numbers have multiplied. Why then, did Chakko migrate to Pakistan? It was an odd decision. Did he go on his own? I don't think so. Was Ilahi Master responsible? The letter seems to indicate this. But I wasn't convinced. Chakko was not a child to be coerced into going. Ilahi Master could not have his way without Chakko's consent. Chakko was simple-minded. His letter suggested that he had acted impulsively, on the spur of the moment.

Now that Chakko was gone I felt all the more drawn towards him.

The door at whose threshold Janva had been sitting a short while ago was still ajar. Maybe the children of the *mohalla* had drawn on the verandah floor weird patterns of circles and squares with pieces of red brick. Ah, nothing seems to work with these street urchins. They are rebuked and reprimanded, but . . . they got on with their games the moment they discovered that I was away. But once the door was thrown open they would disappear into thin air. They were a nuisance.

But on that day the sight of the disfigured floor did not upset me. I felt as if the sketches were drawn by Chakko and me. I felt as if we were engrossed in playing and were oblivious to the world around us. Just then, I could hear *Abba*, chiding us. Chakko fled from the scene. I was inside my room. But *Abba* knew what we were upto. His voice, which used to make my heart quiver with fear, still echoes in my ears. 'Ruffian! Evil-faced. How many times have I told you not to play with menials? But you'll never listen. Next time I'll knock the life out of you!'

The next day I would again play with Chakko in the verandah.

We were Syeds. There were only three or four Syed families in our *mohalla*. The rest were weavers, butchers or tailors. The people of the *mohalla* held us in high esteem. *Abba* was no doubt conscious of his high pedigree but never gave the impression that he was superior to others. If he saw me playing marbles or *gulli-danda* with the urchins, he would be angry but not pull me up in public. He would rebuke me in the house. Once Chakko overheard *Abba* calling him a 'menial'. He was so upset that he stayed away from me for many weeks. He was greatly offended by Abba's innuendos against him, a 'menial'. I was also indignant. He had no right to denigrate my friend so outrageously. He could call me names, hurl abuses at me and insult me. But he had no business to call Chakko a 'menial'. Why hurt his feelings? I lacked the courage to say all this. I merely seethed with anger.

The entire *mohalla* regarded *Abba* as a kindhearted and God-fearing man. He helped people in distress. He offered *namaz* regularly and observed fast. But when he described Chakko as 'menial', I felt he had suddenly fallen from a high pedestal, that he had thrown away his mask and revealed himself and his hideous face.

I tried to pacify Chakko. Those were summer days and we went to school early in the morning. Abba would leave for the court in the morning and return home after midday. He would have lunch and then his usual siesta. As soon as I heard him snoring, I quietly climbed up a chair and unlatched the door. Then, closing the door from the outside, I went out in the verandah. I looked for Chakko in the lane. He was there. I tried to draw his attention.

'I refuse to play with you', he would say. 'You may be a gentleman, but what is that to me? I may be a menial. But how are you concerned? No, I won't play with you.'

Abba's remark still rankled. But how was I to blame? I couldn't shut *Abba*'s mouth. But why was Chakko taking out his anger on me? I never said or did anything to offend him. I often thought of taking up the matter with *Abba*. But I was nervous. He was an angry man and had no control over his temper. Even *Amma* was terrified when he was angry. What could I do? I was reduced to a cipher in his presence.

But one day I mustered courage and shared my thoughts with

him. I awaited the consequences. Luckily, *Abba* was in a good mood that day.

'So that's what's troubling you. Come here,' he said. I was fear-stricken. But he patted me on my back and laughed.

'So Chakko has taken offence at my remark?' he said. 'Don't worry. I'll pacify him.'

The next day was a Sunday. Both the school and Abba's office were closed. Abba woke up as usual early morning, performed his ablutions and his *namaz*.

Taking out a rupee from his pocket, he said, 'Go and fetch a rupee worth of *jalebees* from Vishnu's shop.' On the prayer carpet Abba began reading the *wazifa*. I ran to Vishnu *halwai*'s shop and returned with sizzling hot *jalebees*. In those days one could buy a lot of *jalebees* with one rupee. Dalda and food adulteration were unknown. I was very fond of *jalebees* and was happy. At the same time I wondered what was the occasion. There was no festival, no reason for the treat. And why was *Abba* reciting the *fateha* so early in the morning. Anyway, I was happy with the *jalebees*. *Abba* was still on the prayer carpet when he called out in his loud voice, 'Chakko!'

I don't know whether Chakko heard Abba's voice or not but his father Mahmood Khalifa came running to our verandah.

'What's it, Babu?'

'Send Chakko to me. I have to give him *fateha* sweets.'

Chakko entered the room looking scared. *Abba* asked him to sit by his side. He was affectionate. He then placed twelve pieces of *jalebees* on a plate and gave it to him. 'Here are four for you,' he said, 'four for Janva and four for Benga.' Chakko was about to leave when Abba caressed his head affectionately and said, 'Don't grudge what elders say. The time you waste in playing could well be spent in doing something useful.'

Abba's behaviour proved his greatness. I was greatly pleased. I could tell from Chakko's subdued looks that he too was deeply impressed.

Something strange happened the same night. After dinner we lay down to sleep. It was a moonlit night. The sun had been raining fire throughout the day but now a pleasant westerly wind started blowing, converting hell into heaven. The white bed sheets spread on the beds had a soothing effect. *Amma*'s bed was adjacent to mine. She was cutting arecanuts for the *paans*—the brass, Moradabadi arecanut cutter was shining in the light. *Amma*'s glass bangles jingled as she cut, but the jingling was drowned in the gurgling sound of *Abba*'s *hooqah*. At some distance from our roof, a palm tree was bathed in moonlight. It seemed very beautiful. Suddenly, a loud and horrendous sound boomed in the lane down below. 'Is Saheb Jaan there?' Fearful, I clung to my younger brother. *Amma* also got scared and dropped the half cut arecanut piece between the cutter blades. But *Abba* kept pulling peacefully at his *hooqah*. There was no sign of worry on his face. Sensing our fear he said, 'There's nothing wrong. It's a policeman. He has come to enquire about Saheb Jaan, a *goonda*. The police has to keep an eye on him.'

Saheb Jaan was a notorious character in the *mohalla*, known also in the city for his rowdyism. He was Chakko's maternal uncle but Chakko's father did not like his ways and there was no love lost between the two. Saheb Jaan had his ups and downs: his life seesawed between penury and prosperity. Sometimes he was seen in silk shirts with gold buttons, a silken *lungi* round his waist, a gold watch with a gold chain round his wrist, and a gold chain round his neck. He wore shining pump shoes and smoked Scissors cigarettes, the best brand in those days. He would generously throw eight-anna and four-anna coins at the boys. And then there were times when one saw him wearing a torn undervest and a dirty *lungi*. He would be in utter penury, wondering where his next meal was going to come from. Sometimes he would stray over to our house, asking for a handful of rice or flour. Everyone detested Saheb Jaan but at the same time they stood in awe of him. So much so that even *Abba* did not rub him up the wrong way. The policeman had just gone from the lane when we heard Saheb Jaan's voice down below. He was dead drunk. He used obscene language. I could not grasp much.

Abba called me. 'Son, as they say all people are equal in the eyes of God. But family and prestige have their own place in society. Right from our forefathers down to the present there has not been a drunkard in our family. No gambler either. Saheb Jaan is Chakko's maternal uncle. I concede that Saheb Jaan's and Chakko's fathers have different habits but both belong to the same family. We should avoid their company so that their bad habits do not have an unhealthy effect on us.' Abba sermonized on so many other things and supported his arguments with a Persian couplet whose essence was to avoid bad company.

The next day when *Abba* returned from court he carried a big packet. 'I've brought something for you which will keep you from going outdoors.'

It was a carrom board. I was overjoyed. It was a treasure trove for me. Now when I think of it, I laugh. Childhood pleasures are so simple.

Call it the effect of the carrom board or the effect of *Abba's* sermonizing, I started keeping Chakko at arm's length. There was a time when I stopped playing with him in the afternoon. Instead I would busy myself playing carrom with my younger brother. I would hear the sound of pebbles falling in the verandah. I would hear the faint sound of clapping, even the stamping of feet on the floor. But these sounds were lost in the staccato sound of the carrom board.

The gulf between me and Chakko widened. We would meet in passing and exchange a word or two. Sometimes we wouldn't. There seemed to be a barrier between us. The burden of studies also took me away from Chakko. Games still interested me. I now played football, ring-ball and hockey instead of *gulli-danda* and marbles. I would come home from school, do my home work and then on to the school playground. The school was not far from my home. When I returned my tutor would be waiting. This is how I spent the day. I lived in the *mohalla* but felt as if I did not belong to the place. When I think of my childhood vagaries they seem so strange and so inconsequential. But there is some thin, invisible thread which has strung these memories together. At the slightest pretext they begin to glow like pearls on a string. One of my early memories is of Mahmood Khalifa walking through the lane, the measuring tape dangling from his neck, a pair of scissors held in one hand and a small bundle tucked under his arm. Chakko is walking silently behind his father. Like a prisoner behind a policeman. A blank expression on his face. Suddenly that face is infused with life, as Mahmood Khalifa hurls abuses at him. 'Your mother . . . your sister . . . !'

'*Saala*, so you've also learnt to steal! So you are emulating your maternal uncle!'

It was a routine affair not worth noticing. They were screening *Pukaar* at a local cinema hall. Chakko had taken out some money from his father's pocket and slipped out of the shop. When Mahmood Khalifa discovered the loss he came down hard upon Chakko. I was pleased. Also jealous. I was happy because of the dressing down Chakko received. *Abba* never missed an opportunity of doing the same. So whenever someone was rebuked or condemned I derived vicarious pleasure. I was jealous of Chakko because I could never imagine stealing. Chakko had scored over me. In those days *Pukaar* was a very popular film. People doted on the fairy-faced Naseem, singing songs with gusto. I longed to see the picture but *Abba* wouldn't let me. What was wrong with the film? Some 'hot' stuff? Everybody was watching the film. Why deny me the pleasure? But I couldn't argue with *Abba*. Ironically, even *Abba* had seen the picture. It had made me angry. What was the logic? If the film was bad for me, was it not the same for him? Chakko was indeed lucky. He got a dressing down but saw the picture all right.

Many such incidents come crowding into my mind. Chakko as a bridegroom, wearing a brown waistcoat over a white shirt, sitting erect on the bridal mare, the sound of Sukhi *Mian*'s *shehnai* ringing in the air, Bansi barber standing by his side holding an umbrella over his head, and *mohalla* boys crowding around and blocking his way. And then suddenly a hushed silence falls over the lane, making people restless. The marriage party is leaving but nobody from our house joins it. Set rules and norms governed our world. How then, could members of our family join Chakko's marriage party? Everybody knows this truth, just as they know that the sun rises from the east. Nobody complains, nobody feels hurt. Chakko has scored once more over me.

But when I read Chakko's letter from Pakistan I felt the wall raised between us by *Abba* or the carrom board had crumbled in one stroke. It seemed Chakko had suddenly come closer to me. Even closer than before, the time when I played with him after making those patterns on the ground with pieces of red brick.

Fifteen days later there was another letter from Chakko. It read: '*Salam* to *Abba* and Janva *bua* from Abdur Shakoor. This is to tell you that all is well with me. You people had written that I should not have gone away as I did, leaving you behind. What should I tell you? It is not for me to tell you. I did not want to come here either. But Ilahi Master said something bristling with acrimony. He said he had stood by me but that I was prepared to desert him in his hour of distress. I had to abide by his wishes. I said "Master I am not what you think of me. I'll accompany you. If I don't, may I drink my father's urine." I had to go. I gave him my word. I miss home very much. People here are very different from us. They speak Bengali. They start muttering the moment they set eyes on us. Today is the fourth day of Moharram. The *tazia* procession will come out on the seventh and it will terminate on the tenth. If I had been with you I would have observed the Moharram. Please offer sweets and *sherbet* at the big *imambara* on my behalf. Ask Dahu *Bhaiya* to request *Imam Saheb* to pray for me. How was the *mohalla* procession? Do write to me about it. I hope Ibrahim *Ustad* turned up to supervise the Moharram. How many lamp-bearers were there? Did they erect a gate or not? Write everything in detail. My *salams* to all.'

It was the seventh day of Moharram. The drums boomed and boys wearing green shirts and bright waistcoats moved around in the lane. If Chakko had been here, how he would have gone prancing about in a green shirt and *churidar*, a *cummerbund* round his waist, three or four bells dangling from it. He always joined the *tazia* procession and came home late the next morning. How I longed to go round the city with the procession! But *Abba* would not allow me to do so. Every year when our *mohalla* took out a procession, it first stopped near our house at the corner of the lane facing the big *maidan*. We would view the procession from the street corner of our house.

On that day *Abba* would have a big tub filled with *sherbet*. It was offered to all present at the *akhara*. Before the procession moved on *Abba* would put twenty or thirty rupees in Ibrahim *Ustad's* hand. I had seen Chakko participate in the *akhara* on numerous occasions. He was an expert in *gatka* and *lathi*. Once he grew up, he showed the same skill at *gohar*. He was its best exponent—not letting the opponent's *lathi* even touch his body. I also wanted to participate in the *akhara*. But how could I with *Abba* around? I was a puppet in his hands. I wanted to play the role of a *paek* (courier or messenger of God) but there was no such tradition in our family. I was given an iron brace to wear during Moharram to which a new link was added every year, to indicate that another year had been added to my age. Before giving me the neckbrace, *Abba* would solemnly recite the *fateha*. As part of the ritual, I was given *rewries* (sugar or jaggery candy coated with sesame seeds) to eat and *sherbet* to drink. I did not care much for all this. I also wanted to be a free bird, play the role of a *paek* and have a *cummerbund* round my waist with bells dangling, and roam about the whole night. I wanted to do what Chakko did. But I had no such freedom. I was sent to an uncle's house in the middle of the *bazar* from whose rooftop I could view the entire Moharram spectacle. But there was no fun in being a captive at a vantage point. Roaming around in the streets was such fun.

These are childhood memories. Even today the Moharram *akhara* takes place opposite our house. Even today we offer money to Ibrahim *Ustad*. Even today *sherbet* is offered to those taking part in the *akhara*. But nowadays all this has been reduced to an empty ritual. The fervour of those childhood days is gone. Yet Chakko talks about Moharram with the same passion. And such wistfulness, as if he has some spiritual affinity with it. I still recall how my heart leaped with joy when one day *Abba* brought a carrom board for me. Now the texture of happiness has changed. That simple, unsophisticated joy of childhood is not there any more. But the warp and woof of Chakko's joy is still the same. It was the same with me.

I appeared for the judicial officer's competitive examination and was selected. Before my appointment I was required to go to Patna for my medical examination. On my return another letter from Chakko awaited me.

'Many *salams* for Baba and Janva-*Bua* from Abdur Shakoor. Received your letter. This is to tell you that Ilahi Master's shop is doing well. He has bagged a good contract from the government. Master says he will increase our emoluments and give us a share in the profits. But I do not feel at home here, though I am quite comfortable. Our food, which we share, is cooked in Ilahi Master's common kitchen. I was sorry to learn that this time you had only a three-unit music band for Moharram whereas in previous years you engaged a four-unit band. I hear that no illumination gate was erected at the head of the procession. If I had been there I would not have allowed this to happen. I would have collected sufficient funds to put up a grand show. God-willing, I will attend our *mohalla* Moharram next year and prove my capability to the people. Curse on the people of our *mohalla* who do not care a fig for our *mohalla*'s prestige. You have not written anything about *mehndi*.'

'Tell *Abba* I don't approve of Quresha's engagement with Saheb Jaan's son. I don't. No doubt, Bhura has a steady job but he is the son of a thief. How can I allow my sister to marry the son of a thief and a dacoit? Tell *Baba* on my behalf not to rush in fixing her engagement.'

'Blessings to Zubeda. My blessings to Mustaqeem and Yasin.'

Chakko's letter set me thinking. He lived hundreds of miles away from us. Yet he was so deeply attached to our *mohalla*. I was in the thick of things; yet, I was aloof. What interested Chakko did not interest me anymore. Though Chakko was so far away from us; yet he felt everything on his pulse as if only death could cast him apart from these things. Was it second nature with him or had distance lent enchantment to these goings-on in our *mohalla*? But then, I had also stayed away from home. Yet Moharram and its accompanying observances had not fascinated me. Their memory had never given my heart a wrench. Perhaps I was past the age for taking part in such observances. But the simple and small joys of life were as important to Chakko today as they were to him in his childhood. To me he was the same Chakko who, as a child, went prancing in the lane as God's courier, the bells dangling from his waistband, jingling in the air. Even when he had taken offence at Abba's strictures he remained very much a child. He was still a child at heart when he went to Pakistan at Ilahi Master's behest, tearing himself away from the country of his birth and depriving himself of the atmosphere in which he had grown to manhood. He was like a child weeping for his mother's milk with his mother nowhere in sight.

My first posting as a civil judge was in Purnea. I was transferred to Samastipur after three years. Both these places were in north Bihar on the banks of the Ganga. I would spend the day listening to lawyers' arguments and cross-examining of witnesses. I would remain busy till late writing my judgements. I was so overworked that I went home only once and that too for a day or two. After completing four years of service I availed of two months leave and came home. Two days later, in the morning, I was in my sitting room writing an urgent letter. The door opening into the verandah was ajar.

Suddenly I heard someone calling, 'Is Khaje *Saheb* in?'

'Who's there? Please come in,' I said.

'It's me, Abdur Shakoor.' Chakko walked in and stood in front. He was just the same as he had been years ago except that his hair had a sprinkling of grey.

'When did you return from Pakistan?' I asked.

'I've been here for the last two months, Babu. I feared I may miss you. Then Janva-*Bua* told me that you were here. My good luck, that I've been able to meet you. I'm meeting you after such a long time.'

'How long will you stay here?'

'I must leave today. I had a month's visa which was extended by another month. Ilahi Master is writing regularly asking me to return soon.'

'Have you started liking the place?'

'No, sometimes I feel so wretched that I pine for home.'

'Then why did you go?'

'What can I say, Babu? Ilahi Master deceived me. He made me fill in the passport form without telling me what it was all about.'

'How is your daughter? She must have grown up by now.'

'Yes, Babu, she is twelve. If I can find a suitable boy I'll marry her off. Please look around. Let me know if you come across somebody nice.'

'But you have only one child. Take her along and marry her off there.'

'What are you saying Babu? How can I find a boy from our community there?' Chakko asked innocently.

At eight that night a rickshaw stopped at the corner of our lane. Chakko walked in front of the rickshaw followed by Mahmood Khalifa, Janva, her sons, Mustaqeem and Yasin, Chakko's sister Quresha and her daughter Zubaida. Chakko's gait was just the same. He walked slowly behind his father, as if he was returning after closing his shop for the day. A measuring tape dangled from his neck. He held a pair of scissors in one hand and a bundle was tucked under his arm. But where was he going? Not to his house surely, for he was walking in the opposite direction. Mahmood Khalifa walked in front and Chakko followed him. It seemed as if my spell had broken. Oh, how times have changed! Everything looked so different. Getting down from my verandah I proceeded towards the street corner and saw Chakko climbing into the rickshaw. I had witnessed this scene so many times in the past. Whenever Chakko went to Hazaribagh, Kodarma, Jhumri Talliaya or Calcutta, the rickshaw would stop at the corner of the lane to pick him up. But I never went to see him off. His father, brother, sister bid him farewell. There were no tears in their eyes, though they looked sad. They knew that his coming and going would go on. The people of Chakko's *mohalla* often went to other places in search of work. But his going away was different. Today, Chakko was not in search of a job. So it seemed. He was going away to a far off place. He did not know whether he would return or not.

I stood at the corner of the lane. The rickshaw was parked alongside the steps leading to the house. Chakko's face looked drawn and tense—as if his heart would burst under a storm raging within him. An *Imam-Zamin* rested on his arm. On the footboard, a black tin trunk. On top of it an earthen pot tied in red cloth. There was food for the journey. His widowed sister Janva stood by his side. Chakko's one foot rested on the rickshaw's footboard while the other was rooted on the ground. Janva's tearful words reached my ears, 'May Allah bring you back safe and sound!'

Suddenly Chakko's face crumbled and the storm in his heart burst forth. He slipped from the rickshaw's footboard and hit the ground. He started crying like a child as if something dear had been snatched away. I have not seen Chakko weep so bitterly. I saw his passport: Abdur Shakoor, son of Mahmood Khalifa, citizen of Pakistan. Having studied law I believe in its sanctity. But I don't know why my brain suddenly became numb—as if thick law books were being swamped in Chakko's flood of tears. I realized with intense feelings that Chakko was in reality going to an alien land where everything was an unknown entity to him.

Translated from Hindi by Jai Ratan

His Heap of Rubble
MOHAN RAKESH

Mohan Rakesh (1925-72) was a leading playwright and fictionalist in Hindi. Born in Amritsar, he was educated in Lahore and took degrees in Hindi and Sanskrit. With Kamleshwar and Rajendra Yadav, he is credited with launching the Nai Kahani Movement (New Short Story) in the fifties. His *Adhe-Adhura* is considered a classic of modern Hindi drama.

The story 'His Heap of Rubble' unfolds at two levels. Taking off as a narration of typical incident of partition days it culminates into a rich metaphor of a vivisected community and of an agonized consciousness, in which the conflict over the 'lordship' becomes an interface with the contemporary human situation.

It was after seven and a half years that they had come from Lahore to visit Amritsar. Watching the hockey match was of course an excuse; what they were really keen to see once again were those houses and marketplaces which they had been separated from seven and a half years ago. On every street one could see a group of *Mussulmans* strolling about. They were looking at everything around with such fascination as if this were no ordinary town but a great tourist attraction.

Passing through narrow streets and markets they reminded each other of familiar things and places. Look, O Fatehdin, there aren't half as many shops of crystal sugar left now in this Crystal Sugar Bazar! Over there at that street-corner where were that *panwallah* sits now, Sukhi the Baking Woman had her bakery. And *Khan Saheb*, just mark this Salt Bazar! Every shop-girl here is sultrier than the other!

'Malbe ka Malik' translated by Harish Trivedi in *Breakthrough: Modern Hindi and Urdu Short Stories*, ed. Sukrita Paul Kumar, Indian Institute of Advanced Study, Shimla, 1993, pp. 223-233.

It was after a long while that one saw again in the marketplace tasselled turbans and red *fez* caps. A large proportion of the *Mussulmans* who had come from Lahore were those who had been forced to flee Amritsar at the time of the partition. Looking at all the changes that had inevitably come about during the seven and a half years, their eyes would now fill with wonder and now cloud over with regret. Good Lord! How they have widened Katra Jaimalsingh! Were all the houses on this side burnt down? Hakim Asif Ali had his shop here, no? This cobbler now occupies it, does he?

And occasionally one could also hear a sentence such as: Wali, but this mosque still stands where it did! They haven't turned it into a *gurudwara*!

On whichever road the group of Pakistanis passed, they evoked wonder and curiosity among the people of the town. On seeing the *Mussulmans* approach, some still felt apprehensive and would get out of the way, while others would go up to them and start walking alongside. They would ask the visitors all kinds of questions. So what news of Lahore then? Is the area of Anarkali still as grand as before? They say the Shahalmi Bazar has been completely rebuilt. Is Krishnanagar much the same as ever? And this new Rishwatpura, is it really all built out of *rishwat* [bribes]? I hear the *burqa* has quite disappeared from Pakistan—has it? A feeling of such intimacy lay behind these questions that it might have seemed that Lahore was not so much a city as a dear relative of thousands of people who were eager to have all its news. The visitors from Lahore were the guests of the whole of Amritsar, and every one was delighted to see them and talk with them.

Bazar Bansa is a fairly desolate quarter of Amritsar which mainly housed lower class *Mussulmans* before the partition. It had been full of shops selling bamboos and beams of wood which had been all gutted in the same fire. The fire in Bazar Bansa had been the most terrible fire in all Amritsar; it had seemed at one stage that it would burn the whole city down. Many neigbourhoods around Bazar Bansa had in fact been consumed by that fire. The fire had somehow been put out, but not before it had reduced to ashes half a dozen Hindu houses for each *Mussulman* house. Now, in the seven and half years that had passed, many houses had come up again, but there still lay heaps of rubble here, there and everywhere. Lying in between newly built houses, these heaps of rubble evoked a strange atmosphere.

On that day too, there wasn't much going on in Bazar Bansa. For not only had most of its residents perished with their houses but even among those who had survived and fled, few would have dared come back. Only a solitary old and frail *Mussulman* visited the desolate Bazar that day and, in the midst of all the new and burnt down buildings, found himself in a maze. When he approached the lane leading off to the left, his feet all but led him in, but then he dithered and stood without. It was as if he couldn't believe that was the lane he wanted. At one end of the lane some children were playing hopscotch, and a little further off two women were calling each other names in high-pitched voices.

'Whatever else may have changed, it's still the same tongue!' the old *Mussulman* said softly to himself, and stood leaning on his walkingstick. His knees peeped out of his *pyjama*, and there were patches on his *sherwani* above. A little boy came out of the lane crying. The old man said to him kindly, 'Come here, son! Look what I have got for you!' And he dug his hand into his pocket to see what he could come up with for the child. The child, who had stopped crying for the moment, now pouted and began to howl again. A girl of sixteen or seventeen came scurrying out of the lane, grabbed the child by the arm, and began to drag him back in. On top of his crying, the child now also struggled to get free. The girl picked him up and held him close in her arms and kissing him on the face said, 'Be quiet, you little devil! If you cry this *Mussulman* will grab you and be off with you! Be quiet, I tell you!'

The old *Mussulman* put back into his pocket the coin that he had taken out to give to the child. He took his cap off, scratched his head, and tucked the cap under his arm. His throat had gone dry and his knees trembled a little. He clutched for support at the extended ledge of a closed shop outside the lane and put his cap back on. Opposite the lane where tall beams of wood were stacked once, there now stood a three-storey house. In front on the electric wire two fat kites sat stock still. Near the electric pole there lingered a little patch of sunshine. He watched for a while particles of dust swirling in it. Then he heard himself say, 'Dear God!'

A young man approached the lane twirling a bunch of keys. On seeing the old man standing there he asked, 'Yes, *Miyan-ji*, what brings you here?'

The old *Mussulman* felt a shiver run down his chest and arms.

He passed his tongue over his lips, looked at the young man closely, and said, 'Son, you are Manori, aren't you?'

The young man stopped twirling his bunch of keys, closed his fist over it, and said with some surprise. 'But how do you know my name?'

'You were just this high seven and a half years ago,' said the old man with an attempt to smile.

'Have you come today from Pakistan?'

'Yes, we used to live in this lane,' the old man said. 'My son was Chiragh Din the tailor. Just six months before the partition we had a new house built here.'

'Oh, Ghani *miyan*!' Manori said, with recognition.

'Yes, my son, I am your Ghani *miyan*. I can't have my Chiragh and his wife and children again but I thought, why shouldn't I come and have a look at the state of the house at least.' The old man took off his cap and stroked his head with this hand and held back his tears.

'You yourself had left here a little sooner, hadn't you?' Manori asked, his voice brimming up with sympathy.

'Yes, my son, it was my misfortune that all by myself I had gone away ahead of my family. Had I stayed on I too with them could have....' Even as he began the sentence he realized that perhaps he shouldn't finish it. He held back his words but let flow his tears.

'Never mind, Ghani *miyan*, what's the use of dwelling on it like that?' Manori took Ghani by the arm. 'Come, let me show you your house.'

In the meanwhile, a report had spread in the lane that a *Mussulman* stood outside and was about to snatch away Ramdasi's little child. His sister had gone and pulled the child back just in the nick of time or else the *Mussulman* would have run off with him. As soon as they heard this the women who had been sunning themselves sitting on wooden stools placed in the middle of the lane picked up their stools and retreated within their house. They also called in all the children who had been playing in the lane. When Manori entered the lane leading Ghani in, there was no one left in it except a passing street-vendor, if one did not count Rakkha the Wrestler who was sprawled under the *pipal* tree growing over the well, sleeping. However, from behind doors and windows many faces were peering into the lane. On seeing Manori come into the lane with Ghani a conspiratorial whisper had started up among them. No one had any difficulty recognizing Chiragh Din's old father Abdul Ghani, even though his beard had gone completely grey.

'There, that was your house,' Manori pointed to a heap of rubble at some distance. Ghani stopped short and stared wide-eyed in that direction. He had long ago learnt to accept the death of Chiragh and his family. But he hadn't been ready for the manner in which his flesh now began to creep. His tongue grew drier than before and his knees trembled a little more.

'This heap of rubble?' he asked unbelievingly.

Manori looked at his face drained of all colour. He held his arm tighter and said in a flat tone, 'Your house was burnt down right then.'

Leaning on his stick Ghani somehow reached the heap of rubble. It was all dust now with some broken and burnt up bricks sticking out here and there. All the iron and wood had been pilfered long ago. Only the frame and threshold of a burnt door somehow still remained in place. At the back stood two burnt out cupboards; a hint of a layer of white paint gleamed through the soot covering them. Having examined the rubble closely Ghani said, 'And is this all that is left?' His knees gave way and he sank to the ground holding on to the wooden frame. In a moment his head too came to rest against the threshold and in a plaintive tone he said, 'Oh alas my Chiragh Din!'

Though the threshold of the burnt out door had stood sticking its head up all these seven and a half years, the wood in it had all turned to powder. At the touch of Ghani's head it began to flake off and some of the flakes came and rested on Ghani's own cap and hair. With them also fell off an earthworm which now crawled away on the brick ledge running alongside the open drain at Ghani's feet. It lifted its head now and then to look for some hole in which to hide but not finding one, it beat its head on the ground again and slithered off in another direction.

The number of faces peering from behind windows had now multiplied. A hushed whisper of anticipation ran among them; something or the other was bound to happen today. Chiragh Din's father Ghani was here, and so the whole episode of seven and a half years ago would surely disclose itself. It seemed to everyone watching as if the heap of rubble would itself relate the whole story to Ghani—how Chiragh was having his dinner that evening in the room upstairs when Rakkha the Wrestler had shouted to him to come down and listen to him just for a minute. The Wrestler was then the boss of the lane. Even the Hindus were all under his thumb, to say nothing of Chiragh who was a *Mussulman*. Chiragh had left the morsel in his hand half eaten and come down. His wife Zubaida and the two daughters Kishwar and Sultana had come to the window and looked down. Chiragh had no sooner stepped out across his threshold than the Wrestler had caught him by the collar and pulled him to himself and flung him down in the lane and sat on his chest. Chiragh had grabbed his hand holding the knife and screamed, 'Oh, don't kill me, Rakkha the Wrestler! Someone save me, please!' Zubaida, Kishwar and Sultana too had cried out from upstairs in desperate tones and had come screaming down to the front door. A wrestling disciple of Rakkha's had held down the struggling arm of Chiragh's and as he pressed down Chiragh's thighs with his knees Rakkha had said, 'Why d'you scream, you goddamn sister-fucker. I'm giving you your Pakistan—here, take your Pakistan!' by the time Zubaida, Kishwar and Sultana could get to him, Chiragh had already attained his Pakistan.

The windows of all the neighbouring houses had then promptly shut. The eye-witnesses to the scene had absolved themselves of any responsibility for it by shutting their doors on it. Through their closed doors they could still hear the wailing of Zubaida, Kishwar and Sultana for a long while afterwards. Rakkha the Wrestler and his mates gave them their Pakistan as well that night, but by a more circuitous route. Their bodies were found not in Chiragh's house but in the waters of the canal later.

For a couple of days afterwards Chiragh's house had been thoroughly ransacked. When everything in it had been looted, God knows who had set fire to it. Rakkha the Wrestler had then sworn that he would bury alive the man who had set the house on fire, for had he not decided to kill Chiragh with a view to his house. In fact he had already bought the necessary ingredients for the ritual purification of the *Mussulman*'s house. But to this day, the person who had set the house on fire had not been found out. For all these seven and a half years Rakkha had treated that heap of rubble as his own property where he would not let anyone tether their cattle or let any one set up a vending-stall. No one could help himself to a single brick from the rubble without his permission.

People expected that this whole story would surely somehow

reach Ghani, as if he would come to know it all merely by looking at the rubble. Ghani was turning over with his fingernails the dust from the rubble and pouring it over himself. He had his arms wrapped round the threshold and was wailing. 'Tell me, my Chiragh, tell me, where have you gone, oh where? O Kishwar, O Sultana, O my children, why have you left poor Ghani behind?'

And flakes of wood flew off the crumbly door.

Either someone had gone and woken up Rakkha the Wrestler sleeping under the tree or he had woken up by himself. When he knew that Abdul Ghani from Pakistan had come visiting and was sitting on the rubble of his house, his throat grew thick with spittle which made him cough and which he then spat out on the platform of the well. As he looked at the heap of the rubble a noise like that of a pair of bellows escaped his chest and his lower hip hung out a little.

'Ghani is sitting on his heap of rubble.' his disciple Lachcha the Wrestler came and sat by and told him.

'How's it his heap of rubble? It's my heap of rubble!' the Wrestler said in a voice gruff with spittle.

'But he's sitting there anyhow,' said Lachchha with a secret twinkle in his eye.

'Let him, then, let him. You go and get my *chillum*!' Rakkha spread his legs out a little in front of him and passed his hand over his bare thighs.

'And suppose Manori were to spill the beans?' Lachchha said in his secretive way as he arose to go and get the *chillum*.

'As if Manori doesn't know what's good for him.'

Lachchha went off.

On the platform of the well lay scattered old *pipal* leaves. Rakkha picked them up one by one and crushed them in his hands. Once Lachchha had wrapped the cloth round the lower end of the *chillum* and handed it to him. Rakkha drew on it and asked, 'No one else been talking to Ghani...eh...has any one?'

'No,'

'No,'

'Here,' he coughed and passed the *chillum* down to Lachchha. Manori was seen walking up from the heap of rubble, leading Ghani by the arm. Lachchha squatted on his haunches, and drew long drags on the *chillum*. His eyes would rest for a split second on Rakkha's face and then travel to Ghani's.

Manori was leading Ghani by the arm and walking one step ahead, as if to ensure that Ghani should pass by the well without seeing Rakkha. But the way Rakkha sat sprawling, Ghani could spot him a long way off. As he approached the well he called out, with both his arms spread out before him, 'Rakkha the Wrestler!'

Rakkha lifted his head and screwed his eyes and looked at him. An indistinct gurgle sounded in his throat, but he didn't speak.

'Rakkha the Wrestler, don't you know me?' Ghani asked, dropping his arms, 'I am Ghani, Abdul Ghani, father of Chiragh Din!'

The windows above were abuzz with whispers: the two were at last face to face, now everything must come out... and then my be they will exchange words... Rakkha cannot touch Ghani now. Those days are gone... How he fancied the rubble as his own!... The heap of rubble is in fact neither his nor Ghani's. The rubble is the property of the Government! The rogue does not even let anyone tie his cow there!... What a coward Manori is. Why didn't he tell Ghani it was Rakkha who had killed Chiragh and his family!... Rakkha is not a man, he is a bull! He keeps roaming in the street all day like a bull. How frail has poor Ghani grown. His beard has gone all grey.

Sitting on the plinth of the well Ghani said, 'Rakkha the Wrestler, just look how everything's changed! I had left a flourishing family here and have now come back to see it all turned to dust. This is all that remains of a bustling household. And if you ask me, I don't now want to go away leaving even this heap of dust behind!' His eyes filled up with tears again.

The Wrestler drew in his outspread legs, picked up his towel from the edge of the plinth, and flung it over his shoulder. Lachchha offered him the *chillum*. He drew on it.

'But tell me, Rakkha, how did it all happen?' Ghani asked, straining to hold back his tears, 'All of you were with him. You had all been close together as brothers. Had he wanted couldn't he have hidden with any one of you in your houses? Didn't he have even a little sense?'

'That's how it was.' Rakkha himself could hear the unnatural ring his voice had. His lips were clammy with thick spittle. From under his moustaches sweat trickled on to his lips. On his forehead he felt a pressure and his backbone wanted support.

'And how are you folks in Pakistan?' he asked. His vocal chords were tense. He wiped with his towel the sweat under his armpits, sucked in the spittle in his mouth and then spat it out into the lane.

'What can I say, Rakkha,' Ghani said, leaning with both hands on his stick and with his head bent, 'My Maker alone knows how things are with me. Had I Chiragh with me there it would have been all quite different....How I had tried to persuade him to leave with me. But he wouldn't listen—said he wouldn't leave the new house, for wasn't it our own lane, so how could there be any danger to us. The poor dove never imagined that even if there was no danger from within the lane, danger could come in from without! All four of them gave their lives guarding the house... Rakkha, he had great trust in you. He often said no one could harm him at all so long as you were around. But when it was time for him to go, no one could save him, not even Rakkha.'

Rakkha tried to straighten himself up, for his backbone was hurting like mad. The joints of his waist and thighs seemed under terrible pressure. Something welling up from near his guts was beginning to choke him. His whole body was soaked with perspiration and the soles of his feet were tingling. Before his eyes would descend from above blue sparklers and then they would swim away. Between his tongue and his lips a gap had opened up, he felt. With his towel he wiped the corners of his lips. At the same time there escaped from his lips the words, 'O Lord, there is none but thou but thou but thou!'

Ghani saw that the lips of the Wrestler had gone dry and the rings round his eyes had grown darker. He put a hand on his shoulder and said, 'Well, dear Rakkha, what happened was what had to be, and no one can undo it now. May Allah keep the good in their goodness and forgive the harm that the wicked do. I have been here and I have seen you all so I'll think I have seen Chiragh. May God keep you well!' And he leaned on his stick and got up. As he walked away he said, 'Good bye then, Rakkha the Wrestler!'

Some faint sound escaped Rakkha's lips. His hands still holding the towel came together in farewell. Ghani slowly passed out of the lane casting a longing look all around.

In the windows above, the whispering went on for a little while longer how Manori surely must have told Ghani everything once they were out of the lane... how Rakkha had gone all dry in the mouth when faced with Ghani! And how dare Rakkha now stop any one from tying his cow at the rubble? Poor Zubaida! What a good soul she was! This rogue Rakkha, with neither home or hearth of his own, what did he care about the honour of someone else's wife or daughter?

Presently the housewives descended into the lane again. The children started a game of *gulli-danda*. For some reason known only to themselves two girls of twelve or thirteen got engaged in close combat.

Well into the evening Rakkha sat at the well coughing and smoking his *chillum*. Many passersby stopped and asked. 'Hello there, Rakkha, we hear Ghani came to visit today from Pakistan?'

'So he did,' was Rakkha's reply each time.

'And then?'

'Then nothing. Went away, didn't he?'

When night fell Rakkha moved as he did every day to the extended platform of the shop to the left at the mouth of the lane. Each day he used to call out to all kinds of passersby and have them sit by him and give them tips on betting and on body-building. But this day he spoke only to Lachchha, describing to him the arduous pilgrimage to the shrine on the hill of *Vaishno Devi* on which he had gone some fifteen years ago. When he returned into the lane having seen off Lachchha, he saw Loku Pandit's buffalo near the heap of rubble and began out of habit to shoo it away: 'Whoosh! Tat-tat-tat-tat! Whoosh!'

Having driven the buffalo away he sat down at the threshold in the rubble to catch his breath. All was quiet in the lane. As the municipality had provided no street-lights here, it grew dark in the lane soon after sunset. Water flowed in the open drain by the rubble making a soft sound. A variety of noises arose from the heap of rubble slicing the stillness of the night: cheu cheu cheu... chik chik chik.... kirrr-rrrr-rrrrrr-chirrrr...

A stray crow came flying in and perched on the wooden threshold. This caused some more flakes to scatter. Hardly had the crow alighted when a dog lying in a corner of the heap of rubble rose up growling and began to bark loudly; bow-wow-bow! The crow sat hushed on the threshold for a while and then fluttered off to the *pipal* by the well. Once the crow had flown off, the dog came down the heap and now began barking at the Wrestler. The Wrestler tried to shoo it away by saying in a gruff tone: durr-durr-durray. But the dog only came closer and barked: Bow-wow-bow-bow-bow-bow!

The Wrestler picked up a lump of earth and threw it at the dog. The dog retreated a little but it did not stop barking. The Wrestler called the dog a mother-fucker and got up and slowly went and lay down on the platform of the well. As soon as he had moved off, the dog came down into the lane and faced the well and began barking again. Having barked for a long while, he found that not a soul was stirring in the lane, so he flapped his ears once and returned to the heap of rubble and sat in a corner and began to growl.

Translated from the original Hindi by Harish Trivedi

The Wagah Canal
FIKR TAUNSVI

Wagah.... It is neither located on a plateau nor on a river bank. Neither does it produce cotton to be sent to Vassawar. Nor is it a port for which the British and the French fought for years. Wagah is a plain and simple canal—silent, gentle and calm. It watered the fields before the formation of India and Pakistan and breathed life into swaying fields of corn. But the moment the bugles were blown to herald Independence, it seemed as if the Wagah canal had turned into an arid wasteland. Instead of milky white cascading waters, the troops were stationed there. Guns, cannons and armoured cars brought news of freedom to Wagah and relieved the canal of the burden of cultivating the fields. Henceforth, the fields around Wagah canal were not to wait for the streamlets carrying life-giving nectar. Instead, they were to get used to the weight of cannons and armoured cars. The fields, in any case, were not servile to either the canal or its glistening sweet water. Nor were they bonded to the farmer who ploughed them or to the ears of corn that swayed over them. They were, in reality, only a few pieces of dry land. And land either belongs to God or the King. No one else has any claim over it. And the King, the deputy of God on this earth, can dispose it of any time and anyway he likes. If he so wills, he can destroy the ears of corn and replace them with guns and bullets. He can change the face of the earth. He can turn a jungle into a flourishing country and then divide it into two and call one *Mangal* (Mars) and the other *Sanichar* (Saturn). Having done that he can proclaim before the whole world to the beat of drums that *Mangal* is *Mangal* and *Sanichar* is *Sanichar*. That is why the twain will not be allowed to meet....

And then to emphasize the divide between the two, huge signboards were installed. Colourful flags were hoisted, a green one on this side and a red on the other. Now they had separate names,

'Wagah ki Nehar' from *Satvan Shastra*, pp. 57-66.

separate flags, separate uniforms and separate cannons. That is how the world came to know that the canal which watered the fields, both on the east and west, would now be used to divide east from west, and henceforth historians would call it Wagah.

I could have easily called Wagah, the border between India and Pakistan, but I feared—and I had solid and valid reasons for my apprehensions—that all the leading historians and geographers would have immediately censured me for doing that because, for them the old concept, according to which there used to be only one border between the two countries, had now become redundant. Moreover, a few astrologers in 1947 made the heavenly bodies revolve in such a scientific manner that instead of having one border between them, India and Pakistan had two. Actually the word 'two' had befuddled their minds in such a way that now neither the stars moved in an orderly manner nor did their predictions come true. Exasperated by this very 'two' and swayed by their animosity to 'one' they became oblivious of the fact that the new unit they were trying to create was by itself a derivative of 'one'.

Consequently you may be exasperated or annoyed, but I can't deny the two borders between India and Pakistan. One is Wagah and the other. . . . But what have I to do with the other one? I only want to convey a few things about Wagah crossed by over ninety lakh people during the last few days in the name of safeguarding their religions. I chanced to cross the border three times during the last few days.

The first time my status was of a regular citizen, i.e., I entered the territory of India as a regular refugee, riding a regular army truck, and with proper pomp and show. I say 'pomp and show' because our grand caravan, consisting of trucks, was given a grand reception of a fluttering red and yellow flag, an extensive army camp approbation and applause, and slogans shouted by the refugees themselves. The first thing I did was to try and search for that dividing line. To define it, the pages of the Quran, the Vedas and the Granth Sahib had to be reinterpreted so as to bring out altogether different meanings from what they actually stood for. On this the Prime Minister of Great Britain said: 'It is not merely a line. On the contrary, it is a sacred link which will strengthen the bond of friendship between India and Pakistan.' Consequently I was disappointed when I looked for that strong bond. There was no formidable mountain, sea, river or jungle on the border. But almost

THE WAGAH CANAL

immediately I repented having thought so foolishly, because having a river, a sea or a mountain for a border was a concept associated with the Stone Age. Man was afraid of man then, one state was against the other, and the borders existed as defence barriers against the enemy. Wars were fought to vanquish adversaries and gain dignity and honour. As far as I could understand, there was no earthly reason for India and Pakistan to be enemies. Whenever the elites of the two countries met, they embraced one another like brothers. That the commoners of the two countries always pounced on one another like hungry wolves was an altogether different matter. The downtrodden people are by nature wolves, eternally hungry and bloodthirsty. Why should anyone raise walls for the sake of people like that? Actually the real cause of a war was the clash of interests between the elites. Otherwise, how else can one explain that when the commoners are virtually tearing each other apart like wolves, the elites, overflowing with love and affection for each other, sit together in cozy comfort over tea, rub their snouts with each other like goats, and work out how to bear the crushing burden of the extra millions raked in as profit under the new industrial policy.

I was shocked to see the border guards of both countries indulging in idle gossip-mongering outside their camps. I felt like shouting at them and telling them: 'Aye soldiers! What's the use of posting you here? Don't you know you are there to strike terror in the heart of the enemy? And here you indulge in meaningless chatter, as if you have been trained since childhood just to do that! How comfortable you look playing cards, as if you were born masters.'

But before I could learn more about the Wagah border, our caravan set out on the road to India, the land of paradise. My desires remain unfulfilled.

The next time I went to Wagah on a lorry from Amritsar. This one too, like other lorries, collected a fixed fare from the passengers and took them to the border. The passengers were either Hindus or Sikhs. Almost all were traders. All of them cursed Pakistan during the journey. I got angry several times. One person deliberately picked a quarrel with me when he heard me say that I was going to Wagah to meet Ahmad Nadim Qasmi, a Muslim friend of mine. When I asked him: 'Are you going to Wagah to sell the bundles of Kashmiri cloth to your Muslim friends?' he told me truthfully that the merchant in question was no friend of his. He was just a merchant. And as far as he was concerned there was not even a remote connection between trade and friendship.

This time, I was shocked to see the way the two governments functioned. There was no sign of the Wagah Canal on the border. Nor did I see the flags or the soldiers. There was just a three-mile long sea of people who had swallowed up the marks which demarcated one country from the other. This sea was pulsating with the same people, who until only a year ago were enemies. Now, they could be seen sitting together under the shade of the trees having a friendly chat, sharing a sliced melon, enjoying a joke, guffawing and hugging one another. A man donning a Turkish cap was slicing a mango and offered pieces of it to a Sikh. A Muslim woman had brought homemade *keema-parathas* and was laughing and affectionately feeding a *dhoti*-clad gentleman. Thousands were crossing the border at will without fear of being stopped. I really felt sorry for the way the two governments functioned. What could be more absurd than this: that these thousands of people seemed to have absolutely no feeling and regard for the dignity and honour of their respective governments! They hardly remembered that only a few months ago they did not carry melons, mangoes and *keema-parathas* for one another. Instead, they had daggers, swords and bombs to destroy one another. I wondered how the intensely violent religious hatred in their hearts had subsided. I wished to God they had the sense to keep their religious feelings alive for a few more days so that their respective governments could prove to the world that they were two different people prepared to destroy each other! But that had not happened. Yesterday's enemies were sitting together recounting their tales of woe. The tales of ransacked homes. Tales of how their women were dishonoured, how their flourishing businesses collapsed, how their homes were set on fire, how their children got separated from their mothers and the wives from their husbands. All these tales were shocking and full of anguish. They brought tears of sympathy to every listener and carried with them a faint glimmer of hope that one day they might go back to their homes and live together once more. Now, those tales had no meaning. At the most they could provide raw material to the future historians. And there was also the possibility that future historians might refuse to include them in histories because they had more melons, mangoes and *keema-parathas* in them than daggers and swords. Such nonpolitical aspects had no place in history books.

The history of Wagah of those days is absurd because it was against the basic ideology of a government, and encouraged disloyalty towards the government. And the truth was that the downtrodden people have always rebelled against the ruling classes and betrayed their trust in them. That was why I felt like descending on their camps and giving them a piece of my mind: 'Gentlemen! Stop this cursed friendly intercourse between these people. Otherwise, if people keep on meeting one another like this, they might begin to understand the reality and all that has been achieved so far would go down the drain.'

The most interesting feature of the Wagah border were the shops set up for the organized sale of religion. A bearded *Maulvi* sat there with a huge pile of books, including the Vedas, Shastras, Granthas, Geetas and Upanishads and many more works in Hindi and Sanskrit. Sitting next to him was a Sardarji who sold copies of the Quran *Majeed, Fiqh, Hadith* and dozens of other writings in Arabic. All those books were a part of the loot which the two gentlemen had brought to sell. Otherwise, they would have been at each other's throats by now. But at Wagah they were selling their books peacefully, the Maulvi selling the Hindu scriptures and the Sikh works on Muslim theology. In their heart of hearts they were thinking that once the books were sold, they would sit back and live comfortably for at least a few months. If by selling religion one could have two square meals everyday, what could be better.

Next, I met the writers. They were Muslims. They had come to Wagah from Pakistan. Their group consisted of Sahir Ludhianvi, Ahmad Nadim Qasmi, Ahmed Rahi, Abdul Matin Arif, Ibne Insha, Barkat Ali Chowdhury and Salahuddin Akbar. We just rushed and hugged one another. The earth under our feet did not shake with this. Nor did it protest that the earth which the Hindu and Muslim writers trod was either a part of India or Pakistan. As such it should have cried out in protest against the aliens treading on its bosom. But it remained quiet. How dumb this earth was! Actually, we were totally oblivious of the religion of the soil, stones, straw and grass underneath our feet, though we ought to have been more aware. In fact, if we had made these mute elements conscious of the greatness of their religion and their regional cultures, there was every chance of their revolting against us!

Anyway, we writers were not bothered about the protest or lack of it. Ours was a meeting of writers. So we poked fun at one another's writing and enjoyed *kababs, korma,* rice and tea at an exclusively Muslim hotel. We almost forgot that we were sitting at a place called Wagah which divides Pakistan from India. We laughed at the folly of those thousands who wanted to forge an intimate relationship between the two dominions. Then, we informed one another about the major achievements of our respective governments so that we could convey the information to them and thus perform the literary duties of fifth columnists. All sorts of suggestions were mooted to strengthen each other's governments, so that they could join hands to wage war against the half-naked and the semi-starving masses and suppress them. A couple of writers suggested they should raise a wall of tigers on one bank, and a wall of elephants on the other bank of the Wagah border so that people who regularly sat on either side and devoured melons and mangoes should learn to stay put in their own homes.

Anyway, we noted these absurd and impracticable suggestions and dispersed. The evening was drawing near and the military post on the border had sounded their bugles, warning people to return home. Gradually, the dividing line at Wagah emerged more clearly. We suddenly realized it was time to part, and walked to the border together *Neem* trees were lined on one side of the Grand Trunk Road. One stood bang on the border, almost as if it were a communist, otherwise it might have easily grown a little away, on either side. How boldly it stood there, as if no one could touch it! Had this been reported to the authorities of either country, the tree would have been surely felled. But why do that? Why not divide the leaves and branches equally between India and Pakistan? Why not tell the tree which of its branches and its leaves are Hindu or Muslim?

Sahir said to me: 'Why bother about this tree? Come let us go to Lahore.' And then all the Hindu writers went over to the other side of Wagah to the enemy country.

No one knows which politician forwarded the suggestions we had aired at Wagah just to have some fun at the expense of the lawmakers in both countries. When I went to Wagah for the third time, I was glad to see that the hallmarks, signs and symbols that distinguish one country from the other were in place. There was no trace of melons, mangoes and *keema-parathas.* Silence and desolation prevailed. All those guffaws, echoes of laughter, those tears and tales of woe had retreated to where they belonged. Their place was taken by tigers and elephants. Realizing the special importance of Wagah canal and fearing that this 'beauty' would become world famous and start attracting hordes of lovers from all over, it was hidden from their prying and unwelcome eyes. About half a mile away on this side of the border a lion spotted me and gave me a look which seemed to say: 'Sir, your daily incursions have made the border an object of ridicule. Don't you know, the border came into existence after long and serious deliberations. You should know the difference between taking this fact seriously and mocking at it?'

Following this, I and many other fun-loving people like me raised their heads and fluttering their eyelids attempted to catch a glimpse of the Wagah canal. But we could see nothing except army camps and the outlines of some familiar sights. One of the tigers told me that half a mile away, to the west of Wagah canal, an elephant was an expert in constitutional and international law. He prevented people from crossing over and informed them that the outmoded and uncivilized way of friendly social intercourse among people belonging to different countries was prohibited. Now, only regular passport-holders could touch the 'Wagah beauty'. The government had to be convinced that the person claiming to be a lover was 'genuine' and that he was not a threat to the security of the 'beauty'.

I quietly took the army sentinel aside and asked: 'Well sir, a tree stood on the bank of Wagah canal. Can you tell me whether it has been felled and thrown away or. . . ?'

The sentry pointed his bayonet at me and staring at me said: 'Who are you to interfere in this business which concern the two governments?'

And in the core of my heart I said: 'Listen good man, after all I am a branch of the same tree.'

Translated from Urdu by A.S. Judge and Mushirul Hasan

So the Witnesses Stated
FIKR TAUNSVI

Statement of Dandot Ram Khan Singh, Witness Number 1

Your Honour! No one knows better than you that I am branded as a criminal. There was a time when my robberies, pillage and plunder caused such an uproar that even the King of England sat up and admired my exploits. People call me a *goonda*. I am not only a boozer, but also enjoy smoking drugs like *ganja*, *charas* and *bhang*. You must think it is not good to indulge in such things but. . . .

JUDGE: You have been summoned to testify against a criminal called 'refugee' and not relate your life history.

WITNESS: Sir, I beg your pardon. It was my fault. But Mr. Justice! You have no idea about my revelations. A man in your position should be aware that the activities of this 'refugee' are inextricably connected with my life's story. Now, if I don't tell you about myself, you will never discover the crimes committed by him for centuries. But for me, it would have been difficult, if not impossible, for him to come into existence. I am sure you've read in the newspapers how our eminent leaders tried their best to destroy peace and unleash the forces of destruction and disintegration. They would have been gladdened by a natural catastrophe like floods or a revolution bringing anarchy and disorder in its wake. If that didn't happen, the least they expected were social disturbances and communal riots. But on their own they couldn't bring them about. But now they know that only Dandot Ram Khan Singh can perform wonders and satisfy . . . their political ambitions. Your honour! Have you noticed how this refugee, standing in that enclosure, is looking at me with wrathful eyes? Although it is true that my name is not included in the list

'Gavahon Ne Bayan Diya' from *Satvan Shastra*, pp. 185-202.

of *goondas* and branded criminals and our police and government have made me don the dress of a national leader, I still have the power to strike hard. If I could create hell for him in the past, I can very well charge him with staring at me and send him to the police station.

JUDGE: The honourable witness should not lose his temper. This court assures him that it will give due consideration to his resentment and anger while giving exemplary punishment to the refugee.

WITNESS: Yes, your honour! If the court does not punish him after listening to my testimony, then it would be a blot on the country's name. Kind sir! In a way this refugee too is a blot on the fair name of our country. When I tried to make him into a refugee, he attempted to place all sorts of obstacles in my way. He invoked the values of democracy and freedom. There were times when he wept profusely, talked to nonliving objects like fields. 'My dear fields', he would say, 'I have squeezed the last drop of the sweat from my brow and mixed it with your soil. How can I part with you?' Sometimes he would wander around the streets, taking in their familiar smell and embracing the walls. At times he climbed the roof and hid there. Then suddenly he would start yelling: 'Come what may, I won't go from here!' But your honour! My comrades and I. . . .

JUDGE: Oh, I see. So you also had your comrades with you. Were they also *goondas*?

WITNESS: Yes, they were there with me. Mr. Justice! You are my lord. You know everything. The courage and confidence, the bravery and boldness with which my comrades and I robbed this refugee was a marvel, beyond comparison. One of our national leaders paid us a tribute saying: 'By taking certain clever steps they have not only outdone the glorious traditions of the class that lives on the wages of iniquity and unlawful gains, but also challenged them by setting new standards worthy of being emulated.' You know we *goondas* are endowed with an extraordinary gift. We can fan the feelings of hatred so they spread like wildfire. That is exactly what we did in the case of this refugee. When we were told that our country's leaders have challenged our self-respect and honour and asked us to come out and face the rival community, placing a heroic goal before us, the blood in our veins began to flow faster. And Mr. Justice! May God give you greater perception, desire and determination to send this refugee to his doom! So we came out of our dens into the streets. We held lances, knives, swords, daggers, bombs, guns, pistols. We had drums and the blessings of our leaders with us.

JUDGE: In that case your whole being must have been electrified.

WITNESS: Electrified? More than that. We thundered like clouds, screamed like a storm, advanced like floods, and in the wink of an eye fell upon the enemy. It wasn't mere hooliganism. Your honour! We had a worthy goal. We lobbed bombs, set localities on fire, intimidated people, gave them a good hammering; we dragged people from running *tongas*, stabbed them with daggers, threw small children into swirling and roaring fires, finished off robust young men in a flash. We bruised and battered the velvet bodies of screaming, crying and beseeching women, virgins and young girls. We branded their limbs with sanctified words and slogans. We did not hesitate to strip them and parade them around the streets and bazars. We seized their gold. We ransacked and plundered prosperous homes and spent our ill-gotten wealth on pleasures which are difficult to describe. At this point this thoroughly meanminded person decided to become a 'refugee'. We shudder to think of the hardships we had to bear to accomplish the task. Your honour! If even now this obstinate person refuses to call himself a refugee, then pity on him! Had he a speck of decency in him, he would have accepted his guilt immediately. Oh yes, your honour, you have not told us, under which clause has he been booked?

JUDGE: In this case we will have to add a new clause in the law book. As yet I'm not very clear about the nature of his crime.

WITNESS: That you must do your honour! Otherwise our hard work will go down the drain. At night our big and small leaders can't sleep a wink. They go on mumbling because this wretched creature haunts them like a ghost. There is a limit to everything. He can't remain a refugee all his life. Just look at me. With this white cap, white jacket and a spotless white *kurta-pyjama*, can anyone say this man was once a *goonda*, or is one even now? But look at that fellow. From the sound of his footsteps you can tell that a refugee is coming. Kind sir! Is this how a decent and patriotic person should behave? Your honour, he has no right to make every other citizen's life miserable with his crying. I swear by my newly purchased pistol that this person is a confirmed criminal and should be given exemplary punishment, so that in future. . . .

JUDGE: The witness should conclude his statement. Just by looking at him the court is convinced that his statement is true. Let the witness number two be produced.

Statement of Sangratji Shirazji Bhai, Witness Number 2

JUDGE: Whether you have it or not, you believe in it or not, you read it or not, you swear by your Holy Book that you will speak the truth and nothing but the truth.

WITNESS: My Lord and my friend. Why should I lie and get into trouble? Our leadership does in fact rest on the foundation of lies, but there are all sorts of lies, and no lie can work all the time. And to lie about this criminal refugee would be to contradict my earlier statement about him. After all I am a political leader and not an ordinary person. And this refugee who holds meetings and takes out processions against me everyday threatens me himself and through others. It is more than evident from his activities that he is averse to my popularity. He blames me for creating disturbances to hide his own guilt, although, no one knows better than you, that far from being a criminal, I am an innocent witness. Isn't it true your honour?

JUDGE: Yes, of course! Continue with your statement. But why are you trembling?

WITNESS: There is a reason your honour! Sitting safely in that chair of yours, how can you sense our fears and apprehensions? I wish to God that you too were a leader. Only then you would know why I and my comrades. . . .

JUDGE: Does that mean that you too had comrades like Witness number 1?

WITNESS: Yes, your honour! They say that without comrades you can't succeed in any task; it is next to impossible to perpetuate one's leadership without their support in this age of democracy. Anyway, there was no trace of this refugee when we threw out the foreigners and took over the reins of government. Till then he was indistinguishable from an ordinary person. At this stage our aim was to seize power regardless of whether the earth is drenched with blood, locality after locality is burnt down, fields are devastated, children lose their sleep and women their honour, youth forget about love, and rest becomes impossible for the aged. Or if violence erupts all around us, the country's unity is compromised. We had no idea, we'd end up creating the 'refugee'. Now, you tell us your honour! What is wrong with that?

JUDGE: Anyone who dares to call it wrong is a criminal. Please don't be scared. Continue.

WITNESS: I'll try not to be scared, but your honour, this refugee is looking at me with wrathful eyes. Can't you tie a bandage around his eyes?

JUDGE: A separate application should be filed in this court to make such an arrangements.

WITNESS: That's all right My Lord. If a bandage cannot be arranged immediately, forget it. I will shut my eyes and continue with my statement. Oh yes, your honour, our goal was clear. Now the question arises, why did he become a refugee? This man created a situation, whereby we had to talk to the authorities and take a bold decision for the exchange of population. Call it bad luck or the country's misfortune or the smartness of this criminal that he became a refugee. My Lord! Just imagine the things he did to make us take that decision. He wailed and screamed, handed over his life's earnings to the *goondas*, saw his wife and children being slaughtered with knives and daggers, but didn't utter a sigh. He saw his home engulfed by a raging fire and yet didn't let out a scream. Leaving his swaying fields he wandered around hiding himself. In vulgar haste, he left behind the streets where he once roamed freely and sang songs of love and beauty, appealing desperately, 'Save me! Save me! I will not live here any more!' Now you tell us, your honour, whose heart would not melt on hearing such screams? Consequently, we set up camps for this refugee. Since then he parades around shamelessly and is a pain in the neck. I'm sure he will create more trouble for us in future.

JUDGE: If he does anything like that we'll have to add a new clause to our law book.

WITNESS: Not only that, your honour, his actions have become erratic. We thought that after achieving our goal and handing over this pest to the camps and the department of Rehabilitation, he would quieten down and start living decently. But look at our misfortune and this fellow's perfidy that even though two years have elapsed since we became free, he still calls himself a refugee. Sir! Two years is a long enough period for much to happen; a hen would have laid eggs more than thirty times, a cow would have given birth to two calves, a goat would have yielded more than fifteen maunds of milk. And your honour, in two years, all those sixty-eight years old would reach seventy. But just look at this refugee! In these two years he has done nothing except to wander around aimlessly, shedding tears and beating his breast, searching for his lost relatives, consuming tons of grain in the camps, sending applications and cursing the political leaders. Had this man's head not been crammed with a feeling of disloyalty to this country, had he truly wanted his own salvation, had he a genuine desire to cooperate with the government, he would not have stood here as a criminal. Sir! I appeal to you in the name of God, with due respect to your chair, for the respect of all the honourable, civilized and respectable government officials, that you should give him exemplary punishment. If he continues to create disturbances, we will be left with no choice but to side with him. We will be compelled to confront the government, because, with changing times we have to tailor our political strategy accordingly. Your honour! With that I beg your leave.

JUDGE: All right. But do open your eyes now. You have to sign your statement. . . . Hey peon! Produce the third witness.

Statement of the Camp Commander, Witness Number 3

JUDGE: What is your name?
   WITNESS: Jivan Baksh Ilahi, Camp Commander.
   JUDGE: Your age?
   WITNESS: Seventeen years and nine months.
   JUDGE: Your father's name?
   WITNESS: Seth Buta Ram Ghasita Khan, government contractor.
   JUDGE: What does he do for a living?
   WITNESS: Black market.
JUDGE: In that case I am sure you won't tell a lie. Swear in the name of your respected father and tell us everything that you know about this refugee.
   WITNESS: Sir, when he first came to our camp he looked down and out. He was in tatters. A junior clerk of mine told me that the refugees' boxes were packed with silk clothes. I believed him, because, I too, after all, was a refugee. Like him we too had piles of such silk garments. Seeing his tattered clothes I was

revolted. I felt that by wearing these dirty rags, he was insulting his country.

Sir! In the beginning he was not even aware where he had come from. He kept lying in a dark corner of the camp, withdrawn and muttering nonsense. Occasionally, we heard his screams. Your honour! In his camp lived four families, i.e., thirteen women, twenty-eight children and girls, four old men and seven hefty young men and about half a dozen old women. They lay there all huddled together, howling like wretched dogs. Someone told me that they wanted to convey the impression that they had been wronged.

JUDGE: Your story seems interesting. Why don't you write a book on your experiences?

WITNESS: Your honour! It seems you are mocking at me. I can't write a single sentence. Anyway, to continue, when this refugee realized that he received free water, food and clothes and didn't have to pay for the tent in which he lived, he was happy and his greedy eyes sharpened. It was then, my lord, that he started stealing the stuff that actually belonged to the government. He visited the free kitchen three or four times a day and gorged himself with all that food. And when we opened the ration depots, he entered on the ration card names of relatives who had died during the communal riots. But finally we discovered the fraud and stopped his rations. What else could we do, your honour! After all, our country does not have abundant wheat which could be thrown into the sea to maintain the prices on the market on the one hand, and to feed all these bastards, on the other.

JUDGE: Then why don't we import wheat from other countries?

WITNESS: Where is the money for that, your honour! The number of capitalists in our poor country can be counted on finger tips. How can they raise the money? Moreover, my lord, this refugee refused to work! We did our best to convey our message through the radio and newspaper to these bastards. Do you know, my lord, what this refugee said: 'Tell me, where can I find work?' Now, tell us how could we answer such a difficult question? Not getting a reply this person began enjoying the fruits of idleness. He even started stealing. Personal belongings of many refugees began to disappear from the camps. Along with that, he also started something highly degrading; prostitution of the surviving girls. And, your honour, he sold his eldest girl after bribing the police and with the assistance of our staff. We were then convinced that he was bent upon ruining the centuries-old reputation of this country. So to kill two birds with one stone, we threw him out of the camp.

Your honour! The stench he spread in this camp gives me a splitting headache even now. Once he bought a basket of rotten fruits and started selling them outside the camp. A cholera epidemic broke out. He was responsible for killing hundreds of people. Besides, he sold *pakoras* fried in stinking oil and infected vegetables. At times he bought four annas' worth of jaggery and dissolving it in a pitcher of water, sold it in the name of a refreshing cold drink. Sir, he bred such a large number of flies and mosquitoes that now it is difficult for us to discriminate between flies and refugees. What more should I tell you about this bundle of evil and vice? I think the least you can do is to hang him. If he is allowed to live, then decent and respectable refugees like us would earn a bad name. So said my contractor father.

JUDGE: Hey, court clerk! Note the reference about his respectable father getting a bad name in the file of this case and hey, peon, produce the man in charge of the department of rehabilitation, the fourth witness.

Statement of Zahanat Ram Budhi Bahadur, Witness Number 4

JUDGE: You seem to be the scion of a distinguished family from your appearance. How do you know this scum?

WITNESS: I admire your perception. But I'm disappointed that you've forgotten me so soon. Don't you remember that I am the son of the famous landlord—capitalist of this country, Seth Daulat Ram Dhani Baksh. Once you sent a man to my office in the department [rehabilitation] with your recommendation. Although he was not a refugee and was engaged in business in this city for the last so many years, you recommended a loan of ten or twenty thousand rupees for him out of the money allocated for the refugees.

JUDGE: Well! Well! Now I know. So you are the man who works day and night in that department [rehabilitation] to serve humanity..This is marvellous. Please continue with your statement.

WITNESS: You say day and night! I swear by God that I spend at least one hundred and ten minutes at my office everyday in the service of this evil-incarnate refugee. So much so that my wife was so fed up with my devotion that she left for a hill station to relax. It is a pity I ignored my devoted wife for his sake. You won't believe it, your honour, that my office is so crammed with such people that a refugee who had dozed off one day was nearly crushed under my car, even though he knew it was not the time to sleep. After all ours is the Age of Awakening.

JUDGE: I have also read a poem which runs like this: Ruffling their feathers—All sorts of birds have awakened.

WITNESS: Stop bothering about that your honour! That poem must have been written by some Chinese or Russian poet. Our country is . . . Anyway forget it. First, listen to my statement. Otherwise, I'll be late for lunch. Well, sir! When I took over this department and saw such a huge crowd of refugees, I at once assumed that this huge crowd was nonexistent, i.e., zero just like 'x' which they presume in solving a mathematical problem. My boss was so elated that he toasted me with Scotch whisky. Thousands of refugees kept standing outside the office windows buzzing like flies. I was not bothered. To keep them busy, we made them stand in rows and then asked them to breakup and rearrange themselves in rows on the basis of the districts to which they belonged in Pakistan. Every now and then we ordered them to fill up dozens of forms. We got those forms printed just to keep our office going . . . .

At last one day, while drinking tea, I asked my assistant: 'Is there no way of getting rid of all these people except to rehabilitate them?' My assistant answered: 'Sir, a way has already been found. No need for you to worry.' Just as the big people have taken possession of big properties on their own, similarly. . . .

JUDGE: Did this wretched refugee try to do that?

WITNESS: Yes, your honour! This is exactly what this refugee did. It was only when my assistant told me that I realized they had lightened me of my burden. Your honour! The fact is, the refugee community itself was divided into three categories. One was made up of highly respectable refugees who had taken possession of lands, houses and industries on their own; then they phoned us and requested that permission be sent to them. Sir, they were reasonable and wise. The second category was made up of those who were neither respectable nor dirty. They were neither able to take possession themselves, nor ask anyone to recommend their cases to us. No one knows their whereabouts. Anyway it was good riddance. And the third category was made up of people who were like this evil-faced refugee. They simply didn't have the guts to occupy lands and industries, and fearing the rains, they occupied the homes left behind by the rival community.

In this situation, the only course of action was to punish the refugees belonging to the third category. Every now and then I warned them of the consequences of illegal occupation. We issued countless allotment orders everyday. A house allotted in somebody's name was cancelled the day after, and the allotment order was passed on to some new person. Mr. Justice! Confusion, a stampede and much hue and cry ensued. My wife came down from the hills to see the show. We did not allow any refugee to occupy the property. On the contrary, the system we established eliminated that possibility. You can see our files. My Lord, if a single case of a refugee occupying the place for a full twenty-four hours is found, you can sever the heads of our staff!

JUDGE: Committing a crime is an essential condition for severing a head, and you seem unfit for doing that!

WITNESS: Your honour! I am helpless. How can I commit a crime? To do that you should be as stone-hearted as a refugee. I was born with a silver spoon in my mouth. If I had the power, I would have skinned him for the bad name he brought to this country. We did everything for fun. We picked up his belongings from his unauthorized house everyday and threw them out on the road. The police came along and threatened to seize them. Sir, you know well that with things littered, the traffic comes to a standstill. My car took hours to cover a distance which it otherwise did in minutes. Your honour! We arranged a loan of Rs 20 for him, and when the situation was acute even Rs 30, so that he was gainfully employed. We set up an employment exchange so that he could at least get a promise of a job sometime in the future. We requested the landlords to have him as a tenant. We talked to the industrialists and secured for him wages of up to eight annas a day so that this wretched fellow could live in comfort, buy clothes, pay the rent of his house, and educate his children. Oh! But this person turned out to be thoroughly shameless, indolent, and troublesome to the government. By doling out loans to him and his brethren the government treasury was depleted. How would we maintain our army and defend our country? In short, he has hindered the country's defence, spread diseases because of his dirty habits and filthy existence, and placed the country's reputation in jeopardy.

Today, if some respectable Englishman or a cultured American chanced to visit our country, what would he think of us? In short, my lord, he should be included in the list of people who have betrayed their country and God should be told to have him thrown into the fires of hell. Now, I ask your leave. It is lunch time. And your honour! Do you see how his nostrils have flared at the mention of lunch? See, how he has begun to smack his lips. It seems as if he and not me would be having lunch.

Translated from Urdu by A.S. Judge and Mushirul Hasan

Shadowlines

SURINDER PRAKASH

Surinder Prakash (1930-) is the pen name of Surendra Kumar Oberoi. He was born in Lyallpur, Pakistan. He learnt Urdu from his father who was a small trader. His studies were rudely interrupted by partition and the family had to leave Lyallpur and migrate to Delhi. Surendra Prakash worked for sometime with the All India Radio after which he moved to Bombay. He has written scripts for quite a few successful films. He has published three collections of short stories including *Bazgoi* which won him the Sahitya Akademi award. He has also published an autobiographical novel, *Fasaan*. Many of Prakash's stories evoke a composite past which was shared by Hindus and Muslims living in close proximity and enriching each other's life by internalizing the teachings of Hinduism and Islam. "Shadowlines" evokes this past, weaving a touching narrative that unfolds the tragedy of partition, the struggles of the *muhajirin* in Pakistan, the pangs of exile and, above all, the human bond that survives all this.

It was a day in summer. The courtyard was sprinkled with water and the string cots were laid at their usual places. Baoji was sitting on a wicker chair smoking his *hookah*. After every puff, wreaths of smoke went up from his mouth. He was unusually quiet as was the atmosphere around him. Only the gurgling noise of the *hookah* could be heard from time to time. The cloud of smoke coming from Baoji's mouth filled the rooms and the courtyard and then got dissolved in the atmosphere. All of a sudden he cleared his throat noisily and called out:

"Mohammad Bakhsh! O Mohammad Bakhsh!"

Mohammad Bakhsh's voice came from a distance: "Yes, Baoji?"

"What're you doing, son?" Baoji asked.

'Tadposaiyan', from *Indian Literature* (Delhi), December 1995, Vol. 38, No. 6, pp. 93-103.

"Nothing, Baoji, I'm playing hopscotch."

"Then come son, revive the *hookah*."

Baoji took three or four deep puffs and put away the pipe. Then he muttered, "You are the only One", as he twisted his hands.

Mohammad Bakhsh came and took away the cap and the bottom of the *hookah*. He was dressed in a white *shalwar* and a striped shirt which he had been wearing for the last three days. Maaji's standing instruction was that no member of the house should change his suit before seven days.

Mohammad Bakhsh was almost like a family member. His father, Alladitta, and mother, Hari Begum, were victims of plague when he was four years old. Both the husband and the wife worked in our house. Alladitta looked after the daily shopping while Hari Begum dusted the rooms and wiped the floors etc. I do not know their salary but they were happy. When they sat down to eat they would mutter: "*Ya Allah*, a thousand thanks to you for providing us our meals. May you grant prosperity to him who has given us our bread."

Mohammad Bakhsh was about four years. He would sit cross-legged before Hari Begum who would put lumps of food in his mouth at brief intervals. They lived in a small cottage near the courtyard. In summer they would settle on the cot outside the hut after their meals. Their presence in the dark and their conversation seemed to create an aura of mystery. Mohammad Bakhsh would sleep on the cot beside Hari Begum. One day she asked her husband: "*Oye Datia*, when Mohammad gets a wife he won't sleep besides me, no?"

Alladitta would answer, "Wife, your thinking goes quite far."

"What can I do? I've such a great desire . . ."

Then she would begin to pat the sleeping Mohammad Bakhsh with her hand and her voice would slowly drown in the enveloping darkness.

In the *mohalla* everyone called him Mohammadu which angered Baoji: "Stupid! that is what they are. Mohammad is the name of a great personage who was blessed by God. One should not distort his name like this!" Sometimes he would reproach Mohammad Bakhsh: "Hey Mohammad Bakhsh, why don't you tell people to take your name properly?" Mohammad Bakhsh would lower his head and answer helplessly: "What can I do

Baoji? Who cares what I say? Who'll listen to me?" "Yes, you're right. No one listens to anyone in this world. Everyone goes his own way." Baoji would utter each word distinctly holding the *hookah* pipe in hand.

When Pakistan was created we, like the millions of Hindus in Pakistan, were faced with a grievous problem. For a few days Baoji was totally confused. One day he returned home alongwith several other Hindu gentlemen. They talked in low tones: "So we discover today that *they* are different from *us*." Baoji said: "Fact is, we've become helpless. No one is listening to us. No one wants to know our point of view. We have surrendered to the politicians the right to decide our destinies." Finally it was decided that we should leave our own land and migrate to India. But one issue remained unresolved and its solution was to be found by us and not by politicians. This was Mohammad Bakhsh.

Hari Begum, Mohammad Bakhsh's mother, had died three days before Alladitta's death. She implored her husband to look after Mohammad Bakhsh after her death. After that when Alladitta himself was on his deathbed, he put Mohammad Bakhsh in Maaji's arms. His condition was so serious that he could not utter a word. Only the movement of his eyes conveyed his feelings. Seeing this Baoji put his hands on Mohammad Bakhsh's head and his eyes became moist, Alladitta muttered his own death-prayer and breathed his last.

Baoji and Maaji thus made an implied promise to Alladitta for Mohammad Bakhsh's upbringing. He used to study with me at the Sanathan Dharma High School. He would not attend the period on Hindu religion. Instead he would study the Quran with the *maulvi* of the nearby mosque for two hours everyday. Sometimes he would discuss with Baoji specific points on religion. Baoji would affectionately give his own opinion on the point. He was quite interested in Islamic studies.

So how to resolve the issue? We could not leave him because Mohammad Bakhsh had no one to call his own. As Pakistan was created for Muslims, Mohammad Bakhsh, in principle, should have stayed in Pakistan. But . . . it was difficult for him to stay there. Eventually the matter was put to him. He remained silent for a while, then said: 'who do I have to call my own, Baoji? Who'll give me shelter? I'd better go along with you, wherever you go.'

It was decided that we would take Mohammad Bakhsh along

with us to India. On the following day all the Hindus of the town assembled in the Arya High School where a camp was put up. Close by was the Islamia High School where refugees from India were lodged. The living conditions at both the places were the same. It is futile to describe them. We also reached the camp along with some essential household stuff which we placed in a corner. We made a *chulha* for cooking and began to stay there. Every day military trucks lined up to ferry refugees across to India and the Indian refugees from the Islamia School proceeding to different parts of the town with their belongings. We would silently wait for our turn. The Government of Pakistan had deployed a unit of Baluch army for our security. So there was no fear on that count.

On the penultimate night of our departure an important officer of the Baluch army came to interrogate the refugees about their belongings. He would isolate some articles from their luggage and mark them as forbidden. As he came to us the officer asked:

"What's you name, please?"

"Kirpa Ram," Baoji answered.

"Who else is with you?"

"Me, my wife, three children. And Mohammad Bakhsh . . ."

The officer was startled. "What do you mean?"

"Me, my wife, three children and Mohammad Bakhsh," Baoji repeated.

"Mohammad Bakhsh!" the officer uttered the name with special emphasis indicating surprise. "Who is this Mohammad Bakhsh?" Before Baoji could say anything, Mohammad Bakhsh replied.

"It's me, sir. I'm also going with them."

"But you're a Muslim. Why do you have to go?"

"With whom shall I stay here, sir? I've been with these people since my birth."

"Stay with your parents."

"They are dead. I was then four years old."

"Oh!" the officer began to ponder, then said abruptly: "But why . . . why with them? All the Muslims from there are coming here. And you . . ."

"Sir, I've no one here to call my own. Where shall I stay? How will I manage my food and clothing? And my studies?"

"Everything will be managed. Pakistan will look after everything. This is Pakistan's responsibility. Don't you worry."

"If I don't worry now, dear sir, I'll have to worry throughout my life."

The officer was not impressed. When Mohammad Bakhsh was ordered to sit at a distance from us, he clung to us and wept bitterly. We also wept profusely. We had never thought that a day would come when Mohammad Bakhsh would be separated from us. He had become a part of our daily life . . . A soldier was ordered to take him to the Muslim camp at the Islamia High School. It was a strange scene. He was separated from us as a calf is wrenched from its mother.

The lorry moved on. Baoji was sitting silently. Maaji remonstrated: "What're you pondering over?"

Baoji gave a start and said: "Ram Pyari, I was thinking how people would address Mohammad Bakhsh now—Mohammadu or Mohammad Bakhsh!!"

There was silence again. The lorry moved on—towards India. We reached Amritsar where we had the permit made and then proceeded towards Lucknow. One of Baoji's cousins, Gurdayal Singh, had already reached Lucknow. The day we reached we found Gurdayal Singh at the railway station, his son Gurpreet Singh clutching his hand. He was living in a house abandoned by a Muslim at Ganeshkhand Road. As we reached the house Maaji embraced his wife warmly and both wept bitterly. Then we freshened up, had lunch and went to sleep. We slept till late in the afternoon after a long voyage. When we got up we began to talk about different things. In the midst of the talk Gurdayal Singh asked Baoji how much money he could bring from Pakistan. He told us that a good piece of property was on sale near Aminabad Chowk. He and Baoji went to see the property the next.

There was a big mansion known as 'Haji Mohammad Husain Ki haveli' owned by the Haji's son, Jahandida Husain. Jahandida Husain wanted to leave his homestead and go to Pakistan. He always believed that the Muslims of India should have a homeland. He participated wholeheartedly in the creation of Pakistan. Like many other Muslims he hoped that at least the district of Lucknow, if not the whole of U.P., would be included in Pakistan because it was the nerve centre of Islamic culture. But this did not happen. When the creation of Pakistan was announced, the Muslims of U.P. were sorely disappointed. Haji *saheb* died on August 17, 1947. Now it was October. Jahandida Husain realized that the pomp and grandeur with which he had lived so far would not be possible now. He thought of spending the rest of his life in Pakistan. He would receive some high position and the courtyard of his mansion would remain filled with people seeking his audience. But things went awry. People who regarded him as their natural leader and were ready to sacrifice their lives at his bidding turned away from him. Now they believed that Jahandida Husain was the root cause of their troubles.

Jahandida Husain wanted to sell off his father's mansion but no local Hindu was ready to buy it. They regarded him as the enemy of the composite culture of Lucknow. The impasse continued. The local people scared away any potential buyer from outside Lucknow.

Gurdayal Singh thought of buying the mansion without anyone knowing it. Word would be spread that Jahandida Husain had allowed a hapless Hindu family to stay in his mansion. After tortuous negotiations the deal was struck at twenty-two thousand rupees. Relevant papers, receipts etc. were arranged secretly. Baoji was given the power of attorney and our family shifted to the mansion at night.

Jahandida Husain sold his mansion on one condition: Of the twelve rooms in the mansion he would keep one to store his own things. The doors would be padlocked and he would keep the keys. Baoji agreed without bothering to know what stuff Jahandida Husain had put in the room whose key would remain in Pakistan.

Jahandida Husain was then about thirty, thirty-five years old. Haji *saheb* had a fairly old wife who was married to him in his childhood. He had married twice since. One of the wives gave birth to Jahandida Husain and passed away. Haji *saheb* divorced the third wife after paying off her *mehr*. The first wife, Razia Begum, refused to go to Pakistan with Jahandida Husain and left for Gorakhpur, her old homestead. She had some land there which she inherited from her forefathers.

The family now comprised Jahandida Husain, his wife Naima, and their twin sons, Yaqub Husain and Ayub Husain who were six years old. Besides them there was an old maidservant. All were prepared to leave. There was an interval of three or four days between their departure for Pakistan and our shifting into the mansion. Meanwhile we got acquainted with them. Both Yaqub and Ayub were lovable boys. Both were the same age and looked identical. We could tell one from the other only by the colour of their hair. While one had black hair, the other had grey hair and eyebrows.

We saw them off at the station as they got on the train bound for Delhi. On the railway platform we clasped one another in arms and wept uncontrollably. They cried over their sorrow, we cried over ours. Baoji and Jahandida Husain made a solemn promise to let each other know about the well-being of family members through letters. Finally the trained steamed off—*chugh, chugh, chugh* . . .

We began living in one part of the house. In the front part Baoji opened his traditional dry fruit shop. The business picked up and we lived comfortably. Slowly we started to forget the town we had left behind, its pace of life, trade etc. So much so that Baoji almost forgot Mohammad Bakhsh and the promises.

Then one day came Jahandida Husain's letter from Karachi. He had reached the new land through the grace of Allah. He was allotted a large house and a shop by the government. He had a shop of Lucknawi *Chikan* in Karachi. Several experts in the art of embroidery from Lucknow worked for him. People had begun to fancy the dresses made by them. The family was thriving. Naima was fine, Yaqub Husain and Ayub Husain were in fine fettle. They were admitted to a reputed school. Their old servant, Ruqaia, also sent her greetings.

Baoji replied immediately. He informed that Jahandida Husain's *Badi Amma*, Razia *Begum*, had passed away in the village. The property had been acquired by the custodian and would, in all probability, be allotted to an appropriate person.

No reply to this letter came for quite some time. We got to know that Razia *Begum's* paternal property had been allotted to a Hindu refugee. Jahandida Husain was informed about this in another letter.

One day Baoji said rather abruptly: "It is strange. Mohammad Bakhsh appeared in my dream last night. By God's grace he has grown up to be a hefty young fellow. Having taken up the business left by us he has now become an experienced tradesman.

He is married with children. As I was going to the market he saw me. Immediately he came to me, touched my feet and threw himself into my arms. Then he took me to his house where I met his wife and children. He poured red-coloured *sherbet* into a big glass and offered me to drink. Later we went to his shop. The board hanging from the wall read—'Mohammad Bakhsh and Sons.' I was very happy.

That day Baoji wrote to Jahandida Husain asking him to look for a youngwoman named Mohammad Bakhsh in Karachi. After a long time the reply came that Mohammad Bakhsh could not be traced, that Jahandida Husain had become the leader of the Indian refugees, the *muhajirin*, in Karachi and was active in local politics. Baoji was glad that Jahandida Husain was fighting for the protection of the rights of the refugees though he was quite sad that there was no news of Mohammad Bakhsh.

Then something strange happened one day. Baoji was sitting in the shop looking after the routine business when he called Maaji and said: "Ram Pyari, make a cup of tea please." Maaji prepared the tea and carried it to him. He took a sip, belched . . . then smiled and said, "Alright, I should be on my way. When you come, bring some news of Mohammad Bakhsh." The next moment he died.

Now I, Indernath, look after the family and the trade. I am married with two children—Pinky and Raju. I've got my sister married. She is happy in her house. My younger brother, Jitender, has completed his studies and is an engineer. He is working on a government project. He is married into a good family and has a son, Rajesh, who is too young to go to school.

There was a letter from Karachi to inform that Jahandida Husain was no more. The other members of the family are fine. Maaji passed away without knowing anything about Mohammad Bakhsh. Things have changed considerably in our house. Ayub *Bhai*'s letters come frequently from Karachi to which I reply regularly. Of course the language has changed. Formerly they were in Urdu, now they are written in English. Well, what difference does it make? One can understand the meaning of words in any case. Now he dictates his letters to his secretary who types them out and posts them like other business letters. About Yaqub *Bhai* he informed that he is quite a name in local politics, that the people of Pakistan do not take to the *muhajirin* kindly.

Yaqub *Bhai* also brings out a weekly, *Al Muhajir*, in both Urdu and English. This paper has become quite popular with Indian refugees and may soon be published as a daily. Yaqub Husain himself will be its chief editor. The children of Yaqub Husain and Ayub Husain are fine and send their greetings.

I am thinking—one generation has passed away. The second is at an advanced stage. And the third generation has just begun to blossom forth in our courtyards and is sending across greetings. My son, Raju, has returned from school and is sitting by me in the shop. He tenderly massages my feet and asks:

"Daddy, how's the pain in your leg?"

"There's a slight improvement," I answer.

"Why don't you consult a specialist? Get a general check up done as well. You'll get to know the actual cause of pain."

"You're right. I should know the cause of the pain." Then he looks towards the almirah at the corner where Baoji's ornate *hookah* was kept. I also follow his gaze. I seem to hear the growling noise of the *hookah* of which Raju seems unaware.

"What's this contraption, daddy?" asks Raju still looking at the *hooqah*.

"This . . . is *hookah*, son. Its lower part is filled with water and its cap is made of clay. Tobacco is put in the cap and then live embers are placed on the tobacco. Your gandpa used to smoke it. Mohammad Bakhsh used to prepare the *hooqah* for him!"

"Then?"

"Then smoke would come out of his mouth."

"What a funny thing!" he says and proceeds towards the inner apartments. He stops at the door and says: "Daddy, I'll be back after my homework." He does not ask about Mohammad Bakhsh. Perhaps he is not interested in knowing about him.

For a long time no letters have come from Ayub *Bhai*. Perhaps he is too busy. *Al Muhajir* must have become a daily now. Yaqub *Bhai* may have become a known political figure. I carefully go through newspapers, especially if there is any news about Pakistan. Besides, there is one Farooqi *Saheb* among my friends whose sister and sister-in-law live in Karachi along with their children. Sometimes they phone up Farooqi *Saheb* who tells me everything in detail. One day he asked abruptly:

"Inder *Bhai*, why do you take so much interest in Pakistan? Who is there after all that you feel so concerned?"

"Mohammad Bakhsh."

"Mohammad Bakhsh! Who is he?"

"Well, Mohammad Bakhsh is Mohammad Bakhsh; that's all." He is taken aback by my reply.

From the newspaper the strained relations between the two countries is apparent. Pakistan has closed its consulate in Bombay where the consul general was Shahryar Rashid. He was the son of N.M. Rashid, the pioneer of new poetry in Urdu. I still remember N.M. Rashid's poem and its title, 'A stranger in Iran.' Time passes imperceptibly and we automatically move on our destined way. Pistachios do not come from Afghanistan *via* Pakistan anymore. They now come through other routes.

A letter from Ayub *Bhai*. Quite unexpectedly from London and not from Karachi. He is in London with all the members of the family and wants to come to India. I wrote back promptly urging him to come. Me, my wife Anuradha and our two children, Pinky and Raju, would eagerly await their arrival.

We tidied up the house. Two rooms were earmarked for them. Foodstuff was arranged from the market. The driver was asked to get the car cleaned and serviced. Then one night the telephone rang. Anuradha picked up the receiver and said to me, "for you, from London." I took the receiver from Anuradha and listened intently. Ayub *Bhai* was on the phone. He informed me that he was reaching Delhi by an Air India flight after three days and would reach Lucknow on his own. But I was so eager to meet him that I drove to Delhi along with my wife and children.

When the airbus touched the runaway, I missed a heartbeat. Then the door opened and the passengers began to come out. I could not identify Ayub *Bhai* and was almost in tears. The passengers picked up their bags and began to leave. I saw a handsome man of my age with grey hair and eyebrows come out and look around anxiously. I ran towards him and, to make sure, asked: "Ayub *Bhai*?" He took me in his arms and pressed me to his chest while he muttered: "By God, I knew that we'd meet in Delhi. Aha, what bliss!"

An unusual aroma came from Ayub *Bhai*'s body. I felt the same warmth in his hug as I once experienced when embracing my father, brother or Mohammad Bakhsh. "I could not stay at home", I replied slowly. We disengaged ourselves and began to stare at each other. Then I realized that there were two women and five children accompanying him. He introduced them to me:

"These are my two children and these three are the children of late Yaqub *Bhai*. This is your *Bhabhi*, and this is Yaqub Bhai's widow. I was thunderstruck.

"What do you mean, Ayub *Bhai*?" I asked.

"I'll tell you," he said sorrowfully and we were on our way. We hired two cars from Delhi and proceeded towards Lucknow.

On the way Ayub *Bhai* told me that in Karachi tension between the local people and the *muhajirin* had mounted. Bloodshed and arson was common. Since Yaqub *Bhai* was in the forefront of the movement spearheaded by the Indians and brought out two dailies, he became an eyesore to the opponents. During the last riots in Karachi, a group of musclemen attacked his house and press. Yaqub *Bhai* did not care for his personal safety and faced them unarmed. Three shots pierced through his chest and he died instantly. His security guards also fired in return and then the mobile police force reached there. By then it was too late. His house, office and press were wrecked. For their personal safety it was necessary to leave the country. No other course was open. London seemed to be the safest place. Then he thought of Lucknow, the land of his forefathers.

"Oh God! the pity of it!" I said regretfully.

"Yes, something has gone wrong with the world. Everywhere Muslims have become thirsty for the blood of their own brethren," said Ayub *Bhai* looking out through the windsreen. Perhaps he was watching the harvest field which spread far and wide.

When we reached Lucknow my own relatives and the relatives of Haji *Saheb* and Jahandida Husain converged on my house. After the reunion some became sorrowful while others, willy-nilly, burst into tears. There were some who whispered among themselves.

The following day Ayub *Bhai* took the key from his wife and opened the room where his father had kept some of his belongings. He went in along with other members of his family and children. Some moments later we heard them crying. I peeped in to see what was the matter. There were old books, photographs and dresses spread before them. A big portrait was lying on one side. It was Wajid Ali Shah in Kathak *mudra*.

After weeping copiously for sometime they came out. Their

eyes were still moist. They did not close the room. The widow of Yaqub *Bhai* said: "Inder *Bhai*, this room needs tidying up".

"Sure, *Bhabhi sabeha*, it'll be done immediately," responded my wife.

Next day they went to the tomb of Hazrat *Bibi* and visited all the old places and *imambaras* of Lucknow. They read *fateha* at each place. The cycle of prayers continues till today. From the *haveli* of Haji Mohammad Husain, built at the spot where Ganesh Khand Road ends and Aminabad begins, some mysterious shadows come out at the crack of dawn everyday and can be seen returning to it at sundown.

Translated from Urdu by M. Asaduddin.

Roots

ISMAT CHUGHTAI

Ismat Chughtai (1915-1992), the *enfante terrible* of Urdu fiction, was born in Budaun. Her milieu was the Muslim middle class of U.P. She depicts this class and mercilessly exposes its hypocrisy. A born iconoclast, Chughtai is known for her 'unconventional' views on man-woman relationship and religion. She has a special place among her illustrious contemporaries like Saadat Hasan Manto, Rajinder Singh Bedi and Krishan Chander inasmuch as she brought into the ambit of Urdu literature the complex and forbidden terrains of female sensibility treating it with a candidness that is still unmatched. Though she is known primarily as a short story writer, she has written quite a few novels as well, *Terhi Lakir* being the undisputed masterpiece. Among her stories, the most celebrated are—"Lihaf" and "Chauti ka Jora". M.S. Sathyu's famous film on India's partition *Garam Hawa* was based on one of her unpublished stories.

The faces were pale. No food was cooked in the house. It was the sixth day of the forced holiday from school for children who were making life miserable for the inmates in the house—the same childish tiffs, wrangles, noise and somersaults as though the fifteenth August did not come at all. The wretched urchins did not realize that the English had left and while leaving, they inflicted such a deadly wound that would fester for years to come. India was operated upon by such clumsy hands and blunt knives that thousands of arteries were left open. Rivers of blood flowed and no one had the strength left to stitch the wounds.

Had it been a usual day the little devils would have been shooed away from the house to make mischief outside. But for the last

'Jarein', from *Fasadaat ke Afsane*, ed. Zubair Rizvi (Delhi: Zahn-i-Jadid, 1995), pp. 55-61.

couple of days the atmosphere had become so foul that the Muslims of the city were living under virtual siege. The houses were padlocked and the police patrolled outside. So the children were free to let loose their terror in the house. Of course, the Civil Lines was quiet as usual. In any case the filth spreads where there is a surfeit of children, poverty and ignorance—the preying ground for religious fanaticism. This had already been provoked. On top of it the swelling number of refugees from Punjab created panic among the minorities. The garbage dump was being scratched and the filth had come on to the road.

There were open skirmishes at two places. However, in the state of Marwar Hindus and Muslims had so much in common and could not be distinguished from one another by their names, features and dresses. Those Muslims who came from outside Marwar could be identified easily: they had already crossed the border to Pakistan at the whiff of what was to happen on the fifteenth of August. As far as the old inhabitants of the state were concerned, they had neither the sense nor the status for anyone to talk to them about the complicated India-Pakistan problem. Those who had any sense, understood the situation and had become secure. Among the rest were those who were tempted to go to Pakistan by the rumours that four seers of wheat cost only one rupee there and a cubit-long *naan* only four annas. They were returning as they realized that to buy four seers of wheat they needed one rupee and though a cubit-long *naan* cost a quarter, it still had to be paid for. And those rupees and coins were neither sold nor did they grow in fields. To aquire them was as difficult as was the struggle for existence.

So a serious problem arose when it was openly decided to throw out members of the minority community. The Thakurs told the officer in clear terms: "Look, the people are so intermingled that for combing Muslims out you need staff which involves wasteful expense. However if you want to buy a plot of land for the refugees, that can be arranged. Only animals live in the forest and they can be driven away any moment".

Only a few select families remained—they were mostly in the employ of the Maharaja and there was no question of their leaving. There were also those who were packing their bags and preparing to leave. Ours was one such family. As long as *Bare Bhai* did not return from Ajmer, there was no urgency. But as soon as he returned, he caused panic; yet no one paid heed. As a matter of fact no one would have taken him seriously if Chabban *Mian*—may Allah grant him prosperity—had not played the trick. Having tried in vain to persuade his family to emigrate to Pakistan, *Bare Bhai* had almost given up when Chabban *Mian* decided to inscribe 'Pakistan *Zindabad*' on the school wall. Roopchandji's children were up in arms and wrote *Akhand Hindustan*. This led to a fight, to intimidation and death threats. As the matter got out of hand, the police were called in and the few Muslim children on the spot were put into a lorry and sent home.

Now behold! When these children reached home their mothers who were always too ready to curse them invoking cholera and plague on their head, ran out of their houses solicitously and held them to their bosom. In normal circumstances if Chabba had come home after a fight with Roopchand*ji*'s children, Dulhan *Bhabhi* would have served him a few resounding slaps and sent him to Roopchandji for administering castor oil and quinine mixture. Roopchandji was not only our family doctor but was Abba's long-standing friend as well. His sons were my brothers' friends and his daughters-in-law were friends of my sisters-in-law. This close friendship extended to the children. The two families were so close to each other over three generations that no one had the slightest suspicion that the country's partition would rupture their relationship.

There were of course members of the Muslim League, the Congress and the Hindu Mahasabha in both the families who held fierce debates on religious and political matters. But it was more like a football or a cricket match. If Abba was a *Congressi*, Doctor *Saheb* and *Bare Bhai* were supporters of the League. Gyan Chand was a *Mahasabhai* while *Manjhle Bhai* was a communist and Gulab Chand a socialist. Women and children supported the party patronized by their husband/the father. When an argument ensued, usually the Congress supporters tilted the balance. Abuses were hurled at the socialists and the communists but they would end up siding with the Congress. That would leave the League and the Mahasabha to act in unison. They were each other's enemy but invariably combined in attacking the Congress.

However over the last couple of years, there was a groundswell of support for both the League and the Mahasabha. The Congress was in disarray. The entire new crop of the family, with the exception of one or two impartial Congressmen, spruced themselves up like the National Guards under the command of *Bare Bhai*. On the other side a small group of Sevak Sangh was raised under Gyan Chand's leadership. But this did not strain mutual affection and friendship.

"My Lallu will marry none else than Munni", the *Mahasabhai* Gyan Chand would tell Munni's father, the Leaguer. "We'll bring gold anklets for her."

"*Yaar* I hope they won't be simply gold plated", *Bare Bhai* would have a dig at Gyan Chand's trade.

If the National Guards wrote *Pakistan Zindabad* on the walls, the party of Sevak Sangh would wipe it out and write *Akhand Hindustan*. This was the time when the formation of Pakistan was still a matter of jokes and jibes.

Abba and Roopchand*ji* would listen to all this and smile. They would make plans for a united Asia.

Untouched by politics, *Amma* and *Chachi* would talk of spices like coriander and turmeric and their daughters' dowries. The daughters-in-law were busy aping each other's fashion. Besides salt, pepper etc., medicines also came from Doctor Saheb's place. If someone sneezed, he'd run there. If anyone fell sick, *Amma* would make *rotis* thick with pulses and *dahivadas*. Invitation would be sent to Doctor *Saheb* who would arrive holding the hands of his grandsons.

His wife would say, "Don't eat there, did you hear?"

" And how would I collect my fees, then? Listen, send Lala and Chunni as well". "*Hai Ram*, you've no shame"—*Chachi* would mutter.

It was great fun when *Ammi* fell sick. "No, I'll not allow this joker to treat me"—she would say. But who would go to call in a doctor from the city when there was one at home. Doctor *Saheb* would come as soon as he heard of *Ammi*'s illness.

He'd tease—"If you gobble up all *pulao-zarda*, how can you avoid falling ill ?" *Ammi* would retort from behind the *purdah*, "Everyone's not like you."

"Well, why make excuses? If you want to see me, just send word and I'll be here. You need not fake sickness!" He'd say with a mischievous smile. *Amma* would jerk her hand back in mock anger and mutter curses. *Abba* would smile indulgently.

If Doctor *Saheb* came to see a patient, everyone else would line up for a check up. If one had stomach problems, another a pimple;

a pimple; others had either an inflammation of the ear or a swollen nose.

"What nuisance, Deputy *Saheb*! I'll give poison to one or two. Do you take me for a vat that you pounce on me like hordes of animals?"— Doctor *Saheb* would go on muttering while examining them.

Whenever he came to know that a new baby was expected, he would explode—"*Hunh*! the doctor's for free. Procreate as many and make my life miserable!"

But as soon as the labour pain started, he would pace restlessly between our verandah and his. He caused panic with his screams and shouts rendering it difficult for the neighbours to come. The would-be father would be slapped vigorously and castigated for his foolhardiness.

But as soon as the new born's cry reached his ear he would leap from the verandah to the door and then into the room, followed by *Abba* in a state of flutter. The women would resent and curse and then go behind the *purdah*. He would examine the pulse of the mother and pat her back, "Good show, my lioness". Then he would cut the umbilical cord and bathe the baby. *Abba* would nervously act as a clumsy nurse to him. Then *Amma* would start screaming: "God's curse! These men have no business to be here." Under the circumstances, both would slink away like two chastened children.

When *Abba* was paralyzed Roopchand*ji* had retired and his medical practice was restricted to his own house and ours. *Abba* was being treated by some other doctors but Roopchand*ji* would keep constant vigil along with *Amma* and the nurses.... After *Abba*'s passing away, he felt a new sense of responsibility besides the affection he had towards the members of our family. He would go to the children's school to get the fees waived, prevent Gyan Chand from charging on the girls' dowry. In the house nothing was done without consulting him. So much so that when it was suggested that two rooms be added to the western wing of the house, the plan was scrapped at Doctor *Saheb*'s instance.

"Why don't you build two rooms upstairs, instead" he suggested and it was acted upon. Fajjan was not ready to opt for science in F.A.; Doctor *Saheb* thrashed him with his shoes and the issue was resolved. When Farida fought with her husband and returned home, her husband sought Doctor *Saheb*'s help. As Sheela came to his family as the wife of his younger son, the problem of a hunt for midwife was solved. She would run from the hospital as soon as word was sent. Not to talk of charging a fee, sh'd present the baby with a cap and a *kurta* on the sixth day.

But today when Chabba returned after the fight, he was feted as a crusader, a *mard-i-ghazi* having won a battle. Everyone asked him about his daring acts. Only *Amma* was mute as she had been from the fifteenth of August when the tricolour was hoisted on the roof of Doctor *Saheb*'s house and the Muslim League on ours. Between these two flags there was a gulf, miles long. *Ammi* would look at its bottomless depth with her melancholy eyes and shudder. Then, like a deluge, refugees began to arrive. As the relatives of the oldest daughter-in-law arrived from Bhawalpur losing all their possession and somehow escaping with their lives, the chasm widened. And then, when the in-laws of Nirmala arrived from Bhawalpur in a half-dead state, the chasm became filled with venom-spewing snakes.

When *Choti Bhabhi* sent word that her son had stomach ailment, Sheela *Bhabhi* drove the servant away. No one made any comment. Neither did anyone speak about his own ailment in the house. *Bari Bhabhi* forgot her fits of hysteria and began to pack up her belongings in haste.

"Don't touch my trunk", *Amma* at last broke her silence. Everyone was stunned.

"Aren't you coming with us?" *Bare Bhai* asked sharply.

"No. Do you think I'll go to die among those Sindhis. God's curse on them! They wander about in flowing *burqas* [sic] and *pyjamas*."

"Why doesn't she go to the younger son in Dhaka?"

"*Aye*, why should she go to Dhaka? Those head-hunting Bengalis knead rice in their hands and then slurp it down"— taunted *Mumani Bi*, the mother-in-law of *Sanjhle Bhai*.

"Then go and stay with Farida at Rawalpindi", Khala suggested.

"*Tobah*! May *Allah* save us from the Punjabis. They speak like the denizens of hell." My taciturn *Amma* was rather voluble that day.

"*Ay bua*, you're acting like a woman who would rather sit in wilderness than seek shelter in anyone's house. *Ay bi*, stop throwing tantrums as though the emperor has invited you... that he has sent elephants that would amble along.... that he has sent black horses that would go trot-trotting... and throw away kicks... In spite of the grim atmosphere, peals of laughter rang out. *Amma*'s face fell further.

"Stop behaving like children", Sardar Ali, the leader of the National Guards reprimanded.

"You're talking nonsense. Do you want us to stay back and get killed?"

"You all go. As for me, where shall I go at this age?"

"At the end, do you want your ruin at the hands of these *kuffar*?"

Khala-bi kept count of her luggage. Alongside gold and silver she also stuffed bone powder, dry fenugreek and Multani *mitti* in bundles. She was taking them along with such care as though the Sterling reserves in Pakistani banks would fall without them. Getting angry, *Bare Bhai* threw away these bundles three times but she screamed so loudly as though Pakistan would become poor if this wealth was not taken. Eventually one had to take out the cotton from mattresses soaked with children's urine and pack them in bundles. Utensils were stuffed into gunny bags, beds dismantled and their legs tied together with ropes. Right before our eyes the well-equipped house slowly turned into misshapen bundles and boxes.

Now the luggage seemed to have grown legs and danced through the house.

Amma's trunk, however, rested immobile.

"If you have decided to die here, no one can stop you", *Bhai Saheb* said finally. And my simple, innocent-looking *Amma* stared at the sky with her wandering eyes as though asking herself—'who could kill me? When?'

"*Amma* has become senile. She's not quite sane"—*Manjhle Bhai* whispered.

"What does she know how the *kuffar* have tortured the innocents! At least, life and property will be safe if we have a land of our own."

If my taciturn *Amma* had a sharp tongue, she would have retorted: "What's this strange bird called 'our land'? Tell me where's that land? This is the place where one was born, one grew up in body and mind. If this cannot be one's own land then how can the place where one simply goes and settles down for a couple of days be one's own? And who knows whether one won't be driven out from there as well and be told—'Go and inhabit a new land'?

I'm like a lamp in its last gasp. A mild gust of wind and all this fuss about choosing a land will be over. After all, this game of one's land vanishing and inhabiting a new land is not very interesting. There was a time when the Mughals left their country to inhabit a new country. And today you want to establish a new one. As though the land is no better than a pair of shoes—if it gets a little tight, throw it away and get a new one." But she was silent and her face looked weary than before, as though she, after her quest for a land over centuries, felt exhausted. And she seemed to have lost her self in that quest.

Time passed on, but *Amma* stayed steadfast in her position like a banyan tree that stands upright in storms and blizzards. But when the caravan consisting of her sons and daughters, sons-in-law, daughters-in-law and grandchildren passed through the big gate and got on to the lorries under police supervision, her heart fluttered. Her restless eyes gazed helplessly towards the other side of the chasm. The house on the other side seemed as far removed as a fleeting cloud on the distant sky. The verandah of Roopchand*ji*'s house was desolate. Once or twice when the children came out, they were dragged in quickly. But *Amma*'s tearful eyes could glimpse those eyes ranged behind door-holes and *chik* curtains that were brimming over the tears.

When the lorries left kicking up a lot of dust, some dead soul on the left side seemed to take a breather. The door opened and Roopchand*ji* emerged with heavy steps and gazed at the vacant house like a thief. For sometime he tried to trace the images of those who had left in the dust haze. Failing, his gaze wandered for a while in the desolation and got fixed to the ground.

Having surrendered all the assets of her life to the mercy of God, *Amma* stood on the desolate courtyard. Her heart sank and she got scared like a small child as though ghosts would pounce on her from all sides. She felt giddy and supported herself against a pillar. As she turned to the room in front, her heart came to her mouth. It was here that the *ghunghat* was lifted from the moon-like face of the young and timorous bride who had surrendered her life to her husband. In the room on the other side her eldest daughter was born whose remembrance pierced through her heart like lightning. There, in the corner, her umbilical cord was buried . . . In fact all her children had their umbilical cords buried there. Ten images of flesh and blood i.e., ten human beings were born in that hallowed room from the sacred womb which they had left behind that day. As though they hung her in thorns like an old snake-slough and made good their escape. In search of peace and contentment, looking for the place where wheat was sold for four seers a rupee. The voices of her children filled the room. She ran towards it with outstretched arms but her lap was empty. The lap which newly-wedded brides touched with devotion so that their wombs would not remain barren. The room lay desolate and she returned, terror-stricken.

However she could not stop the flight of her imagination. Tottering, she ran to another room, the one where her life-partner had breathed his last after fifty years of conjugal life. Wrapped in the shroud, his body was kept near the door. The whole family had stood around it. He was fortunate to have passed away, lamented by his dear ones. But he left me behind who is lying here today like an enshrouded corpse, uncared for. Her legs gave way and she slumped at the spot where the head of her dead husband rested and where she had been lighting lamps with trembling hands for the last ten years. But there was no oil in the lamp that day and the wick had burnt out.

Roopchand*ji* was pacing up and down his verandah. He was cursing everyone—his wife, children, the government and the silent street that stretched before him—also the bricks and stones, the knives and daggers. Indeed the whole universe seemed to be afraid and cringe before his torrent of curses. His special target was the vacant house that stood across the road and seemed to taunt him as though he had broken it, brick by brick, with his own hands. He was wrenching the things which had got entrenched in his existence like deep-seated roots, but felt as though his flesh would come off his body with them. Eventually he gave up the effort with a groan and his curses stopped abruptly. He stopped pacing, sat in the car and sped away.

As night descended and the street corner became desolate, Roopchand*ji*'s wife entered our house stealthily through the back door holding two trays of food. The two old women sat across each other silently. They were mute, but the eyes communicated everything. The food trays remained untouched. When two women indulge in backbiting their tongues run like scissors, but when they are overwhelmed with emotion their lips get sealed, as it were.

Alone in the house, she was oppressed by painful thoughts

throughout the night. 'I hope they won't be done away with on the way. Nowadays, whole trainloads of people are being slaughtered'—so ran her thoughts. She had nursed the crop with her heart's blood through fifty years and that day it had been exiled from its own land to find a new land. 'Who knows whether the new soil will be conducive to these saplings or make them wilt. These poor saplings! *Choti Bahu*—may *Allah* protect her—her baby is due any moment. Who knows in which wilderness she will deliver it. They left everything—their homestead, job, business. Have the vultures left anything for them in the new land? Or will they have to return soon? When they return, will they get the opportunity to develop their roots again? Who knows whether this old skeleton of mine will be a witness to the return of spring?'

She kept on muttering to herself for hours clutching the walls and parapets of the house. Then she slumped on the floor. There was no question of sleep amidst nightmare in which she saw the mutilated corpses of her youthful daughter, her young daughter-in-law being paraded naked and the grandchildren being cut to pieces. Perhaps she had just dropped off to a moment of oblivion when she heard a great commotion at the door. One may not care for one's life, but even a lamp whose oil has run out shudders before its final gasp. 'Is the natural death less terrifying that it should come in the form of men who have turned demons? People say that they catch even old women by their locks and drag them along the street so violently that their skin comes off revealing the bones. And then, the horrors of the world are let loose in such a manner that the horrors of hell pale into insignificance!'

There were violent knockings on the doors. *Malik-ul-Maut*, the angel of death, seemed to be in a hurry. Then automatically all the door chains came loose. The lights came on. A voice came from afar, as though from the bottom of a well. Perhaps the eldest son was calling out. No, it seemed like the voice of the younger ones from some hidden corner of the other world.

So everyone has reached the new land? So fast? She could clearly see the younger son and the youngest standing along with their wives and children. Then, all of a sudden, the whole house came back to life. The souls came alive and stood around the grieving mother. The hands of the old and the young touched her tenderly. Soft smiles spread on her dry lips. Apprehensions swirled and vanished in the overwhelming tumult of happiness.

As she opened her eyes, she felt the touch of familiar fingers on her pulse. "*Arrey Bhabhi*, if you want to see me, just send word and I'll be here. You need not fake sickness!" Roopchand*ji* said from behind the curtain. "*Bhabhi*, today I must be paid my fees. Look, I have brought back your good-for-nothing children from Loni junction. Scoundrels! They were running away. They were not ready to trust even the police superintendent."

Again a smile blossomed forth on the old lips. She sat up. There was silence for a while. Then two pearls of warm tears trickled down and fell on Roopchand*ji*'s wrinkled hands.

Translated from Urdu by M. Asaduddin

The Vultures of the Parsi Cemetery
ALI IMAM NAQVI

Ali Imam Naqvi was born in 1945 in Bombay, where he received his early education. He has authored two story collections and a novel. The following story is a comment on continuing communal violence after independence and partition.

It was all so unexpected. They were stunned. They put the stretcher down abruptly, gawked at the dead body, and then looked at each other with a million questions stirring in their eyes. Their eyeballs moved dumbly in their sockets for quite some time, and when they stopped, the two shrugged their shoulders uncomprehendingly. Then, simultaneously, they grimaced, severely straining their neck veins and let their gaze hover over the dense trees of the Parsi cemetery. Not a single vulture! Not even as far as one could see! This was absolutely the first time it had happened. The bell had gone off two hours earlier to put them on alert. And sure enough, a quarter-of-an-hour later the attendants of *Bagli* No. 2* were handing the corpse over to them. The two had pulled the corpse into the *bawli* area and closed the doors behind them. Later Pheroze Bhatina, after he had opened the small window in the door and questioned the funeral attendants outside about the relatives of the deceased, asked one of them, 'How about the tips—did they give any?'

The attendant had smiled and flashed two ten-rupee notes at Bhatina, who promptly snatched them, stuffed one in the pocket

---

'Dongarvari Ke Gidh' Translated by Muhammad Umar Menon in *The Colour of Nothingness: Modern Urdu Short Stories*, ed. M.U. Memon (New Delhi: Penguin Books, 1991), pp.138-43.

*One of the several rooms in a Parsi mortuary where the corpse undergoes its final rites before being handed over to the caretakers for its ultimate disposal.

of his *dagla** and gave the other to his companion, Hormoz. Then they shut the window.

'Good Lord,' Hormoz lifted his head and thankfully looked at the stretch of sky peeping in from the thick foliage of tall trees. Then he motioned to Bhatina with his eyes. The two bent over, picked up the stretcher, and started to walk towards the *bawli* well.

'Pheroze,' Hormoz addressed his companion, walking along.

'Yes.'

'How long . . . I mean how long will we go on doing this sort of work?'

'Cut it out.'

'*Yaar*, is it the only thing we're good for?'

'So what do you think'

'Nothing, really. I was merely asking.'

'That's all?'

'That's all. I swear by Zaratushtara.' He looked up at the sky.

After a brief silence Bhatina said, 'Look, Hormoz. The Parsi Council took care of us, didn't it? Let's just say we were the unlucky ones. Right? What do you say?'

'Same story. Not much difference. But the truth is, I'm fed up. I'm just fed up.'

Their conversation was cut short, as they had reached the *bawli* enclosure. A single kick of Hormoz's foot opened the door and the very next instant they took their places by the corpse, one standing by the corpse's head, the other by its feet. The corpse's face, which had been smeared with yoghurt, was absolutely white. Hormoz lifted the corpse's head a little and Bhatina quickly pulled the shroud clean out from under it. By turns they reverentially touched the corpse's feet, touched their hands to their eyes and chests as a sign of respect, and got up. A handkerchief had been put around the waist with the ritual *kasti*-string ... to cover the corpse's nakedness. They left it alone. Then they came to their quarters in the corner of the *bawli* compound and sat down at a table. After some time Hormoz set a wine bottle on the table and the two filled their glasses. Pheroze Bhatina popped a piece of *arvi* roll into his mouth and said, 'Hormoz'.

*A knee-length garment, like a long coat, made of *malmal* (muslin), worn by Parsis on special occasions such as weddings and funerals.

'Yes, what?'
'What a life.'
'What's the matter?'
'*Bagli* No. 1, 2, 4 . . . the bell . . . son-of-a-*bitch* . . . and. . . .'
'And?'
'Yeah, and . . .'
'And—what?'
'Corpses . . . still more corpses . . .'
'I don't understand.'
'Just look. Look at the life of a Parsi.'
'Life?'
'Yes.'
'What about it?'
'His youth runs superfast but his old age merely crawls along like a freight train.'
'True, brother, absolutely true.'
'Yes, absolutely true.'
They kept up the litany of 'true, true' for quite a while as they continued to drink, breaking somewhat later into fits of sobs. After an hour or so the bell went off again. This time the corpse was coming from *Bagli* No. 4.
'There, Lord Zaratushtara's provided for more wine.'
'Come on, *yaar*, let's get going.'
They made their way over to the *bawli's* main gate. The door opened a second time. They slid the empty stretcher out. Moments later it was pushed back in with the corpse from *Bagli* No. 4. One of the attendants tossed two ten-rupee notes at them once again. But this time Hormoz stepped forward to collect the money. Then they closed the door, picked up the stretcher and started off toward the *bawli*.
'Hormoz?'
'Yes, what?'
'One day we too will end up dead, just like this, no?'
Hormoz stopped, turned his head to look at Pheroze Bhatina, and then asked him rather harshly: 'Now what makes you ask a question like that?'
'Everyone has to die.'
'True. But I'm not planning on dying quite yet.'
'Planning? What the hell do you mean?'
'Shut up, fool. What have we seen in life so far? Dead bodies,

more dead bodies, and vultures. At the most, a little wine now and then from that fucking Sitara Road liquor store . . . crude, mixed with ammonium chloride . . . ten-rupee notes. I ask: is this what you call life?'

Pheroze didn't answer, he just kept looking at Hormoz.

'Come on, brother, is it life?'

'What can I say. All I know is this: when the call comes, I must go. Somebody else will take my place. When you go, somebody else will take your place too.'

'Shut up, fool! Bastard! Pig!' Hormoz shouted.

'Don't make so much noise. Stop talking about life. Look, we've got a corpse to take care of.'

They shut up. Walked over to the *bawli* in silence. And when they opened the door. . . .

It was all so unexpected. They were stunned. They put the stretcher down abruptly, gawked at the dead body, and then looked at each other with a million questions stirring in their eyes. Their eyeballs moved dumbly in their sockets for quite some time, and when they stopped, the two shrugged their shoulders uncomprehendingly. . . . And then they let their gaze hover over the dense trees of the Parsi cemetery. There was not a single vulture anywhere in sight.

This was absolutely the first time it had happened. Corpses, but no vultures in sight anywhere. Usually though, after Hormoz and Pheroze had dragged a corpse to the *bawli*, the vultures made short work of it within minutes. As they saw the vultures return, they would come back to the *bawli*, douse the skeleton with acid, which would then crumble like fine dust into the depths of the *bawli*-well—gone forever, who knows where? Or it happened that no dead body was brought in for days on end. But on such occasions the Parsi Council would buy a goat and have it delivered to Hormoz and Bhatina who would then feed it to the vultures, lest hunger drive them away for ever. But this? Corpses—a shoal of them, so to speak—ready but no vultures around to finish them off!

Both gawked at each other with peeled eyes. After they had stood there dumbly for some time they put the second corpse on the netting as well, then they covered the mouth of the *bawli* and gave each other a deep questioning look.

'What do you think? Shall I go and let Keqabad know?'

'Yes. Go!'

Bhatina went into his room and pressed the emergency button. The red bulb on the wall of the office of the Parsi cemetery began to blink. The clerks scampered out—confused, shocked. Similar bulbs also went on in the *Baglis*. The clerics stopped the holy recitation from the *Avesta*. Dogs wandering about in the *Baglis* were suddenly gripped by fear and slunk into corners. Mournful relatives accompanying their dear departed stepped out of the *Baglis* in a state of prodigious nervousness. Everywhere there was a single question: What's happened?

Keqabad bounded out, looked at the sky closely and promptly went back in. People hemmed him in, noisily asking the same question, 'What's happened?' In response Keqabad announced, 'The vultures have gone away!'

'Vultures've gone away?'
'Vultures've gone away?'
'But why?'
'Something's bound to happen!'
'But what?'

The secretary of the Parsi Council received Keqabad's phone-call. His forehead began to wrinkle. After he had heard it all he returned the receiver to its cradle, turned on the intercom and informed the director of the matter. Right away an emergency meeting was called. The matter was presented before the board of directors. But the question persisted: Where did the vultures disappear to?

'What did you say, the vultures have disappeared?' the police commissioner asked with a trace of surprise in his voice.

'Yes, our vultures have disappeared,' the chairman of the Parsi Council confirmed, stressing each syllable. In rapt attention he listened to all the police commissioner had to say, his face turning one colour after another. He listened to him for a long time. After the commissioner had hung up, the chairman too had returned the receiver to the cradle and looked at the directors and found their gaze intent upon him with a single question. He apprised them of the substance of his talk with the commissioner. Each of the participants left the meeting with prodigious worry and only a slight feeling of reassurance. The secretary rang up the cemetery. Then Keqabad briefly summed up the substance of the exchange between the police commissioner and the chairman to the revered clerics and others present. From the clerics the news travelled down to the attendants of the *Baglis* and from them ultimately to Pheroze Bhatina and Hormoz. Bhatina listened to the whole thing very carefully. He then looked at the sky, clearly visible from random openings in the dense foliage: there was not even a crow anywhere, or a kite, let alone a vulture!

All of a sudden they flinched. The bell had gone off again. A corpse was being sent from *Bagli* No. 3. Once again they were standing at the door. The corpse arrived. This time, though, the attendant thrust two fifty-rupee notes at Bhatina. After Bhatina and Hormoz had pulled the corpse inside, the latter grimaced and said 'Hormoz!'

'Yes, what is it?'

'Why in hell have all the Parsis decided to die only today?'

Hormoz didn't answer. He just went on looking at the sky.

'To start with, no vultures in sight; then corpse after corpse comes our way.'

'Where have the vultures disappeared to?'

'The police commissioner said the vultures, all of them, are flocking to the Kharki, Raviwar Peth and Somwar Peth neighbourhoods.

'What for?'

'Oh these idiot Hindus and Muslims are at each other's throats again. There's been a riot. The bastards, they've torched everything: houses, shops, even ambulances and hearses, the whole lot. The street is littered with corpses. One right on top of the other. Piled high. Our vultures—well, they're having a field day there. And that police commissioner . . . he said that after the street's been cleaned up, the vultures will come back of their own accord.'

'Even if the street's cleaned up—so what? What makes you think the vultures will return? This fucking India . . . there is a riot every day here, every day a fire, every day people die. The vultures'll come back? The hell they will!'